NAVIGATING
THE
SOCIAL WORLD

A Curriculum for Individuals with
Asperger's Syndrome, High Functioning Autism
and Related Disorders

Jeanette L. McAfee, M.D.

FUTURE HORIZONS INC.

Navigating The Social World

All marketing and publishing rights guaranteed to and reserved by

FUTURE HORIZONS INC.

721 W. Abram Street
Arlington, TX 76013
800.489.0727 Toll Free
817.277.0727
817.277.2270 Fax
www.FHautism.com
info@FHautism.com

Printed in Canada

ISBN 10:   1-885477-82-1
ISBN 13:   978-1-885477-82-8

We should not live in the clouds, on a superficial level. We should dedicate ourselves to understanding our brothers and sisters.

Mother Theresa

This book is dedicated to my daughter, Rachel.

You have been my inspiration.

I could not have asked for a better teacher than you.

CONTENTS

FOREWORD

When Jeanette and Keith's daughter was diagnosed as having high functioning autism, their long search for an accurate diagnosis was over. However, they began a new search for knowledge on how to help her. They were determined to learn more about high functioning autism and Asperger's Syndrome and how to provide effective programs for their daughter. They attended workshops and read the research journals and books that describe these conditions, but soon realized that there is remarkably little knowledge on remedial programs. Jeanette began to seek out other people who had worked with individuals with these disorders. She tapped into the experience of a variety of such people, including parents, teachers, speech therapists, occupational therapists, psychologists and applied behavioral therapists. She combined this knowledge with eleven years of experience working with her own daughter and with her training in pediatrics, and began writing social, behavioral, and abstract thinking skills programs for her daughter. These programs later became the foundation of this book.

It was while presenting a workshop in California that I met Jeanette. Her determination to learn more about AS, HFA, and treatment interventions included moving the whole family to Australia for three months to participate in the programs I was developing in Brisbane. While in Australia, Jeanette studied with me at my autism clinic and with two autism advisory teachers in the Brisbane region. In addition, we spent many hours assessing her daughter's unusual profile of abilities and designing and implementing programs. We generated many new ideas that combined our respective experience. Jeanette subsequently incorporated many of these strategies into *Navigating the Social World*.

This "how to" book is written both for the novice and experienced professional and will be of enormous value to parents, teachers, and therapists. Jeanette has undertaken considerable work in designing handouts, worksheets and tracking forms that provide a structured, logical and progressive approach. There are clear explanations of the relevant issues for each goal and the activities are consistent with the theoretical models of autism and Asperger's Syndrome. After reading this book you can immediately start a program at home or school.

There is a special focus on recognizing and coping with emotions, communication, social understanding, and abstract thinking with practical examples and quotations from individuals with Asperger's Syndrome and High Functioning Autism. Jeanette adopts a common sense approach and I strongly recommend this book for parents, teachers and other professionals.

Dr Tony Attwood
August 2001

AUTHOR'S NOTE

When I originally started writing, this book was not even an idea in my mind. I wrote simply to provide a social skills and emotions program for my then ten-year-old daughter, Rachel. Rachel had just been diagnosed with high functioning autism (HFA) after years of puzzling physicians, teachers and my husband and me with her unique combination of strengths and special needs. After years of uncertainty about both her diagnosis and how to best help her with the multiple problems she faced, my husband and I reacted to the news of Rachel's HFA diagnosis with relief. We believed we finally would be able to find an appropriate treatment program for her. However, we soon discovered that such a program was not going to be easy to find. Asperger's Syndrome (AS) had only been recognized as a distinct diagnosis under the umbrella of Pervasive Developmental Disorders (PDD) in the DSM IV[1] in 1994. Thus it was no wonder that little was known about its diagnosis and etiology, and even less about how to treat it. In fact, my husband and I, both physicians, had never heard of either HFA or AS during our medical training. So we were sympathetic when the physicians and psychologists who diagnosed our daughter sent us on our way with the diagnosis, but were unable to suggest specific treatment programs for her. We turned to the next logical place for program options—our local school district—and found that the special education team, including special education teachers and speech and language pathologists, faced the same dilemma. They had little or no knowledge of this new diagnostic category and had had essentially no training in its remediation. Over the last few years we have spoken with many other families and professionals from different parts of the country who have faced the same lack of trained professionals and available programs for children with AS/HFA. It is this need that has motivated me to write *Navigating the Social World*.

---

[1] Diagnostic and Statistical Manual IV (4th edition), published by the American Psychiatric Association. This widely used manual defines neuropsychiatric disorders and lists diagnostic criteria for each diagnosis.

Curricula designed specifically to teach social/emotional, abstract thinking, and behavior management skills to individuals with AS/HFA and related disorders are only now beginning to appear. Many of the ideas in this book have been adapted from teaching and counseling methods that have been in existence for years to meet the specific needs of these students. Other ideas in this text are new. At this point in time most, if not all, programs designed to help individuals with AS/HFA are, of necessity, at the cutting edge of the field. There simply has not been adequate time to develop and test a wide range of treatment approaches in order to ascertain which of them works best. In short, we are still in the research and development phase of treatment for this very complex and often puzzling group of disorders. This is certainly the case with *Navigating the Social World*. For this reason, any input that you, the reader, can give about your experiences using the programs would be greatly appreciated. I hope to use feedback from readers to improve the programs in the future and to provide a forum for sharing ideas. I strongly believe that the more we work together to share ideas and experiences, the better we will be able to help our students, clients, and loved ones with Asperger's Syndrome, high-functioning autism and related disorders to live happier and more productive lives.

Jeanie McAfee
August, 2001

For further information or to send comments, please visit the following website: www.jeaniemcafee.com

ACKNOWLEDGEMENTS

While working on the book I had the privilege of spending three months studying with Dr. Tony Attwood in Brisbane, Australia. With his kind permission, I have included many of his ideas in this book.[2] It is difficult to adequately thank Dr. Attwood for so freely sharing his wealth of knowledge and expertise in the field of Asperger's Syndrome and high functioning autism. Dr. Attwood's passion for his work, and devotion to the individuals with autism spectrum disorders with whom he works, are an inspiration to the people who know him.

I also wish to thank Trevor Beasly, an autism advisory visiting teacher for the Queensland Department of Education in Australia, for so generously allowing me to follow him on his school rounds, and for showing me many of his tricks of the trade. Many thanks to Beth Saggers, also an advisory visiting teacher in Queensland, who shared her time and ideas as well. Carol Gray has been kind enough to allow me to use some of her excellent material on compliments and I have much appreciated her input. Her Social Stories and Comic Strip Conversations also have been invaluable tools in explaining how to interpret other people's actions and words. Autism Partnership in Los Angeles provided me with an excellent foundation for a behaviorally based program for my daughter, Rachel, and other students like her, particularly in the areas of stress management, compliance, applied behavioral analysis and reinforcement techniques. Speech and language pathologists Rolleen Singlecarry and Cathy Hoey both gave me invaluable guidance when I first began searching for approaches to teaching social skills and pragmatics. Jane Germ lent her expertise in speech and language pathology to critiquing the book, and Wes Peterson and Diane Youtsey gave helpful feedback from the perspective of special education teachers.

---

[2] Please also refer to Dr. Attwood's upcoming book with Carol Gray on AS: *Making Friends and Managing Feelings*.

My deep appreciation for the time they have taken out of their busy schedules to read and critique the manuscript goes to Dr. Adrianna Schuler, Dr. Robin Hanson, Dr. Linda Lotspeich, Dr. Marjorie Solomon, Dr. Edward Hallowell, and Dr. Fred Volkmar.

Rodger Stein, who is both friend and advisor, has taught me more than I ever thought I would want to know about applied behavioral therapy. He has been there throughout the writing of this book with honest feedback, support and humor, and has been one of my biggest cheerleaders. My daughter's special education aide, Mary Foster, has worked side by side with me as I have written the book, trying out each new program and helping me immensely with her input. Her love for children, her great sense of humor, and her willingness to try new ideas have been a shining light over the last three years. Many thanks also to my dear friend, Belinda Chamness, for her help with the manuscript and for single-handedly holding down the fort while my family and I were in Australia. I deeply appreciate Bob and Gini McAfee for making it possible to study in Australia, and for their skill and patience in proof reading.

After years of reading acknowledgements devoted to spouses, I finally can say I understand why authors repeat the same words time after time. My long-suffering husband has washed more dishes, given more baths, put more kids in bed and cleaned up more dog, cat and baby poop than most men would ever dream of doing in their worst nightmares. And it goes on from there. He has created charts at one in the morning, retrieved lost programs while comforting his hysterical wife, and given his honest feedback in spite of the knowledge that he was taking his life in his hands in doing so. Through all of this he has put up with five grumpy females in the household, two of whom are bumping through the ups and downs of puberty, and another who is a three-year-old redhead with the personality of a tigress.

To Kim, Dana and Jody who have endured so much—thank you. You are wonderful.

Rachel, who loves lights of any kind, has faithfully lit a beautifully scented candle for me in our home office each time I sit down to work. She always says, "Mom, this is to help you write." Rachel's candles have become for me a symbol of the light inside each person on the autism spectrum. My hope is that this book will help them all shine brighter.

INTRODUCTION

This book was written primarily for people who live with or work with individuals who have *Asperger's Syndrome or high functioning autism (AS/HFA)* and who have limited experience in providing programs for these children. In addition, the book also will be useful for those who work with individuals with related disorders such as *pervasive development disorder-not otherwise specified (PDD-NOS), nonverbal learning disorder,* and *semantic pragmatic disorder.*[3] I have not intended to present a lengthy treatise on the history, diagnosis, or possible etiologies of these disorders. Rather, this book is offered to those professionals, paraprofessionals, and parents who have done some background reading and possibly have attended lectures and workshops on the subject of AS/HFA and related disorders, but who then face the challenge of how to apply what they have learned to real-life teaching situations. In other words, when the research is done, one still has to sit down with the child at some point and actually run a program. It is at this step that people usually stumble. This book is intended to help with that step.

Currently, the rate of diagnosis of AS/HFA is rising at such a rapid pace in most countries that it is outstripping the availability of quality programming for these individuals. Considering that the diagnosis of AS was first published in the DSM IV only in 1994, it is not surprising that the rate of diagnosis is increasing so quickly, as individuals who previously would have been mislabeled are now being identified. It also is not surprising that most research to date has focused on a) refining the diagnostic criteria, and b) searching for possible etiologies of AS/HFA. However, along with the increasing number of identified cases there has been a consequent rise in the demand for appropriate remediation programs. Because the diagnosis is so new, there has been little time to create and study

---

[3] "AS/HFA" is used throughout the book to designate Asperger's Syndrome/high functioning autism.

treatment programs specifically designed for these higher-functioning students. In particular, programs designed to address social and pragmatics skills and the management of emotions and stress are few and far between. This shortage has put school districts in the difficult position of attempting to fulfill their mandate to provide appropriate individual educational plans without the availability of suitable programs for these students.

What information does exist for professionals, paraprofessionals, and parents who wish to learn more about how to help their children, students, clients, or patients with HFA or AS? Until very recently, most medical schools and degree programs in psychology and education have not been able to provide training in this area to their students. Many training institutions are still lagging behind in providing this information. Therefore, a majority of specialists in the field have gained their knowledge and experience through on-the-job training in the traditional mentor/apprentice model. In Australia, for example, the Queensland Department of Education recently put this model to excellent use in their autism Advisory Visiting Teacher (AVT) Program. Although the mentor/apprentice model can be very effective, there is a shortage of knowledgeable mentors in most places. There are some excellent books and papers on AS and HFA, but most, of necessity, focus on diagnosis and *general* approaches to treatment. Few, to date, present a "how to" approach that a novice can put to use without requiring significantly more extensive training. There also are many dedicated professionals who have begun to give much-needed workshops and lectures to share their knowledge. These training sessions are absolutely necessary. They provide not only a huge amount of information, but also access to the specialists presenting the information. However, this access is limited. Attendees often leave the conference or workshop with a head packed full of ideas, but without a clear idea of how to put the newly acquired information to work in the classroom or at home. This is the missing link that motivated the writing of *Navigating the Social World*.

In this book, the reader will find ideas and techniques from several different disciplines, including the fields of cognitive behavioral therapy, applied behavioral therapy, education, and occupational therapy, among others. Some of these techniques have existed for a long time, are widely used in a variety of applications, and essentially have become part of the public domain. Other techniques, developed more recently, were designed specifically for use with individuals with AS/HFA. I have credited the original sources for those techniques that fall into the latter category. Finally, many of the ideas in this book were inspired by my own beautiful daughter and a handful of other children with AS/HFA with whom I have had the great pleasure to work.

The lack of specific, hands-on programs designed to address the deficits in social, emotional, and organizational skills in students with AS/HFA is one of the major missing links in the area of Pervasive Developmental Disorders today. *Navigating the Social World* provides a number of user-friendly programs to address social and emotional delays in these students. While not intended to be an exhaustive work, it hopefully will serve as a springboard to help parents, teachers, and aids "get off the ground" in beginning their work with their student or child. Indeed, it is my hope that this book will not only get the reader off to a good start, but will stimulate more work in the area of programming for this very special group of individuals.

HOW TO USE THIS BOOK

Navigating the Social World was written for parents, professionals, and paraprofessionals who would like specific information on how to provide an intensive social-emotional skills program for their child, client, or student with Asperger's Syndrome, high functioning autism (AS/HFA), or related disorders such as PDD-NOS, semantic-pragmatic disorder and nonverbal learning disorder. It has been written so that readers without extensive experience in this area can understand and apply the information contained in each program. However, it also may be helpful to those who already have significant experience working with this group of individuals by providing new program ideas or by offering different ways of approaching the deficits common to these disorders. In addition, adults with AS/HFA or related disorders who are looking for help in the areas of social and emotional skills may find this book useful, either as a general reference or as a curriculum resource to be used in a more structured setting with a mentor, counselor or other professional. It should be noted that some of the programs in the book (such as Program 7, Basic Conversational Responses) are most useful for students who need more basic instruction. Other programs (such as Program 18, Resolving Conflicts) are more applicable to older, very high functioning students. The majority of programs fall somewhere between these two categories, and most can easily be adapted to fit the needs and skill levels of the individual student.

Many of the general social skills and emotion management programs currently on the market present discreet, single lessons on isolated skills that are designed to be covered in one or two sessions per skill. While this approach may work for students who are not on the autism spectrum, it is becoming increasingly clear that brief, isolated teaching sessions such as this do not produce lasting, long-term gains in social and emotional management skills in individuals with AS/HFA.[4]   In response to this problem, the programs in this book are designed to provide in-depth teaching with reinforcement through repetition and skill building over a period of months to years. Each step should be practiced until the student has mastered it (i.e. can correctly perform that step 80-90% of the time) and then should be reviewed intermittently to ensure that the student retains the skills he has gained. Also, when being used with children and teens, the programs in this book are intended to be used in conjunction with a solid reinforcement system.   (The subject of reinforcement is addressed in Section 4.   There also are helpful hints regarding reinforcement techniques throughout the text.)

To encourage *generalization* (see glossary for definition) of learned skills to real-life situations, it is critical that the skills learned in school or clinic are reinforced consistently at home, and vice-versa. To get the most benefit from the programs in this book, parents, other caregivers, clinicians and teaching staff need to work together as a team. Each team member should be familiar with the programs on which the student is actively working, and should employ like techniques as much as possible. The team should meet on a regular basis to share information and ideas. Taking a flexible approach to implementing the programs (i.e. changing what does not work, capitalizing on what does work, and searching for ways to improve the program) will ensure the best possible results.

The basic principle underlying each of these programs is the tried and true teaching method of breaking tasks down into small, incremental steps (sometimes called "chunking"). Teachers have long known that this system works consistently for both neurotypical students and for those students with neurodevelopmental challenges.   In the case of individuals with AS/HFA and other related developmental problems, it is critical to break into small steps those tasks that are challenging to them. These students do not learn by

---

[4] Saggers, Beth. PhD Thesis Results. Brisbane. 2000.

simple observation or by "osmosis," particularly if the task they are learning involves social-pragmatic skills, the understanding and management of emotions, or organizational skills. Many of these children have experienced repeated failure when presented with more information than they can process in the realm of social/emotional skills. This accumulation of failures is not only damaging to their self-esteem, but also can cause them to withdraw from further attempts to understand information presented to them in these areas. Chunking the material into small, manageable parts allows them to succeed, thus improving their self-esteem and their willingness to tackle increasingly complex social and emotional problems.

In general, the programs within each section have been designed to be taught in the order in which they are presented. However, the user may choose to start with any section or use only selected programs for individual students. Within a program, each step is built upon the skills learned in previous steps. This can be adapted to the needs of the individual student by starting the program at a later step if the student clearly has already acquired the skills covered in preceding steps.

Most of the programs in this book can be used either in individual work with a single student or in a small group setting. However, in many cases it will be most effective and efficient in the long run to spend some time at the beginning of a program working one-on-one with the student. This provides an opportunity to assess his skill levels and assure that he understands the basic concepts to be covered, before having him work in a group.

When working with students on the autism spectrum, it is important to teach them not only those skills that will help them fit in with their current peer group, but also to focus on skills and habits they will need over a lifetime. Keep in mind that once these students have learned to do something one way, it may be very difficult for them to change the way they do it in the future. For example, a student who learns the jargon that his peers use at age nine may still be using that same jargon at age nineteen if he is not helped to learn more age-appropriate language as he gets older. Likewise, a sixteen year-old student may continue to use the same methods of dealing with anger or frustration that were deemed "normal for his age" when he was five years old, but are socially unacceptable for a teenager. Therefore, it is important to plan for the future when teaching social/emotional skills to students with AS/HFA. Keep in mind that it invariably takes much longer for these students to acquire such skills. If the teacher is not careful, the student may end up learning skills that are no longer age-appropriate by the time he finally masters them. In fact, particularly when working with students in mid- to late adolescence, it is wise to make sure that the student's program presents language, manners, and behaviors that will be appropriate when he is an adult.

Appendices B, C and D contain student handouts, templates, and program tracking forms that may be photocopied for individual use by parents or professionals. Appendix A provides a list of additional resources that may be helpful to the reader. Appendix E is a glossary of terms found in this book and in the field of autism in general.

A note on videotaping: Many programs in this book use videotapes of the student as he practices various skills. This allows him to see specifically what he is doing well and gives the teacher a chance to point out those elements of the skill that need more work. Although students may initially act silly or shy when being videotaped, most of them will adapt to the process quite rapidly if the taping is treated in a matter of fact way. Note that giving the student an opportunity to videotape *you* and then discuss your performance as well as his when reviewing the tape will help the student feel less "singled-out." It also will give you the opportunity to model positive ways of self-correction and acceptance of feedback.

Note: For the sake of simplicity and clarity the term *"teacher"* is used in this book to mean *anyone who works with, lives with, instructs, mentors, or cares for an individual with AS/HFA*. This includes parents and professionals. Likewise, the term *"student"* refers to any individual with AS/HFA or a related condition who participates in the learning experiences described in this book. Having said that, I immediately am compelled to apologize for this artificial split between teacher and student. In truth, more often than not it is the person with AS/HFA who has more to teach, and the rest of us who have the most to learn.

(To protect the privacy of the students mentioned in this book, their names and identities have been changed.)

BRIEF OVERVIEW OF ASPERGER'S SYNDROME AND HIGH FUNCTIONING AUTISM

What are Asperger's Syndrome and high functioning autism (AS/HFA)?

Asperger's Syndrome and high functioning autism are two terms that commonly are used to refer to higher-functioning autism, a pervasive, neurodevelopmental disorder of the brain that affects a number of abilities. These include the abilities to communicate, make and keep friends, carry out everyday social interactions, and deal with change. People with these disorders typically have repetitive behaviors and intense or unusual interests in certain subjects. Also, they often have problems with abstract thinking, motor and coordination skills, and recognizing and coping with emotions. Many are plagued with atypical sensitivity to sensory input (i.e. uncomfortable or even painful responses to everyday sounds, lighting, touch, smells, tastes, or textures of certain foods).

It is crucial to recognize that there is no single blueprint for AS/HFA. Each person with one of these conditions is a unique individual, and will have varying degrees of function or dysfunction in the areas listed above. For example, one person with AS/HFA may have extreme problems dealing with change, repetitive behaviors, and moderate difficulties with nonverbal communication. Another person with the same diagnosis may be able to tolerate change fairly well, but may ask frequent, repetitive questions and have severe problems communicating in a socially appropriate way. A common pitfall for people newly acquainted with the diagnosis is to employ a definition of AS/HFA that is stereotyped or too narrow in scope, and to rule out the diagnosis if the individual in question does not fit every aspect of this definition to equal degree. Another common mistake is the use of the criteria for classic, or Kanner's, autism when evaluating a person for possible AS/HFA. By these criteria, for example, if a person has superficially normal speech and language, and average cognitive abilities, they may be disqualified for receiving services even though they *do* meet all the criteria for Asperger's Syndrome.

Are Asperger's Syndrome and high functioning autism the same or different?

A debate currently exists in the field of autism about whether Asperger's Syndrome and high functioning autism are two different entities or are indeed one and the same thing. Good arguments exist on either side of this debate, and although the question is an interesting one, the answer simply is not yet available. Perhaps more importantly, both terms describe conditions that are more alike than different. For this reason, and because the treatment approach to both is the same for the purposes of this book, the two terms are used interchangeably herein, and they are referred to together as Asperger's Syndrome/ high functioning autism, or "AS/HFA."

A Summary of Diagnostic Criteria

As it is much easier to find a clear definition of Asperger's Syndrome than of HFA, the diagnostic criteria for Asperger's Syndrome will be used to cover both terms. However, even within the diagnosis of Asperger's Syndrome, the diagnostic criteria differ somewhat depending on the source. Two of the most widely used sets of diagnostic criteria for AS are those listed in the World Health Organization's ICD 10[5] and the American Psychiatric Association's DSM IV.[6] Two other sets of diagnostic criteria specific to AS include those by

---

[5] World Health Organization (1992). <u>International Classification of Diseases</u>. (10th edition). *Diagnostic Criteria for Research*. Geneva: WHO.

[6] American Psychiatric Association (1994). <u>Diagnostic and Statistical Manual of Mental Disorders</u>. (4th edition). Washington DC: APA.

Gillberg and Gillberg[7] and by Szatmari, Bremner and Nagy.[8] All four of these sources list the following key criteria: 1) problems with developing normal peer relationships, 2) impaired ability to recognize or use appropriate nonverbal communication, and 3) impairments in social interaction, such as problems recognizing and responding to other people's emotions, inappropriate social and emotional behavior, and failure to seek out interaction with peers. With the exception of the Szatmari group, all sources also mention remarkably restricted and intense interests in certain subjects or activities, as well as stereotyped, repetitive routines. There is less agreement on whether or not the syndrome includes problems with language development. Gillberg and Gillberg include delayed speech and language development as present in some individuals with AS, whereas the DSM IV and the ICD 10 require that there be *no* significant general delay in language development. Also, both the Gillberg and Szatmari criteria mention certain oddities of speech and language that may be present, such as pedantic speech, odd prosody, and comprehension problems (including literal, concrete interpretation of metaphorical speech). Finally, both the DSM IV and the ICD 10 require that there be no significant delay in cognitive development in order for the diagnosis of AS to apply.

Asperger's Syndrome and High functioning Autism as Part of a Continuum

It is now widely accepted that autism is not a single entity, but is instead a spectrum of disorders. The features that are present throughout the spectrum include problems with communication and social interaction, and narrow, repetitive patterns of interests, activities, and behavior. At one end of this spectrum are individuals with classic autism, or "Kanner's Syndrome" (based on the work of Leo Kanner, published in 1943). These individuals have

[7] Gillberg, C. and Gillberg, I.C., (1989) "Asperger syndrome – Some epidemiological considerations: A research note", J. Child Psychology and Psychiatry 30, 632-638.

[8] Szatmari, P., Bremner, R. and Nagy, J. (1989) "Asperger's Syndrome: A review of clinical features." Canadian J. Psychiatry 34, 554-560.

more severe problems, including significant cognitive and speech delays. At the other end are those individuals with Asperger's Syndrome (first described in a doctoral thesis by Hans Asperger in 1944), a diagnosis that implies near normal to above-average cognitive abilities and at least superficially normal expressive and receptive language abilities. Some workers in the field use the term "high functioning autism" for those individuals who fit the criteria for classic autism as infants and young children, but later develop some basic social skills, speech that includes complex sentence structure, and intelligence within the normal range.[9]

Pervasive Developmental Disorders

The DSM IV uses "Pervasive Developmental Disorder" (PDD) as an umbrella category under which there are five subcategories. These include Autistic Disorder (i.e., classic autism) and Asperger's Disorder (or Asperger's Syndrome) as described above. Also included are two rare neurodevelopmental disorders, Rett's Disorder and Childhood Disintegrative Disorder, which share some of the features of autistic disorders. Finally, a fifth subcategory, called Pervasive Developmental Disorder–Not Otherwise Specified (PDD-NOS), describes cases in which the child clearly appears to have a pervasive developmental disorder but does not fit neatly into one of the other four subcategories.

Possible Causes of AS/HFA

While it is now clear that autistic disorders are neurologically based, the exact cause or causes are as yet unknown. It is widely accepted that genetic factors play a definite role in the etiology of autism, although which genes are involved and the exact mode of transmission are still under investigation. One theory is that environmental factors such as

---

[9] See Attwood, T. (1998). *Asperger's Syndrome, A Guide for Parents and Professionals*. Jessica Kingsley, p. 150.

exposure to infection or a potentially toxic substance may trigger the activation of the errant gene or genes. (For example, the question of whether some cases of autism may be vaccine-induced is a subject that is currently under intense debate.) An old theory introduced by Bettelheim[10] during the heyday of psychoanalysis in the 1960's, blamed the development of autism on emotionally detached "refrigerator mothers." While this theory has been clearly shown to be wrong, remnants of it unfortunately still emerge from time to time, leaving parents, particularly mothers, to carry the burden of blame for their child's autism.

Other Issues

Theory of Mind

"Theory of mind" is a phrase which means the ability to recognize other people's feelings, thoughts, beliefs, and intentions and to respond to the other person accordingly. All individuals with AS/HFA are lacking in this skill to varying degrees. In practical terms, this inability to "mind-read"[11] means that they have problems understanding why people feel, think, and do the things they do. As a result, they are poor at predicting how another person might respond to them and what the other person is likely to do next in a given situation. Some researchers believe that this poor ability to mind read is the central deficit in autism, and that it is the cause of the severe problems with social interactions found in individuals with AS/HFA.[12]

[10] Bettelheim, B. (1967). *The Empty Fortress: Infantile Autism and the Birth of the Self*. New York: Free Press.
[11] Howlin, P., Baron-Cohen, S. and Hadwin, J. (1999). *Teaching Children with Autism to Mind-Read*. Wiley & Sons. p.2-3.
[12] Baron-Cohen, S., Leslie, A.M., and Frith, U. (1985). "Does the autistic child have a theory of mind?" Cognition, 21. p. 37-46. In Howlin, P. (1998). *Children with Autism and Asperger Syndrome*. Wiley.

Executive Functioning

Many people with AS/HFA have deficits in executive functioning. "Executive functioning" is a technical term that refers to the ability to plan and organize tasks, monitor one's own performance, inhibit inappropriate responses, utilize feedback, and suppress distracting stimuli. Deficits in executive functioning can cause major difficulties in accomplishing school or work assignments and self-help tasks.

Abstract Thinking

The ability to understand abstract concepts is compromised in a large percentage of people with AS/HFA. These individuals often think in very concrete terms, and while they may excel at remembering the minutest details about a subject that interests them, they often fail to understand abstract or metaphorical concepts. Parents often report that their child takes figures of speech literally (for example watching out the window for small pets falling from the sky after someone remarks that it is "raining cats and dogs"). Likewise, their inability to grasp abstract concepts may make it very difficult for them to do school assignments that require them to come up with the main idea of a story or to compare and contrast two events.

Recognizing and Coping with Emotions

To varying degrees, many people with AS/HFA have trouble with identifying, quantifying, expressing, and controlling their emotions. Some may appear on the surface to have few emotions because they don't show those emotions in the same way a neurotypical person might show them. In contrast, others may express a higher degree of emotion than they actually feel. For example, annoyance might be expressed as fury, or mildly happy might be expressed as overjoyed.

Stress

As a result of the pervasive nature of their deficits, many individuals with AS/HFA are under a great deal of stress during most of their waking hours. In light of their struggle to understand even the most elementary social and communication skills, to cope with problems with planning and organizing, and to deal with major difficulties understanding emotions and abstract concepts, it is easy to appreciate why many of these individuals are chronically stressed. In fact, it is truly remarkable when someone with AS/HFA does *not* suffer from chronic, high-level stress. It is also easy to understand why children with AS/HFA sometimes develop problem behaviors (such as acting out) in response to that stress.

SECTION ONE

RECOGNIZING AND COPING
WITH ONE'S
OWN EMOTIONS

INTRODUCTION

Recognizing and Coping with One's Own Emotions

The world of emotions can be puzzling and often overwhelming to individuals with AS/ HFA. They often have difficulties recognizing and labeling their own emotions effectively. Furthermore, they may not understand that there are varying degrees of feeling within a particular emotion. They may appear to be overly emotional because they express their feelings in an all-on or all-off fashion; the slightest irritation comes out as rage and the mildest contentment comes out as elation. On the other hand, they may appear to be uncaring or lacking in emotion because they fail to express their feelings appropriately. Because emotions are not logical and do not lend themselves to straightforward, consistent definitions and rules, people with AS/HFA may find feelings extremely confusing and even frightening. This fear can lead them to over-react or under-react to their feelings. For example, a child who one moment is overjoyed to receive a long-wished-for present, may in the next instant dissolve into tears because her own feelings of happiness frightened and overwhelmed her. With such hurdles to face, it is not surprising that people with AS/HFA often find it very difficult indeed to understand and cope with emotions.

Stress is a feeling with which most people with AS/HFA are all too familiar. The difficulties that many of them face on a daily basis trying to communicate effectively, fit in socially, and navigate their own and other people's emotions are enough to cause an extraordinary degree of stress in many of these individuals. This stress can take a huge toll on the individual's emotional and physical health and can wreak havoc on his ability to learn, play, and enjoy life. It can also take a huge secondary toll on those who live and work with that individual. For these reasons, it is critical that stress management be given top priority when planning programs for people with AS/HFA.

The goals of this section are to 1) teach students to better recognize, label, and quantify their own feelings, 2) help them learn positive ways of dealing with their emotions, and 3) provide them with a reliable set of tools for coping with stress.[13]

---

[13] Several programs in this section were developed in collaboration with Dr. Tony Attwood. In particular, the "happy book" project in Program One was adapted from Dr. Attwood's work with his generous permission. Dr. Attwood also contributed several of the ideas for labeling, quantifying, and expressing emotions found in Programs Two and Three, as well as the design and use of the stress thermometer in Program Five.

PROGRAM 1

RECOGNIZING A SIMPLE EMOTION
REDIRECTING NEGATIVE THOUGHTS TO POSITIVE THOUGHTS

INTRODUCTION

Many people with AS/HFA are much more comfortable in the cut-and-dried world of facts and logic than they are in the nebulous world of emotions. There are few rules to aid one in defining emotions, and words invariably fall miserably short of describing all of the fine shades and subtleties within a particular emotion. It is no small wonder that these individuals, who rely so heavily on rules and definitions to understand the world, may find that emotions are simply too difficult to comprehend, and that it is much easier to ignore the subject altogether. They may not tell loved ones "I love you," or explain when they are feeling confused, afraid, sad, or lonely. Unfortunately, this may lead others to think that the person with AS/HFA lacks those feelings. However, in most cases individuals with AS/HFA have the same range and depth of feelings as do the rest of us and would willingly share their emotions if they understood them better. This program introduces the concept of identifying one's own feelings, starting with the emotion of happiness. (Happiness is presented first because it is a simple and positive emotion.) In addition, the student uses a "pleasures" book and cue cards as a set of visual cues to trigger happier thoughts or direct him to mood-lifting activities.

GOALS

The goals of this program are to:

1. Introduce the concept of identifying and labeling one's own emotions, starting with the simple emotion of happiness.

2. Introduce the concept of redirecting negative thoughts to positive thoughts as a way to cheer oneself up.

3. Introduce the concept of directing oneself to a calming or mood-lifting activity when stressed.

INSTRUCTIONS

Step One: Recognizing happy feelings.

First, help the student to create a scrapbook (or "Pleasures Book") by collecting and entering into the book photos, mementos and diary entries of events or things that make her happy. Items for the scrapbook may vary from written descriptions of happy events to the box label of a favorite game, photos of a special friend, or the lyrics of a special song. More entries can be added to the book at any time.

Step Two: Redirecting negative thoughts to positive thoughts.

Discuss with the student that a common way people deal with sadness or loneliness is to redirect their thinking to something that makes them happy. Then encourage her to use her Pleasures Book to help her redirect her own thoughts when she feels "down." Make sure the book is accessible both at home and at school, and cue her to look through the book at times when she is feeling unhappy. Sometimes, just looking at the entries in her book may be enough to lift her mood. At other times, the entries may cue her to an activity that will help her feel better (such as playing a computer game, taking a warm bath, listening to her favorite music, or going for a walk).

Step Three: Using favorite activities to calm down.

The student and teacher may wish to create cue cards taken from the items in her Pleasures Book. The cue cards can be laminated and carried around in the student's pocket so that she can refer to them for redirection when she is feeling down. Certain cue cards may also be used to unobtrusively communicate to the teacher that the student needs a break. A technique that has been used successfully in many classrooms is *"break time"*: the student hands the teacher a cue card to indicate that she is stressed and is going to a pre-arranged, alternate place for a few minutes until she calms down. For example, the student gives the teacher one of her cue cards showing a computer to indicate that she is stressed and is going to work in the computer lab for a limited time. (Note: This strategy is intended for stress management and is not intended as a means of avoiding non-preferred activities. See *page 38* for more information on break time.)

PROGRAM 2

RECOGNIZING AND LABELING MORE EMOTIONS
LINKING NONVERBAL CLUES TO EMOTIONS

INTRODUCTION

Paul was five years old before he learned to smile. His parents had been told that Paul had atypical attention deficit disorder, but they suspected there was more to it than that. Indeed, they later found out that their son had Asperger's Syndrome. His face was a blank slate most of the time, except when he was angry. He threw temper tantrums several times a day that the neighbors two blocks away could hear. Paul did not smile; his face and body posture rarely showed worry, sadness, pride, or any of the other emotions that five-year-old boys typically feel, even when there was more than enough reason for him to have such feelings. One day his mother grew weary of waiting for her boy to smile and she took things into her own hands. She sat Paul down and showed him pictures of people with smiles, and others with worried, sad, proud, and silly expressions. Then she made the same expressions with her own face and asked her son to copy her expressions. When he had trouble, she held up a mirror for him and pointed out how he needed to change the position of his lips or eyebrows, or the way he held his body. They did the same thing day after day until Paul could model, without help, the emotions his mother asked him to show her. As Paul learned how to do this, he also learned the words for the emotions he had been feeling all along. Little by little, he began to tell people how he felt. But the best part of all, his mother thought, was that now he smiled.

The above story about Paul and his mother is a common one. Often parents realize that their child with AS/HFA needs more specific instruction than do other children in recognizing and expressing their own feelings. By following their instincts, many parents teach their child how to do so. It is not unusual to find parents who have patiently taught their son or daughter with AS/HFA to make eye contact, smile, and give words to their feelings, even before they knew their child's diagnosis. However, even children who have received this help often will benefit from further work in this area. In particular, explicitly teaching these students about the messages conveyed by body language, facial expression, and tone of voice gives them a concrete set of external signals (or "clues") that they can use to express their feelings. In later programs, the student will be shown how to use these same signals to help decipher what other people may be feeling.

GOALS

The goals of this program are to:

1. Expand the student's ability to recognize and label his own positive and negative emotions.
2. Introduce nonverbal, tone of voice and situational clues to feelings.

INSTRUCTIONS

(An empty photo album and access to a Polaroid camera, video camera and television will be needed for this project.)

Step One: Identify and label emotions using photographs.

Using a Polaroid camera, take candid photos of the student displaying a variety of naturally occurring emotions, both positive and negative, in as many environments as possible (parents, aid and/or teacher should all take part in this project, if possible). Immediately after taking a photo (or as soon as the student is calm enough), help him label his emotion. To help expand the student's "emotional vocabulary," let him choose from the list of emotions and related terms at the end of this program. *(See figure 2a, page 13. Also, a student copy is included in Appendix B.)* Alternatively, if he has a wide vocabulary, ask him to come up with the most precise word he can think of to label the emotion. Redirect to a more accurate label if necessary. Have the student glue or tape the photo into the album and label the photo with the name of the emotion. *(See example on page 14, figure 2b.)*

Step Two: Identify and label nonverbal clues and situational clues using photographs. [14]

Using the photographs from Step One, help the student identify the nonverbal clues found in his facial expression and body language that convey what he is feeling to observers. Also, ask him to look for situational clues that have been captured in the photograph (such as other students who may have been engaging him in some way, a workman in the background, a spill on the floor, a photocopy machine in the background, etc.) Have him label the photograph with the nonverbal and situational clues he has found in the photograph. *(See figure 2b.)*

Step Three: Identify and label emotions and related nonverbal, tone of voice, and situational clues using role-play.

Using the skills gained in Steps One and Two, role-play different emotions and their corresponding nonverbal, tone of voice, and situational clues. Start by working one-on-one with the student, taking turns doing the role-play, and

---

[14] See also Program 8. This program addresses recognizing situational and nonverbal clues in *other* people.

guessing the emotion. "Freeze the action" to point out facial expression, body language, tone of voice, and situational clues. The student may find it helpful to use a mirror to work on his facial expression and body language. When the student is competent in this activity (this may require anywhere from a few days to several weeks, depending on the skill level of the student), repeat the role-play game in a small group setting. Continue to practice this skill until mastered. [15]

Step Four: Identify and label emotions and nonverbal, tone of voice,[16] and situational clues using videos.

Videotape the student showing different naturally occurring emotions in various settings. Again, it will work best if parents and the teacher or aide take part in this program. Freeze the tape to show the emotion, and help the student to label it appropriately. Encourage the student to assign the most specific label possible to the emotion. He may refer to the list of emotions (*figure 2a*) if needed. Redirect to a more accurate label if necessary. Also, work with the student to identify the nonverbal clues (body language and facial expression), tone of voice clues, and situational clues that correspond to the emotions he has identified. Review the role of nonverbal clues and how they relate important messages to others about our moods and feelings. Also review how situational clues can help an observer guess what the other person may be thinking and feeling. To keep this activity fun and to ease pressure on the student to "perform," consider allowing the student to videotape you as you demonstrate emotions. When reviewing the tape with the student, make sure you ask for his feedback on how *you* did.

---

[15] For the purposes of this book, mastery of a task or skill is defined as that point at which the student can perform the task correctly in nine out of ten trials.

[16] See also Program 12. This program addresses the recognition and use of tone of voice clues.

Step Five: Follow-up

After completing this project, continue to help the student label his emotions, both in and out of school. Restate the emotion to him, as well as his comments on why he feels that way. For example, if Jason says that he feels angry because John never returned the money he borrowed, state back to Jason, "I can see that you are feeling angry because John hasn't paid you back yet." Try to avoid passing judgment. This technique of non-judgmentally reflecting back what the student says about his feelings and their causes not only will reinforce his attempts to talk about his feelings, but it also can be a very effective method of stress reduction. (*See Program 5, page 33 for more information about stress reduction techniques.*) "Talking it over" with a sympathetic listener is a skill which students with AS/HFA often do not acquire without training in how to do so.

List of Emotions

AFRAID

Afraid
Anxious/Worried
Cautious
Frightened
Terrified
Uncertain

ANGRY

Angry
Enraged
Exasperated
Frustrated
Irritated

CONFIDENT

Confident
Courageous
Optimistic
Smug

CONFUSED

Confused
Perplexed
Puzzled

CURIOUS

Curious
Fascinated
Interested

HAPPY

Amused
Blissful
Contented
Ecstatic
Enthusiastic
Excited
Happy
Proud
Relieved
Satisfied
Silly

MISCELLANEOUS EMOTIONS

Bashful
Bored
Disgusted/Grossed out
Embarrassed/Sheepish
Guilty
Hopeful
Indifferent
Innocent
Jealous/ Envious
Love struck
Pleading
Self-conscious
Shocked
Shy

MENTAL STATE OF BEING

Arrogant/Vain
Bored
Concentrating
Determined
Disapproving
Disbelieving
Mischievous
Stubborn
Thoughtful

PHYSICAL STATE OF BEING

Cold
Exhausted
Hot
Miserable
Nauseated/Ill
Relaxed
Sleepy

SAD

Depressed
Disappointed
Grieving
Hurt
Lonely
Sorry
Sad

Figure 2a. List of emotions for use with Program 2. Note that this is a fairly lengthy list. The student is not expected to learn or use every item on it. Rather, the list is intended to be used as a reference from which the student and/or teacher can choose a term that best fits a particular emotion.

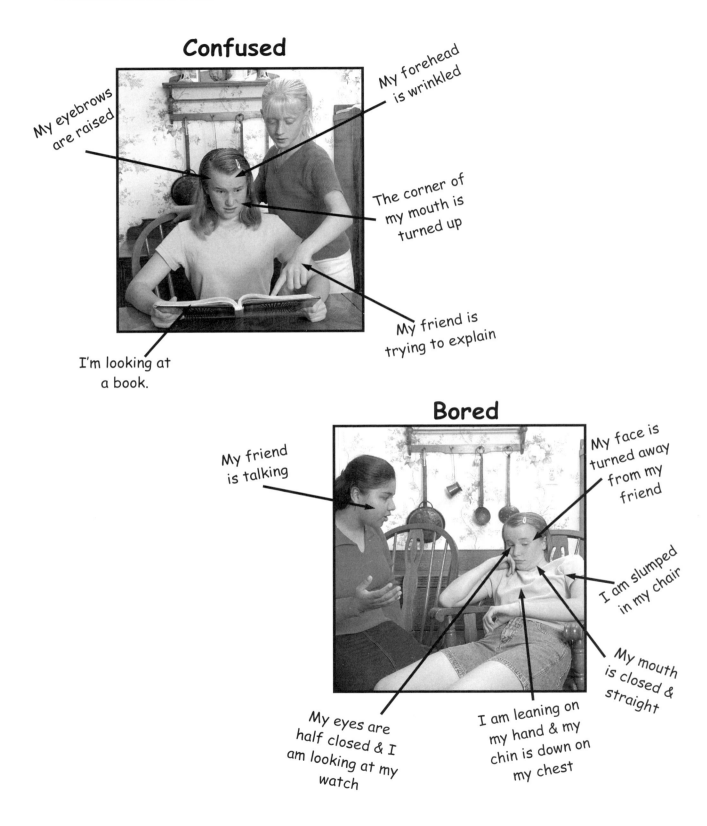

Figure 2b. An example of a page from a student's emotions photograph album, with the nonverbal and situational clues labeled.

Photos by Jim DeWeese

Overjoyed

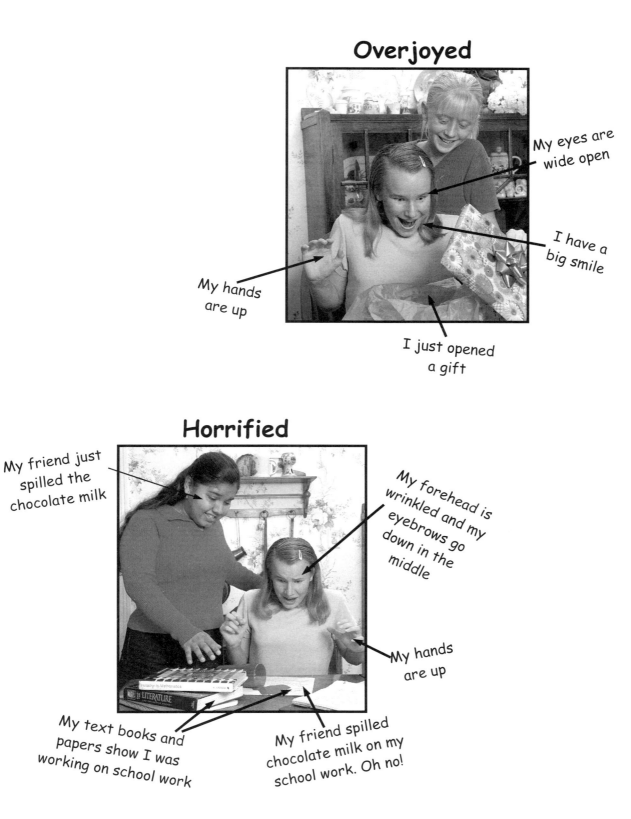

My eyes are wide open

I have a big smile

My hands are up

I just opened a gift

Horrified

My friend just spilled the chocolate milk

My forehead is wrinkled and my eyebrows go down in the middle

My hands are up

My text books and papers show I was working on school work

My friend spilled chocolate milk on my school work. Oh no!

PROGRAM 3

EXPRESSING EMOTIONS. QUANTIFYING EMOTIONS ON A CONTINUUM.

INTRODUCTION

Individuals with AS, HFA and related disorders often lack the ability to recognize and accurately express the *level* of their feelings. They may have trouble both *assigning different levels of intensity* to their feelings and *expressing these varying levels of intensity* in their use of words and nonverbal clues. This can lead them to communicate their emotions in a full-on or full-off fashion. For example, John, an eleven-year-old student with HFA, tended to react with what appeared to be exaggerated anger over relatively small incidents. This was partly due to his level of background stress at those moments, as well as to other contributing factors. However, John also responded in an exaggerated fashion because he did not have the tools to accurately quantify or express varying levels of emotions. In these situations, John may have been feeling only somewhat frustrated but erroneously expressed full-fledged anger instead. This state of affairs caused frequent difficulties for both John and the people around him.

In addition to problems with quantifying and expressing emotions, people with AS/ HFA may not know how to handle intense emotions, regardless of whether those emotions are negative *or positive.* Danielle, a thirteen-year-old girl with HFA, puzzled both parents and teachers when she would dissolve into tears five minutes after being extremely excited or pleased over a positive event in her life. Upon consultation with an experienced therapist, both Danielle and the people who supported her came to understand that experiencing any kind of intense emotion, be it negative or positive, was stressful to her. With time, Danielle learned to recognize when her feelings were approaching a high intensity, and to employ stress management techniques at such times. (See Program 5, *page 33* for more information on stress management skills.)

In this program the student will construct an Anger Thermometer and a set of "emotions scales" to help him recognize, quantify, and express differing levels of anger and other emotions.

GOALS

The goals of this program are to:

1. Help the student understand that there are *degrees* of feeling within one emotion.

2. Assist the student with assigning appropriate values to different degrees of anger.

3. Help the student to accurately express her feelings through her use of words and nonverbal clues.

4. Help the student recognize and manage her reactions to intense emotions.

INSTRUCTIONS

Step One: Construct an Anger Thermometer.

Refer to the example of a completed Anger Thermometer before starting this step (*see figure 3a, page 21*). Using the Anger Thermometer template found in

Appendix C, help the student label the thermometer on the left side with words that express different levels of anger. For example, she might choose to label a zero as "calm", a four as "irritated" and a ten as "furious" or "enraged". Some students enjoy adding words that relate to a special interest. For example, if the student is fascinated with weather, she might choose to label a zero as "cool and breezy" and a ten as a "class five tornado" or "cyclone." In addition, the student may wish to add colors of her choice to represent different levels of anger (e.g., white for calm, red for furious, etc.)

Step Two: Quantify *angry emotions* using the Anger Thermometer. Use discussion, role-play, and videotaping to correct errors in labeling and expressing varying levels of anger.

When the student feels angry, direct her to decide where this level of anger fits on the Anger Thermometer. Wait until she has calmed down if necessary, but try to have her do this as soon after the incident as possible. Have her write a brief description (one to five words) of the situation that caused her anger on a small slip of paper (Post-It page tabs work well), and attach it to the right side of the thermometer as a visual cue. Leave several of the tabs on at a time to help her visualize how different situations can cause different levels of anger. As the student becomes familiar with using this program, cue her to *visualize* the Anger Thermometer at times when it is not available to look at directly.

Sometimes a child with AS/HFA will react to a situation with words, tone of voice clues, and/or nonverbal clues that clearly misrepresent her *actual* level of emotion. If this occurs, help her choose words from her Anger Thermometer that better express her actual level of anger. Then, coach her in the use of body language, facial expression, and tone and volume of voice that better match her true level of anger. (See the preceding program for more help with using nonverbal clues.) It can be very helpful to role-play the situation that caused the anger as soon after the incident as possible. First, help the student find her actual level of anger on the Anger Thermometer. Next, re-enact for the student her original words, tone of voice, and nonverbal clues, and then act out a version that more accurately reflects her actual level of anger. Then have the student enact both versions. You may need to work on one element at a time. For example, you might address the student's choice of words, and then go over tone of voice and nonverbal clues separately. It can help to have the student look in a mirror to help her correct errors in facial expression and body language. Also, when possible try videotaping the sessions and playing them back to allow the student to see and hear her own nonverbal clues, words, and tone of voice.

Step Three: Quantify *other emotions*. Play *emotions charades*.

Using the **Emotions Scales** template found in Appendix C, have the student label and color the scales with her choice of words and colors. As in the previous program, the student may enjoy using words that relate to one of her special interests. *(See example on page 22, figure 3b.)*

Play **emotions charades**. Using terms from the student's Emotions Scales or from the list of emotions and related terms in Program 2 *(page 8)*, write a different emotion and a number from one to ten to represent a level of that emotion on each of several slips of paper. Take turns drawing one of the slips of paper from a container and acting out the emotion, while the other person or people present guess which emotion and level of that emotion is being portrayed. The game can be played by using only nonverbal clues, or alternatively by having the actor use words and tone of voice clues as well. If you have access to a drama teacher, having him or her help coach the students in using body language, facial expression, and tone of voice clues can help immensely. Start with simple emotions and progress to more difficult ones as the student gains skill. This game can be played in pairs or in small groups. If desired, it also can be played by competing teams in the style of traditional charades.

Step Four: Use videotapes to help the student label and quantify his or her own emotions.

Review the videotapes from Step Four of Program 2 with the student. Freeze the tape at various points and ask her to rank the level of each emotion using her Emotions Scales. Elicit help from the other students if the activity is being done in a small group setting.

Step Five: Label and quantify emotions in real life situations.

Watch for various emotions displayed by the student in different environments. When possible, briefly stop the student and help her label and quantify the level of her feeling on the appropriate scale. Be sure to call attention to positive emotions at least as frequently as to negative emotions.

ANGER THERMOMETER

For: _Sam F._

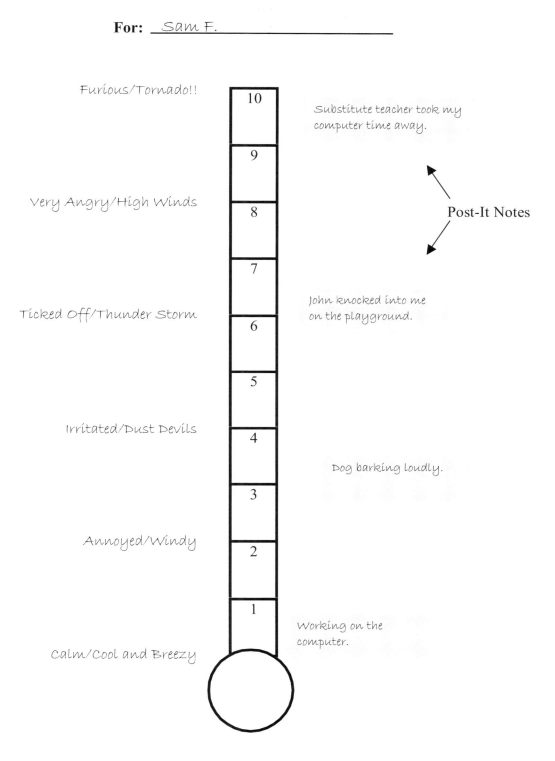

Furious/Tornado!!

Substitute teacher took my computer time away.

Post-It Notes

Very Angry/High Winds

Ticked Off/Thunder Storm

John knocked into me on the playground.

Irritated/Dust Devils

Dog barking loudly.

Annoyed/Windy

Working on the computer.

Calm/Cool and Breezy

Figure 3a. Example of a completed Anger Thermometer. The student has chosen her own set of words to match different levels of anger. Next, with the teacher's help, she has recorded several different events on post-it notes & has placed them on the thermometer to match her level of anger. (Note: the student may also wish to color each section of the thermometer a different color to represent her anger levels.)

EMOTIONS SCALES

For: Kim S.

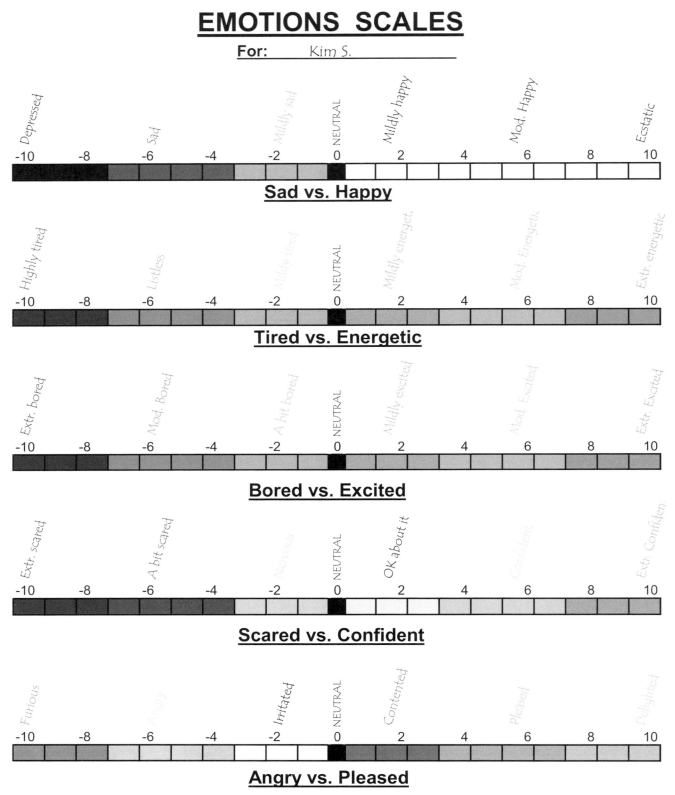

Figure 3b. An example of completed emotions scales. The scales show 5 different groups of emotions, each on a continuum. The student has labeled the scales with her own choice of words and colors, which correspond to the various emotions.

PROGRAM 4

STRESS 1 – DATA COLLECTION; RECOGNIZING STRESS SIGNALS AND CAUSES AND EFFECTS OF STRESS

INTRODUCTION

Each person has his own set of internal and external signals that occur when he is stressed. With age and maturity, most people recognize those signals, can read their own stress levels fairly accurately, and have learned a variety of ways to cope with stress. However, many people with AS/HFA do not develop these skills without help. Individuals with these diagnoses often misread their own stress signals, responding to their stress in ineffective and even detrimental ways. Particularly in children and teens with AS/HFA, the stress may manifest itself as problem behaviors. Unfortunately, this often leads parents and professionals to a *reactive* approach to the problem behavior, instead of a *proactive* approach to the stress itself. Teachers and caregivers may find themselves unwillingly caught in a frustrating cycle: they react to problem behaviors by imposing negative consequences, which in turn often adds to the student's stress level and poor self-esteem, thereby causing more stress and more negative behaviors, and so on.

Ethan, a thirteen-year-old boy with HFA, had daily "blow-ups" which seemed to occur out of the blue for no apparent reason. His behavior at such times included yelling at other students and teachers and occasionally hitting or shoving peers. A behavior program was put into place in which natural consequences were delivered for such behaviors. In addition, he was reinforced when he avoided problem behaviors for a set amount of time. This program, however, was only marginally successful.

The parents and school staff began to carefully track Ethan's behavior throughout the day. They looked for verbal and nonverbal clues and physical symptoms that indicated that Ethan's stress level was rising, and ranked these signals as corresponding to mild, moderate, and high levels of stress. During this program, the people working with Ethan also collected data on common triggers and underlying or "hidden" stressors. They found, for example, that being asked to stop a task before it was finished, or not having his own assigned seat in the classroom, were previously unrecognized stressors that could lead to an unexplained blow up. The data collected was used in subsequent programs to help Ethan recognize his own stress signals, rank his level of stress, and employ different stress reduction techniques according to his level of stress. In addition, his parents and teachers were able to make changes in Ethan's surroundings to reduce environmental stressors. In time, Ethan's problem behaviors began to decrease, both in magnitude and frequency.

The purpose of this program is to collect and summarize data about the student's stress. (The summarized data will be used in three subsequent programs, which develop an individualized approach to stress recognition and management.) In the *first step* of this program, teachers and parents collect the following data for each stressful event: the precipitating event (or trigger), underlying stressors and related emotions, the level of stress, and the outcome of the event. They also collect the student's stress signals, including verbal and nonverbal clues observed by teachers and parents, and physical symptoms of stress as reported by the student. In the *second step*, the teacher will analyze the data and create two summary charts: the first chart will correlate the student's stress level with his verbal and nonverbal stress signals and stress symptoms. This chart subsequently will be used in Programs 5 and 6. The second chart will correlate the student's stress level with underlying stressors and triggers. This chart will be used later in Programs 6 and 7.

GOALS

The purpose of this program is to collect and analyze data regarding stress in the individual student. This information will be used in the three subsequent programs on stress recognition and management. More specifically, the goals of this program are to:

1. Identify the common causes and effects of stress in the individual student, including:
   - underlying or hidden stressors
   - triggering events
   - outcomes

2. Identify stress signals commonly manifested by the student, including:
   - *outward signs*: body language, facial expression, and verbal clues
   - *physical symptoms*: e.g., increased heart rate, sweating, churning stomach, etc.

INSTRUCTIONS

Step One: Collect data and record on stress tracking form.

(See examples on pages 29-30, figures 4a and 4b. Also, a blank template can be found in Appendix C.)

Preparation

1. Students, teachers, aides, and parents should participate in this step to ensure that enough data is collected to identify recurring patterns of stress across environments. It will be helpful for the staff to have one copy of the tracking form at school and for the parents to have a separate copy for home and other environments.

2. The nature of this program requires that the student and the teacher be ready to stop other activities mid-stream in order to collect and record data *while* the student is experiencing stress (or as soon thereafter as possible). While it can be a challenging task to interrupt an activity in order to collect data, it clearly is a more effective approach than asking the student to recall specific information at a later time. The exception to this is when a student is out of control. *In such cases, wait until the student is completely calm before asking him for input.*

3. Prepare the student, in advance, by letting him know that you may be interrupting his activities at times when you notice he is becoming stressed. At those times you will be asking him questions to help you complete his stress tracking form. Explain that the reason for collecting this information is to find out what situations are stressful for him, and what can be done to reduce his stress. During the program, be sure to reinforce the student for giving his input, as this may be quite a difficult thing for him to do.

Data collection

Plan to spend approximately one to two weeks collecting data. Complete the stress tracking forms, using as many forms as needed. ***For each entry, record the following information:***

1. **The** *trigger* (the precipitating event immediately preceding an undesirable behavior). *Determined by student or teacher report.*

2. ***Underlying or hidden stressors* and related emotions** (such as fatigue, anger, confusion, sadness, or a negative event that occurred earlier in the day, etc.) *Determined by student and teacher investigation.*

In the majority of cases of unexplained negative behaviors in students with AS/HFA, there is an underlying or hidden stressor that sets the student up to lose control the next time something goes even a little wrong. Unfortunately, these underlying stressors often are not obvious and it may be necessary to do some detective work to solve the puzzle. For example, the underlying stress may have been caused by a minor change in routine or he may have been teased on the bus earlier that day. Similarly, the student may be stressed by sitting near a noisy, high traffic flow area in the classroom. Missing a hidden or underlying stressor can lead to misunderstanding and mismanagement of the student's behavior. Therefore, in cases where the underlying stressors are not obvious, it is important to take extra time to search for them.

3. **Student's nonverbal and verbal** *stress signals* (body language, facial expression, tone of voice & verbal clues). *Determined by teacher observations.*

Examples of stress signals might include voice changes (e.g., higher-pitched, more rapid or tighter sounding speech), clenched jaw or fists, pacing, asking repetitive questions, and so on. The stress signals vary with each student, but often follow a set pattern in a particular student. Pay special attention to subtle, early signs of stress because your ultimate goal is to teach the student to catch his own stress in its early phases. Once the student is able to recognize his stress early on, it will be much easier for him to use stress management techniques to calm down and avoid outbursts and other problem behaviors.

4. *Physical symptoms* of stress (e.g., sweaty palms, increased heart rate, etc.) *Determined by student.*

During stressful events, ask the student what physical symptoms he is experiencing, such as clenched teeth or fists, increased heart rate, palpitations, sweaty palms, etc.

5. *Stress level* (low, moderate or high). *Determined by student and teacher observation.*

Rank the student's level of stress using your own observations and the student's input. Record the level as mild, moderate, or high.

6. *Outcome* of the incident. *Determined by teacher observation.*

Record the student's specific actions and the immediate consequences.

Step Two: Analyze and condense data. Complete summary charts. *(See examples on pages 31 and 32, figures 4c and 4d. Also, blank templates can be found in Appendix C.)*

Analyze the data from Steps One and Two to identify those stress signals, physical symptoms, underlying stressors, and triggers that occur most frequently. Record this information on the two summary charts as indicated.

Stress Tracking Chart

Home/**School**   Student: __Scott W.__

Date & Time	Precipitating event (trigger)	Underlying or "hidden" stressor(s) & related emotions	Stress signals		Stress level: -Low -Moderate -High	Outcome
			Body language, facial expressions & verbal clues (as observed)	Physical symptoms (by student report)		
4/1/00 9:30 am	Ian sat in Scott's usual chair during art class	Anxiety due to schedule changes that week	Playing with hair Humming	Not obtainable	Moderate	Shoved Ian → Sent to Principal
4/2/00 10:10 am	Joe borrowed Scott's pencil & then lost it	Angry because he was teased on the school bus that morning	Jaws & teeth clenched Squinting	Muscles tense Increased heart rate	High	Shouted swear word Threw homework on floor → Sent to principal
4/5/00 2:30 pm	Scott didn't finish math problems before class ended	Frustrated, unable to concentrate due to noise from photocopy machine in next room.	Humming Tapping on desk Playing with hair	Headache Stomach ache	Moderate	Shouted at teacher that he "had to finish" → Points taken off math grade
4/6/00 1:30 pm	Bill accidentally bumped into Scott on playground at lunch	On playground for entire lunchtime. Difficulty joining in with other kids. Frustrated, lonely.	Humming Glaring	Not obtainable	Moderate	Yelled at Bill and complained to playground aid → No further consequences
4/7/00 10:05 am	Teacher gently corrected Scott's verbal answer in class.	Some other students had giggled last period when Scott was reading report in front of class	Teeth & fists clenched Squinting Talking loud and fast	Face hot Heart pounding Breathing fast	High	Fumed out of room yelling, "I don't like any of you!" → Discussion with teacher
4/8/00 3:15 pm	Joe slapped Scott on the back as a nice "hello" in hall	Group art project in afternoon	Hunched over	Headache Muscles tense Stomach ache	Low	Scowled at other student → No further consequences
4/9/00 12:30 pm	Working on grammar assignment	Photocopy machine in next room	Glazed expression Quiet	Shoulder muscles tense Mild headache	Low	Unable to focus on work

Figure 4a: Example of a Stress Tracking Chart completed by school staff. Consistent & recurrent entries will be listed on the Stress Summary Charts (see Fig 4c & 4d, pg 31-32).

Stress Tracking Chart

(Home)/School   Student: __Scott W.__

Date & Time	Precipitating Event (trigger)	Underlying or "hidden" stressor(s) & related emotions	Stress signals		Stress level: -Low -Moderate -High	Outcome
			Body language, facial expressions & verbal clues (as observed)	Physical symptoms (by student report)		
5/2/00 3:40 pm	Mom asked Scott to show her his homework assignments.	Got teased on the afternoon bus.	Teeth and fists clenched Squinting Pacing	Muscles very tense Breathing fast	High	Shouted, "No, I'm not going to do it!" Then ran out, slamming door. → Sent to his room.
5/3/00 4:55 pm	Al (Scott's brother) accidentally bumped into Scott going to the kitchen.	Family dog had been barking all afternoon at the construction workers at the neighbor's house.	Humming Glaring at family members	Muscles tense Stomach ache	Moderate	Shouted at and shoved brother. → Mother intervened, separating the two boys.
5/5/00 7:35 pm	Zipper on Scott's jacket got caught in the jacket lining.	Family friends had been over for dinner. Worked very hard at avoiding socially inappropriate topics.	Humming Playing with hair	Not obtainable	Moderate	Shouted, "I hate this jacket!" and shoved nearby chair. → Sent to room (with jacket on).
4/6/00 4:40 pm	Scott saw two other boys on his little league team whispering as he walked by.	Had been followed and teased by a group of kids on his way to the ballpark.	Teeth and fists clenched Squinting Pacing	Muscles very tense Sweaty palms Stomach ache	High	Ran to coach in tears, saying, "Everybody hates me—I quit!" → Sent to sidelines. Comforted by teammate's mother.
4/7/00 7:50 pm	Haley, Scott's sister asked to borrow his CD player.	Furniture in living room had been rearranged	Whining voice Hunched over posture	Shoulder muscles tense	Low	Mumbled, "Go away." Then ignored his sister. → Discussion with father.
4/8/00 4:10 pm	Mom asked Scott to start his social studies homework.	Has been working in school on two very challenging subjects on daily basis. No breaks provided. Trouble keeping up with work.	Humming Playing with hair	Muscles tense Headache Stomach ache	Moderate	Slumped over. "I'm so stupid I might as well die." Rebuffed encouragement from mom. Unable to start homework. →Went to quiet room to read book and unwind.
4/9/00 7:45 am	Mom was a bit cross when rushing Scott to get ready.	Slept poorly last night.	Whining voice Hunched over posture	Shoulder muscles tense Mild headache	Low	Irritable and abrupt all morning. Complained that everyone always picks on him.

Figure 4b. Example of a Stress Tracking Chart completed by parents. Consistent & recurrent entries will be listed on the two Stress Summary Charts (see Fig. 4c & 4d, pages 31-32.)

Summary of Stress Signals

Student: _____ _Scott W_

	Low stress	Moderate stress	High stress
Verbal & nonverbal clues Body language, facial expressions & verbal clues (As observed by others. Data from Stress Tracking Charts)	Hunched over posture Quiet, high-pitched voice Glazed expression	Humming Playing with hair Glares Tapping fingers on desk	Teeth clenched Fists clenched Squinting Talks loud & fast Pacing
Physical symptoms (As reported by student. Data from Stress Tracking Charts)	Shoulder muscles tense Mild headache	Muscles tense generally Stomach ache Headache	Muscles very tense Stomach ache Sweaty palms Breathing very fast Increased heart rate Face hot

Figure 4c. An example of a completed Summary of Stress Signals chart. This data is used to fill in the left side of the Stress Thermometer (*see Figure 5d, page 47*).

Summary of Common Stressors

Student: _____ *Scott W.*

	Low stress	**Moderate stress**	**High stress**
Common stressors	Environmental change at home (furniture rearranged) Lack of sleep Group art project (with social demands) Photocopy machine noise in background	When expected to take part in lengthy social functions or stay on playground Teased by other kids Work overload at school (2 hard subjects back to back without a break) Dog barking (or loud background noises)	Teased by other kids on bus Teased by other kids on way to ballpark Other children laughed while Scott gave oral report (not necessarily at him)

Figure 4d. An example of a completed Summary of Common Stressors chart. This data is used in Program 6: Stress Prevention (see page 48).

PROGRAM 5

STRESS II - SELF-MONITORING STRESS LEVELS; RELAXATION STRATEGIES

INTRODUCTION

Stress is an innate part of human existence. Some people are naturally good at relaxing and letting things roll off their shoulders. For others, this is more of a challenge; they need to make a conscious effort to learn to relax under stress. This is especially true for many people with AS/HFA and related diagnoses. Many of them are under an enormous amount of stress for most of their waking hours. To illustrate, imagine finding yourself on another planet where you understand only half of the words spoken by everyone else. You strain to catch the meaning of each and every conversation. Long before the end of the day you reach "system overload," only to have to keep on trying in order to just survive. This is the daily experience of most people with AS/HFA. When a person with AS/HFA tries, yet fails, to understand the unspoken, nonverbal nuances that carry so much meaning in human interactions, when she is faced with emotions that confuse her, and when she cannot predict the effect her words and actions will have on other people, she must feel like a person dropped off on a strange planet. At times it must seem like she will never catch up with this mysterious, unattainable world of mind reading and social language that seems to come so easily to everyone else.

The individual with AS/HFA most often faces other challenges as well. She may have a sensory system that responds with pain to certain types of sounds and touch, or that causes various tastes and smells to sicken her. She may struggle with focusing, attending, learning disabilities, or compulsions that at times seem to control her behavior. She is apt to have trouble understanding and controlling her own feelings. Compounding this, she is likely to be misunderstood, targeted, and disliked because she is different. These conditions, among others, virtually assure that a person with AS/HFA will be significantly stressed a great deal of the time.

This same individual is likely to have very little inherent ability to deal with stress, or even *recognize* her own signs of stress. The latter is particularly true at lower levels of stress. However, it is exactly at these lower levels that we need to help our students "catch" their stress, because as stress levels build, so does the risk of a negative outcome. If the student learns to recognize her stress at the lowest level possible, she will have a much easier time dealing with it (and so, of course, will the people around her).

Ethan was a thirteen-year-old boy with Asperger's Syndrome. From the time he was an infant, he was easily upset. He cried inconsolably, long after the age for colic had passed. In preschool, his teachers and parents were puzzled when he dissolved into tears or wound up on the floor in a full-blown tantrum with no apparent provocation.

When Ethan entered grade school, his tears were replaced by shouting at teachers and peers alike. As time progressed, hitting, shoving, and throwing things at other people became an all too frequent problem. The smallest incidents could set him off. He would punch another student who inadvertently bumped into him in the hallway, or throw a ball hard at another child's head after the mis-aimed ball had accidentally hit him. A program using logical consequences was tried but seemed to have little effect on Ethan's behavior. Over the next few years, Ethan was suspended multiple times for behavior problems. Eventually he was placed in an SED (severely emotionally disturbed) classroom. In this setting, his already high stress levels worsened when the other students targeted him mercilessly. Like most children with AS/ HFA, he had had problems learning the more subtle and complex components of appropriate social behavior. Unfortunately, the more blatant and dysfunctional behaviors displayed by the other students in the SED classroom were much easier to imitate and he soon began to mimic these behaviors. When his parents observed that Ethan's behavior was actually worsening in this placement, he was returned to a general education setting. Nevertheless, his problems continued, and he was ultimately expelled after shouting obscenities at one of his teachers.

Ethan's parents enrolled him in a different school. Fortunately, a consultant at the new school took a special interest in him. After observing Ethan in various settings, he became convinced that the majority of Ethan's problem behaviors stemmed from his extremely high stress load and lack of stress management skills. The consultant introduced Ethan to the stress monitoring and management techniques detailed in this program. Although his problem behaviors did not completely stop, over time they decreased considerably in frequency and magnitude.

Danielle, a thirteen-year-old girl with HFA, experienced a high level of stress on almost a daily basis. When stressed, she would scream at classmates, siblings and parents. On a bad day she sometimes hit or pushed her younger siblings. Soon after such outbursts, Danielle consistently felt remorseful and ashamed that she could not better control her behavior. It was clear that she needed to learn how to better manage her stress. The first step was to teach her to self-monitor her level of tension. In order to do this, Danielle's common stress signals and symptoms first had to be identified. Using the process outlined in Program Four, the people working with her carefully tracked Danielle's stress. At the end of that program they had identified a set of "inner signals" or symptoms, such as tightening of her shoulder muscles, a dry mouth, etc., and "outer signals" such as talking faster or hunching her shoulders that correlated with low, moderate, and high levels of stress in Danielle.

Subsequently, Danielle's teachers helped her to choose relaxation techniques (such as taking deep breaths, visualizing a favorite activity, playing a computer game, taking a quiet walk, etc.) to use at low, moderate, and high levels of stress. She initially practiced these techniques when *not* stressed, during five-minute sessions five times a week for a few weeks, until she was comfortable using each of them. She was provided with a reinforcer after each session for participating in the practice sessions.

Following this, a team consisting of Danielle's teacher, aide, and parents created a written "Stress Hierarchy"[17] (see figure 5c, page 46) in which they listed activities that she was capable of doing but were stressful to her (with the exception that to encourage her participation, the first item on the list was a task Danielle could do quite comfortably). Successive items described increasingly stressful activities. At the end of the list was a task that was almost guaranteed to produce a high level of stress in Danielle.

Finally, Danielle was reinforced for completing the tasks on the hierarchy, starting with Step One and moving up the hierarchy. She was given one task to do during each session. Reinforcement was given for either 1) completing the task without stress, or 2) if she became stressed, successfully using one of her chosen relaxation techniques and then going on to complete the task. A task was considered mastered when she had met either of these criteria three times over three sessions (or in nine out of ten trials if more repetition was required). She then moved on to the next step on the hierarchy. *Note: the emphasis in this program was on Danielle using her chosen*

---

[17] Adapted with permission from Autism Partnership, Long Beach, CA.

stress management techniques, not necessarily on the quality of her work. Danielle was asked to learn to use her stress management techniques only in very small, incremental steps. This guaranteed that she experienced success at each step and encouraged her to continue taking on progressively more difficult challenges. She was finally able to complete the last item on her hierarchy by using her stress management techniques. Over time, Danielle slowly began to transfer her relaxation techniques to naturally occurring situations in the classroom, first with prompting by her aide, and then on her own. Needless to say, her parents were very happy when she later began to use the relaxation techniques at home.

GOALS

The goals of this program are to:

1. Help the student choose and practice a set of relaxation techniques that she can use in situations that cause varying levels of stress.

2. Help the student learn to recognize her early signs of stress, rank the level of her stress, and use one of her chosen relaxation techniques in response.

INSTRUCTIONS

Step One: Develop a preliminary list of *potential relaxation techniques.*

Working with your student, make a list of relaxation techniques that *might* work for her. Divide the list into relaxation techniques for low, moderate, and high levels of stress. Include techniques that would be appropriate in home, community, and classroom environments. List techniques that the student currently uses, as well as some new ones. *(See example on page 44, figure 5a.)* Note that it may be helpful for the teacher to make (and use!) her own list of relaxation techniques as a model for the student. Brief guidelines follow for choosing relaxation techniques for the three levels of stress.

Relaxation techniques for low levels of stress

At low levels of stress, relaxation techniques generally will require less time and often can be done while the student remains seated at her work area. Simple techniques such as deep breathing, closing one's eyes and counting to five, putting one's head down, and so forth, may be all that is needed.

Relaxation techniques for moderate levels of stress

As a general rule, as the stress level increases, so does the amount of time the student needs to diffuse the stress. At moderate stress levels, the student may need to leave the environment where the stress occurred. Techniques might include listening to calming music or looking through one's Pleasures Book. *(See Program 1, page 5.)*

"Break time" is another useful technique. The student and teacher agree, in advance, on a quiet place where the student can go for a brief period of time to work on a favored activity or simply to be quiet. The student has access to laminated cards carrying the message "computer room" or "art room," etc. When she needs a break, the student simply hands one of the cards to the teacher to signal where she is going, without having to disrupt the class. (Other examples include the library for reading time, or a pre-designated "quiet room".) Some schools have rooms equipped with mats, swings, and other sensory integration equipment. These rooms can be an excellent place to which students with AS/HFA or other students with sensory integration problems can go to relieve stress. The strength of this approach is that the student learns to manage her own stress in a socially appropriate way *before* losing emotional control. This requires that

the student be able to accurately judge her own level of stress, has rehearsed exactly where to go, knows with whom to check in, and so on. (Note: a common concern about this system is that the student may misuse it to avoid non-preferred activities. In practice this rarely happens, as long as the student and all staff members involved agree on the basic rules and take time to carefully plan the process beforehand.)

Relaxation techniques for higher levels of stress

Higher levels of stress often require physically active relaxation techniques. While they vary from student to student, the most effective techniques involve activities such as tearing paper, crushing cans, swinging, running, jumping, or going for a silent walk. When the child's stress level becomes high, stay as calm as possible and maintain physical distance. Also, **this generally is not the time to talk**. Accusing words and a raised voice, or even discussions and explanations in a calm voice, may exacerbate the student's stress and provoke a full-blown outburst. Keep directions short and to the point. One successful technique is "walk, not talk." In this method, the student is allowed to walk and talk freely (if she chooses), but the adult accompanying her says little or nothing. If a response is necessary, the adult uses brief encouragement or reflecting back statements, such as "I can see that you are upset about the change in assignments right now." Continue to use this approach until the student has calmed down completely. Once the student is calm, discuss the event as needed. Note: after a full-fledged outburst it is very important to make sure that the student has had enough time to calm down completely before attempting to discuss the situation or resume the previous activity. Generally, after a person has a blow-up, she goes through a period during which her stress level falls, and her mood falls along with the stress. Often at this point the individual becomes remorseful about her behavior. This process typically follows a predictable course. However, if others attempt to start a discussion or another activity and thereby interrupt this process prematurely, the result can be a second, equally or more traumatic outburst.

Step Two: Practice relaxation techniques *when the student is not stressed.* Choose techniques for the final relaxation menu.

Choose a time during the day when your student is relaxed, and have her try one or two of the relaxation techniques she has written down. Spend five to ten minutes per session and repeat it three to five days a week, until she has tried out each technique two or three times. Reinforce the student after each session for participating. *(See Section Four, Behavioral Issues, for information on reinforcement techniques.)* After the student has tried all of the techniques, help her narrow her list down to two to four techniques each for low, moderate and high levels of stress. This will be the student's *final menu of relaxation techniques*. Make sure that she has listed techniques that would be appropriate for classroom, home, and community situations. *(See example on page 45, figure 5b.)*

Step Three: Practice chosen relaxation techniques *when relaxed.*

Have your student spend five to ten minutes a day practicing the relaxation strategies that she chose for her final menu of techniques. Do this *only* at times when the student is already relaxed. *Do not try at this point to use the techniques during stressful situations. The student needs to be well versed in using the strategies in non-stressful situations before she will be ready to start using them in stressful situations.* Reinforce the student for participating in the activity. Practice five days a week if possible. When the student demonstrates that she can use the relaxation techniques easily when not stressed, move on to Step Four.

Step Four: Complete the Stress Hierarchy form.

Complete a Stress Hierarchy form with the student. *(See example of a completed form on page 46, figure 5c. Also, a blank template can be found in Appendix C.) Enlisting the student's input,* list a very mildly stressful activity as number one, a slightly more stressful activity as number two, and so forth, ending with an activity that induces a significant amount of stress in the student. (It is helpful to do this in pencil so that you can make changes later if necessary.) Additions to the hierarchy can be made at any time. Items on the list should be activities that can be realistically carried out in a controlled setting at school or at home.

Step Five: Create a Stress Thermometer.

Using her *Summary of Stress Signals* from Program 4 *(page 23)* and the final menu of relaxation techniques from Step Two above, complete a *Stress Thermometer.* *(See example of a completed Stress Thermometer on page 47, figure 5d. A blank template can be found in Appendix C.)* Have the student label the Stress Thermometer with her stress signals on the left side and her chosen relaxation techniques for each stress level on the right side. Also have her choose her own words to identify her stress levels on the thermometer. Many students enjoy using words from a special area of interest to label their stress levels. For example, the student represented in figure 5d used terms from his favorite subject, weather, to illustrate different levels of stress.

Step Six: Gradually teach the use of relaxation techniques in *artificially induced* stressful situations, using the Stress Hierarchy and Stress Thermometer as guides.

1. Discuss the use of the Stress Thermometer with the student.

Choose a time when the student is relaxed. Explain to her that the purpose of this exercise is to help her learn to use her chosen relaxation techniques to deal with stress when it occurs, first in practice situations, and later in real life. To help her do this, she will be asked to refer to her Stress Thermometer to identify her level of stress and choose a corresponding relaxation technique. Clearly state that the purpose of this step is for her to practice 1) watching for her own stress signals and 2) using her relaxation techniques when (and if) she feels stressed during the exercise. Explain that you will be working with her to help her catch her stress as early as possible; discuss why it is important to do so. Note: the emphasis here is not on the quality of the student's work. Instead, the goal is for her to practice catching her stress at the lowest level possible and then to use an appropriate relaxation technique to calm down.

2. Use the Stress Thermometer in *practice* situations.

Referring to the student's Stress Thermometer, review with her the signals she gives at low, moderate, and high levels of stress. Next, ask the student to do the first activity on her Stress Hierarchy. During this activity, if the student becomes stressed, prompt[18] her to:

a) Recognize her stress signals (if any) *at the lowest possible level.* Ask the student to point out her level of stress on the Stress Thermometer.

b) Choose and use one of her designated relaxation techniques from the Stress Thermometer.

*During or after the activity, **reinforce the student** for 1) recognizing and ranking her stress, 2) using one of her relaxation techniques to calm down, or 3) staying calm. Repeat item one on subsequent days until she has either remained calm or has*

---

[18] For a definition of prompting, see page 343.

successfully used her relaxation techniques during this task for three consecutive sessions.

Repeat the above process with each subsequent item on the hierarchy. Slowly decrease the use of prompts when possible. During the training period, do not prompt the student to use her relaxation techniques in response to real life stressors. (If she is asked to use these techniques in uncontrolled situations before she has had enough practice in controlled situations, she may fail at it and lose confidence in her ability to succeed.) However, if the student spontaneously uses the techniques in response to a real life stressor, be certain to reinforce this strongly. This means that she is beginning to generalize her stress management skills to the "real world." In other words, she is beginning to learn how to successfully deal with stress!

Step Seven: Use the Stress Thermometer in naturally occurring situations.

Keep a copy of the Stress Thermometer near the student throughout the day (e.g., have a copy on her desk or posted on the refrigerator at home). Also, the student may find it helpful to carry in her pocket a shortened version of the thermometer on a laminated index card. When the student becomes stressed, cue her to find her level of stress on the thermometer and to use one of the corresponding stress reduction techniques. Reinforce the student for her efforts to use the Stress Thermometer. Fade the use of cues slowly, but continue to reinforce her for using her stress reduction techniques.

List of Potential Relaxation Techniques for Scott W.

For low levels of stress:

1. 3-5 deep breaths with eyes closed
2. visualize being at the beach
3. visualize being at the train station
4. put head down on desk, close eyes
5. count to five
6. squeeze sponge ball
7. shoulder and neck rolls
8. touch worry stone in pocket (a polished stone with word "relax" written on it) while slowly spelling out r-e-l-a-x

For Moderate levels of stress:

1. break time -- go to quiet place
2. listen to favorite music
3. play computer game for 5-10 mins.
4. rock (in private area)
5. work with molding clay
6. read for 10 mins.
7. talk to trusted person
8. ask for massage

For high levels of stress:

1. "Walk, no talk"
2. break time -- go to quiet place
2. crush aluminum cans
3. shoot baskets
4. tear paper
5. swing
6. go for a run
7. jump rope
8. rock (in private area)

Figure 5a. An example of an initial List of Potential Relaxation Techniques suggested by a team consisting of the student, teachers, and parents. The term "rock" refers to the student's use of rocking from side to side to relax. The student tried out all of the relaxation techniques on this list before narrowing down his choices to two to four items per stress level. (See Final Menu of Relaxation Techniques, page 45.)

Final Menu of Relaxation Techniques for Scott W.

For Low-level stress

1. close eyes, put head down on desk
2. visualize being at the beach
3. roll shoulders and neck

For moderate stress

1. rock (only in private, or around family)
2. listen to relaxing music
3. use molding clay
4. break time -- go to quiet place

For high-level stress

1. walk, no talk
2. swing
3. break time -- go to quiet place

Figure 5b. An example of a Final Menu of Relaxation Techniques. The student has chosen three to four items for each level of stress after trying out several techniques from a larger list. Note that the term "rock" refers to the student rocking from side to side to help him relax. He has designated that he will use rocking only in certain, socially acceptable circumstances. The data from this menu is used to fill in the right side of the student's Stress Thermometer *(see Figure 5d, page 47)*.

Student: Scott W.

STRESS HIERARCHY

1. Fun reading, one paragraph

2. Dull reading, one paragraph

3. Dull reading, one paragraph, then write one fact

4. Math: 3-digit addition, 5 problems

5. Math: 3-digit addition, 10 problems

6. Math: 3-digit addition, 15 problems

7. Math: 1-digit division, 3 problems

8. Math: 1-digit division, 6 problems

9. Math: 1-digit division, 10 problems

10. Writing: 2 simple sentences   (Note: For some, writing might be less stressful than math.)

11. Writing: 4 simple sentences

12. Writing: One paragraph

13. Timed math: Multiplication facts, 1 minute   (Note: Being timed is very stressful for this student.)

14. Timed math: Multiplication facts, 2 minutes

15. Timed math: Multiplication facts, 5 minutes

16. Timed math: Multiplication facts, 10 minutes

17. _____

18. _____

Instructions for completing the Stress Hierarchy Form: List a non-stressful activity as #1, a very mildly stressful activity as #2, a slightly more stressful activity as #3, and so forth. The last item should be an activity that induces a significant amount of stress in the student. Items on the list should be activities that can be realistically carried out in a controlled setting at home and/or school. It is helpful to fill out this form in pencil to allow for changes later on. Additions to the list can be made at any time.

Figure 5c: An example of a completed Stress Hierarchy Form.

STRESS THERMOMETER

For: _Scott W._

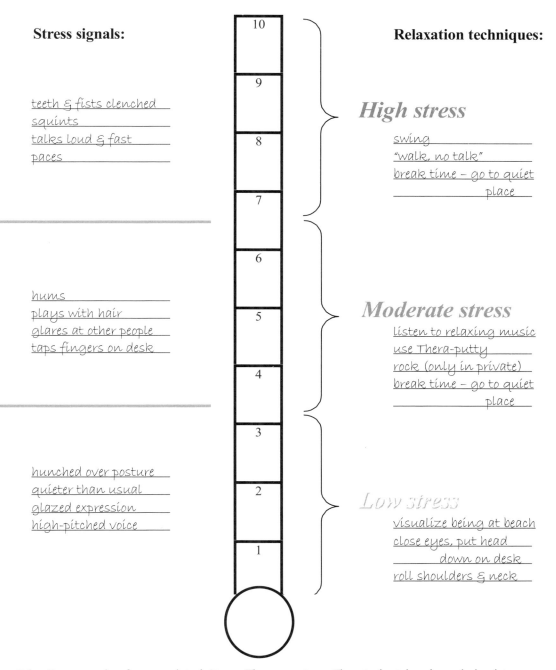

Stress signals:

teeth & fists clenched
squints
talks loud & fast
paces

hums
plays with hair
glares at other people
taps fingers on desk

hunched over posture
quieter than usual
glazed expression
high-pitched voice

Relaxation techniques:

High stress

swing
"walk, no talk"
break time – go to quiet
place

Moderate stress

listen to relaxing music
use Thera-putty
rock (only in private)
break time – go to quiet
place

Low stress

visualize being at beach
close eyes, put head
down on desk
roll shoulders & neck

Figure 5d. An example of a completed Stress Thermometer. The student has been helped to recognize his own stress signals and to choose stress-reducing activities for each level of stress. Copies of the thermometer can be enlarged to poster size or reduced to make a make a laminated pocket card, and the student can be taught to refer to the thermometer when needed. Items on the left are from the completed Summary of Stress Signals chart (see Figure 4c, page 31). Items on the right are from the Final Menu of Relaxation Techniques (see Figure 5b, page 45).

PROGRAM 6
STRESS III – STRESS PREVENTION

INTRODUCTION

Individuals with autism and related disorders are susceptible to certain categories of stressors that are common to these diagnoses. This often-overlooked fact can be very helpful in planning an effective stress prevention program. Generally, it is useful to divide these stressors into four main categories: social stressors, communication stressors, environmental/sensory stressors, and "overload" stressors. Some examples of how stress prevention strategies worked for children with AS/HFA follow.

Jon was an eleven-year-old boy with high functioning autism who, like most people with AS/HFA, often found many social and communication skills to be beyond his grasp. Try as he might to communicate and socialize, he was met with constant roadblocks. He missed the nonverbal cues that would have alerted him to his listeners' boredom when he talked too much about his favorite subject, Star Trek movies. He constantly got into trouble for, as he saw it, telling the truth. He couldn't understand what was wrong with telling someone he didn't like their looks, or correcting teachers and classmates when they broke minor rules. He barged into conversations and couldn't appreciate why this was annoying to others. In short, the multitude of unspoken rules that people use to communicate and socialize with each other were a mystery to Jon. His inability to understand and use these rules isolated him and was an ever-present source of stress in his life. Even worse, some of his peers picked up on his weaknesses and vulnerability, making him the target of their teasing and bullying. They set him up to "act out" just when the teacher would be looking his way, and then sat back to enjoy the ensuing show. Eventually, the combination of being targeted and his failure at communication and social skills became so hard for him that he became severely depressed and required treatment with anti-depressant medication. About this time, a support team made up of his parents and school staff decided to work together to pinpoint the situations that were the most socially stressful for Jon. Then they made some simple changes in the social demands on him. For example, they held a few sessions with Jon's classmates to go over HFA and its effects on social skills. They also watched for situations in which Jon was being teased or set up by the other children. In these cases, the perpetrators were given appropriate consequences. In addition, the team determined that the student lunchroom was simply too overwhelming for Jon and allowed him to eat his lunch in the learning center. At home, Jon was given the option of retiring to his room after a brief conversation with visitors if he found the demand to communicate was too much to handle. These and other simple steps taken to reduce social and communication stressors helped Jon's general stress level and his secondary depression significantly.

.

Paul, a nine-year-old boy with Asperger's Syndrome, was noted for being a good student, particularly in math and science. As he had no major behavioral problems, his teacher became puzzled by an odd behavior change that seemed to occur intermittently during afternoon math lessons. During these episodes he would become irritable and fidgety, and sometimes would sit hunched up with his hands over his ears, seemingly unable to focus on his work. After tracking his behavior, his teacher discovered that these episodes only occurred on Wednesday afternoons. With a little more detective work, she realized that the gardener always worked on Wednesday afternoons, edging the lawn right outside of Paul's classroom. The high-pitched noise had been bothering Paul, leaving him edgy and unable to focus. However, like many individuals with AS/HFA, Paul was quite stoic, and had not thought to mention his discomfort to his teacher. Once the source of Paul's discomfort was recognized, the teacher arranged to have the gardener do the lawn edging after school hours. This small change in Paul's environment made a huge change in his stress level during Wednesday afternoon math classes. As a result, Paul's performance in math improved as well.

Bridget, a fifteen-year-old girl with HFA, seemed well controlled and quiet during school hours, but fell apart as soon as she walked through the door at home. In addition to the normal stressors that children face, Bridget had learning disabilities in math and reading, and had problems with organizational, social, and communication skills. By the time the school day ended, she was invariably on "system overload" and was literally incapable of successfully doing her homework. This led to a daily battle between Bridget and her parents, who were understandably concerned that her grades would suffer if she failed to turn in the required amount of homework. The daily battles over homework led to even more stress for Bridget (and her parents), and the result was often a full- fledged blow-up. Fortunately, at this point Bridget's parents and teachers realized that steps needed to be taken to reduce Bridget's stress or things would only get worse. In response, the teachers agreed to decrease the amount of homework assigned to Bridget. For their part, her parents agreed to make sure that Bridget had a quiet place where she could go to unwind as soon as she arrived home, *before* she was expected to take on the responsibilities of homework, chores, and communicating with family members. This approach worked well to relieve Bridget's stress when she arrived home in the afternoon, and made life much more pleasant for all concerned.

Each of these examples illustrates how eliminating specific stressors can create a better quality of life for the child and those around him. Furthermore, stress reduction will almost always improve the student's performance in both academics and in the social-emotional arena.

GOALS

In contrast to the preceding programs that deal with the treatment of stress *as it occurs*, this program is directed at stress prevention. Specifically, the goals of this program are to help parents, teachers, and the individual with AS/HFA to:

1. Recognize preventable stressors in the following categories:
   - social stressors
   - communication stressors
   - environmental/sensory stressors
   - overload stressors

2. Take steps to prevent these stressors from occurring or to minimize their effects on the individual with AS/HFA.

INSTRUCTIONS

Step One: List social stressors. *(See example on page 55, figure 6a.)*

Referring to the stress tracking charts from Program 4, help the student create a list of those stressors related to his interactions with, or proximity to other people. For example, social situations that often are stressful to people with AS/HFA include interacting with other students on the playground, being introduced to new people, and being in large crowds. Many more examples exist.

Step Two: List communication stressors. *(See example on page 55, figure 6a.)*

Referring to the stress tracking charts from Program 4, help the student create a list of those stressors that are related to communication with other people. For example, the student may have problems maintaining two-way conversations or may interpret other people's words in an overly literal manner.[19] Likewise, he may be stressed by problems with word retrieval and auditory discrimination. Again, many more examples exist.

Step Three: List *environmental/sensory* stressors. *(See example on page 55, figure 6a.)*

Referring to the stress tracking charts from Program 4, help the student create a list of stressors that are related to environmental or sensory stimuli. Common examples include unpleasant or even painful responses to certain types of lighting, sound, or touch. For example, exposure to a fluorescent light or the sound of a refrigerator humming in the background may be both unpleasant and distracting to a particular student. This type of sensitivity to specific sensory input is caused by deficits in the child's sensory integration system. *(For more information on sensory integration issues in individuals with AS/HFA, please refer to Appendix A, Additional Resource Materials.)*

Step Four: List *overload* stressors *(see example on page 55, figure 6a).*

Referring to the stress tracking charts from Program 4, help the student create a list of stressors related to overload. Individuals with AS/HFA can become severely stressed by the intense amount of concentration they must employ simply to function in day-to-day life. For example, although they may have no trouble focusing on a topic of special interest, these individuals may spend an inordinate

---

[19] Because sensory integration problems are very common in this population of children, it is very helpful to obtain input from an occupational therapist with experience evaluating and treating sensory integration problems.

amount of energy on attempts to focus on non-preferred topics. *It is important to note that attempts to avoid non-preferred activities may be due not to laziness or irresponsibility, but to genuine difficulty in focusing attention on such activities.* Research suggests that individuals with AS/HFA have neurological deficits in parts of the brain usually responsible for social, communicative, and executive functioning. As a result, other parts of the brain may be diverted from their normal functions, doing "double duty" to compensate for this gap. By the time a student with AS/HFA arrives home from school, he literally may be on "brain overload" and essentially incapable of social interaction, completing homework assignments, or meeting other demands. The same problem also can occur during the school day. Therefore, workloads at school may need to be modified to amounts that are reasonable for the individual student, and homework may need to be minimized or even eliminated. (See Step Five.)

Step Five: Create and implement *modifications* to reduce social, communication, environmental/sensory, and overload stressors.

In this step, the student and his teachers and caregivers work together to find ways to reduce or eliminate the preventable stressors at school, in the home and community that were identified in Steps One through Four. For example, homework may need to be reduced to only those areas in which the student needs more practice, perhaps with the option of completing the homework during a study period at school. If the student is sensitive to fluorescent lighting, an alternate form of light source may be needed. If being around other children on the playground at lunchtime causes stress, the student may be allowed to spend part or all of his lunchtime in the library. Making simple modifications such as these, at school and at home, can greatly reduce the student's stress level. In turn, this will decrease the number and intensity of problem behaviors and increase the child's ability to learn in the school environment. (Note that it is important to list all school-related modifications in the student's Individualized Education Plan to assure that everyone on the child's team is aware of them.)

Student Name: _Scott W._

List of Social Stressors

1. interacting with other students on the school bus (exposure to bullying and teasing)
2. interacting with other students on the playground (difficulties with "joining in" and with being bullied and teased)
3. giving oral reports (or speaking in front of a group of people)
4. working on group projects (vs. working alone)
5. walking to and from little league practice (exposure to bullying and teasing by other children)

List of Communication Stressors

1. problems initiating conversations with other students on the playground
2. difficulties communicating with peers due to delays in word retrieval and auditory processing
3. problems staying on topic and carrying on a reciprocal conversation
4. problems understanding metaphorical or idiomatic speech
5. having guests in the home—problems differentiating appropriate vs. inappropriate conversational topics

List of Environmental/Sensory Stressors

1. changes in schedule
2. substitute teacher
3. background noise from photocopy machine, etc.
4. noise of barking dog
5. furniture at home rearranged

List of Overload Stressors

1. working in class on challenging subjects (math and social studies) without sufficient breaks
2. unmodified homework load

Figure 6a. Examples of social, communication, environmental, and overload stressors for a particular student. Data to complete this list was collected in Program Four *(page 23)*, using the student's stress summary charts *(see Figures 4c & 4d, pages 31-32)*.

SECTION TWO

COMMUNICATION
and
SOCIAL SKILLS

INTRODUCTION
Communication and Social Skills

Pronounced difficulties in social and communication skills are hallmarks of all autism spectrum disorders. Effective communication requires a multitude of skills in addition to simply understanding the literal meanings of words in a conversation. When most of us take part in a conversation, our brain is very busy indeed, keeping track of a myriad of information pouring into it from several directions at once. First, as our ears pick up the words coming at us, our brains need to distinguish these sounds from irrelevant background noise such as traffic noises, the hum of a vacuum cleaner in a nearby room, or the sound of voices from a neighboring conversation. We must then disengage our attention from whatever task with which our brain was busy and redirect that attention to the person speaking to us. Next, different areas of our brain must process the speaker's words as well as his body language, facial expression and tone of voice. This information then is referenced to a huge amount of related data already stored in our memory banks, including information about the individual talking and about *other people* we have observed in similar situations. Finally, we reformat the meanings of the words to reflect our own biases, beliefs, feelings, and opinions. All of this is done in a matter of milliseconds, with very little conscious effort. In short, in addition to the spoken word, there is an underlying *fluid* dimension of communication and social understanding that the average person uses in each and every exchange with other human beings.

In communicating with one another we also depend on a framework of unwritten, but nevertheless very powerful social and conversational rules that we have stored in our memory banks. Although the *content* of the rules varies from culture to culture, the *types* of rules are very similar across cultural boundaries. For example, most of us learn by observation (and less often by direct instruction) that while you might get away with calling your little brother a lazy bum in private, you will not be so lucky if you say the same thing to your aunt Jane! Likewise, with little to no formal instruction, we learn other social rules, like the proper amount of eye contact, how far away to stand, how to change topics, to take turns within a conversation, and so on.

In addition to a framework of unwritten rules, *social scripts* stored in our memory banks add another element of structure to social communication. Within each culture and subculture, there are generally accepted scripts for greeting and taking leave of one another, making introductions, initiating conversations, offering and asking for help, and giving and receiving compliments, among many others. These scripts change over time, and vary from culture to culture and from subculture to subculture. Despite this, the typical child effortlessly incorporates an amazing variety of scripts into his everyday language. For example, in an average American city, the typical five-year-old girl knows to greet the school principal with "Hello, Mrs. Jones," but to greet a classmate with "Hi, Susan, what are you doing?" On the other hand, her ten-year-old brother and his friends are more apt to greet each other with "Hey, what's up?" Her fifteen-year-old brother's peer group uses "Yo dude, what's goin'?" but his twin sister and her friends greet each other with "Hey, girlfriend!" Using the wrong script at the wrong time can cause a child (or an adult, for that matter) to appear rude or out of place and can make him a target for misunderstanding and ostracism from his social group.

Effective social communication requires that the areas of our brain that control communication and social functioning work rapidly and fluidly within a cultural framework of unwritten rules and social scripts. Most children begin to pick up social and communication skills "by osmosis" while they are still infants and toddlers. However, it is exactly this vast realm of communication and social understanding that typically escapes the person with AS/HFA. Without it he flounders in social situations in the same way most of us would struggle if we were dropped off without preparation onto another planet and were expected to communicate effectively with its inhabitants.

The following section contains twelve programs that address some of the social and communication skills that seem to be most troublesome for individuals with AS/HFA. With the exception of conflict resolution, these are skills that the typical person will have picked up early in his or her life with a minimal amount of instruction. However, if as research suggests, the systems within the brain that control communication and social skills do not function conventionally in people with AS/HFA, it makes sense to train other parts of the brain to take over these functions. This process requires breaking communication and social skills down into small steps, teaching these steps with frequent repetition, and "scaffolding" more difficult tasks onto previously learned, simpler tasks. This is the approach followed in this section.

A final word needs to be said about the *purpose* of teaching social and communication skills to people with AS/HFA. The purpose of doing this always should be to give them the skills to function socially at those times when they *choose* to do so or *need* to do so, either out of their own desire for human warmth and companionship or when they must fit in socially in order to survive independently (for example, when they need to conform to social rules in the workplace in order to hold down a job). In contrast, the purpose of social and social skills training should never be to change *who* they are or to make them copies of us. People that fit into the autism spectrum have unique ways of looking at the world and of interacting with its other, non-autistic human inhabitants. This, however, does not mean that an autistic way of looking at life and interacting with people is fundamentally worse than the non-autistic way. In fact, although no two individuals with AS/HFA are alike, most are honest, straightforward, persevering, humorous and fun loving, to mention just a few qualities, and as such they have much to teach the rest of us. Unfortunately, sometimes in our attempt to help our students, friends or loved ones with

AS/HFA, we try to remake them into someone who is not autistic – an effort that is doomed to failure. In attempting to do so, we run the risk of cutting them off from themselves, leaving them in a twilight zone where they are unable to be either autistic or neurotypical. This loss of identity can be devastating to the person with AS/HFA. After working with these individuals for nearly thirty years, Tony Attwood speaks of several patients with AS/HFA who suffered psychotic breaks as a result of the pressure to be "normal" imposed on them by either themselves or by others. Several of these high functioning individuals were left permanently crippled and unable to function independently.[20]

What can be done to prevent placing an inordinate amount of pressure to change on our students with AS/HFA while still giving them the tools to function socially when they desire or need to do so? Some practitioners argue that we should do very little in the way of formal social and communication training but simply should provide relatively unstructured opportunities for socialization. On the surface, this method would appear to minimize social pressure. However, the problem is that if some amount of social and communication skills training is not provided, then the individual with AS/HFA is left to pick up the necessary skills on his own. Unfortunately, this approach usually fails because the inability to learn these skills in a conventional fashion is one of the defining characteristics of all autism spectrum disorders. On the other hand, approaches that have focused on very intense and repetitive training in non-natural settings have been criticized both for inducing undue stress in the students and for producing children with a limited set of social responses that often do not generalize to situations outside of the training environment. Between these two ends of the treatment spectrum there is a middle ground where our students can be taught to use social and communication skills in increasingly natural social settings while maintaining individuality and minimizing stress. There are

---

[20] Attwood, Tony. 2000. Personal communication.

many different ways to accomplish this, but to be effective, any approach must emphasize teaching in a sensitive and caring way, and employ plenty of patience, fun and humor. Also, for the mental and emotional well being of our students, it is critical that they are supported in taking "time off" from the pressures of fitting in. In other words, they need to have regular times scheduled into their days to withdraw from social demands, and to do whatever they need to do to relax [including time for "self-stimulating" behaviors (rocking, etc.) done in socially appropriate ways, if needed].

PROGRAM 7
BASIC CONVERSATIONAL RESPONSES

INTRODUCTION

Bridget, a fifteen-year-old girl with HFA, had read college level texts on her favorite subject, weather, and could deliver lengthy monologues on that topic. Yet, she often failed to respond to other people's questions or statements. Furthermore, she would often stare past the person's shoulder while they were talking, or even walk away, as if she hadn't heard a word. Part of this problem stemmed from Bridget's central auditory processing deficit. This meant that, although her hearing was normal, she needed extra time to process the words entering her brain through the auditory system. Also contributing to her failure to respond was her problem with *shifting attention* from whatever topic was occupying her mind to the other person's words. However, even when these factors were adequately addressed, Bridget still had problems understanding and participating in the give and take of typical conversations. Bridget's teachers began to teach her specific ways to respond to questions and statements. Using a graded approach and carefully chosen reinforcers, they were able to help her learn to make appropriate verbal responses. Subsequently, Bridget's ability to participate in a two-way conversation improved dramatically.

Many students with AS/HFA are quite verbal, but nevertheless have trouble responding to other people's questions or statements. This program teaches the student to recognize and use seven different types of responses that commonly are utilized in conversation. The student will first practice the responses alone, then within practice conversations, and finally in naturally occurring conversations. As with the other programs in this book, it is important that the teacher or parent provide as many sessions as necessary for the student to master these responses. For some, this may mean a session or two. Other students may need months of practice. *These skills lay the groundwork for conversation.* Therefore, the student needs to be comfortable in using them before moving on to more advanced conversational skills.

GOALS

The goals of this program are to teach the student to make the following *types of responses* within a conversation:

1. Answer yes/no questions.
2. Answer simple questions with a one or two word reply.
3. Respond to a statement with a statement.
4. Answer open-ended questions.
5. Respond to a statement with a question.
6. Respond to a question with a brief statement and a reciprocal question.
7. Respond to a statement with a statement followed by a question.

INSTRUCTIONS

Step One: Demonstrate and practice individual target responses.[21]

(Refer to figure 7a, "Examples of Conversational Responses" on page 70 for examples of the seven types of responses covered in this program.)

Note: Starting with "Answer yes/no questions," and proceeding in the order listed, work on one type of response at a time, practicing it with the student

---

[21] The term, "target response" is used in this program to indicate the particular conversational response (of the seven listed above) on which you currently are working.

over as many sessions as he needs for mastery (i.e., until he can successfully use the targeted response nine out of ten times). Make sure the student has mastered the target response before introducing the next type of response. In Steps Two and Three, the student will be using a variety of responses during actual conversations, so it is important that he master all (or the majority of) response types before proceeding to Steps Two and Three.

For each type of conversational response, follow these two steps:

1. Working with an assistant, *demonstrate* the targeted response for the student (or a small group of students, if applicable). For example, when working on yes/no questions the teacher might ask "Are you hungry?" and the assistant would reply with either "Yes" or "No." Demonstrate two or three different examples (or more if needed). If possible, include questions that pertain to the student's special interests.

2. Next, ask the student(s) to *practice* the targeted response. For example, if you are working on item six (question-statement-question), you might ask the student, "What is your favorite theme park?" An appropriate response would be "Disneyland. What is yours?"

Prompt the student as needed, using the least intrusive type of prompt possible. [22] Fade (i.e., slowly decrease the use of) prompts over time.

Step Two: Practice conversational responses in *practice conversations*.

Explain to the student that he will next practice making the targeted response in short practice conversations. Initially, the teacher should work with the student one-on-one to help guide the conversation. Later, this step can be done in a small

---

[22] Refer to page 233 for more information on prompting.

group setting. Begin by helping the student choose a conversational topic that interests him, then review the target response you will be working on. Start with number one and work up to number seven over several sessions. Using the student's topic, start the conversation, "setting up" opportunities for him to use the target response. Be prepared to do most of the talking initially, particularly if the student has significant problems with two-way conversations. Prompt the target response as necessary, fading the prompts over time as noted in Step One. Depending on the skill level of the student, the initial prompts may need to be quite specific, particularly for the more complex responses. To illustrate, if you are working on item five (responding to a statement with a question), you initially may need to prompt the student with the entire response. If the initial statement is "I had the greatest experience yesterday!" you may need to quietly say to the student, "Dave, ask me what happened yesterday." Or, you may even need to model the exact script: "Dave, say: 'Oh, what happened yesterday?'" As the student begins to catch on, your prompts should become less specific, e.g., "Dave, what can you ask me now?" Later on, your prompt may be simply the word "question" or a discreet hand signal to remind the student to reply.

Start this step with brief conversations (thirty to sixty seconds) and progress to longer conversations as the student becomes more competent using a variety of responses. As the student adds more response types to his repertoire, target two or three types of responses to work on within each conversation. Prompt only these response types to avoid confusion. (Reinforce him after the dialogue for using both the targeted and non-targeted response types.) Vary the targeted response type from session to session. When the student can use all of the response types comfortably with the teacher, have him work with another student. The teacher then can prompt both students. (Note: even if the second student has no communication impairment or does not require prompting, let him or her know in advance that you will be prompting both students from time to time so as not to single out either student.)

When the student is comfortable carrying on two to three minute conversations with only brief prompting, begin to **videotape** the practice conversations. Play the tapes back for the student(s), keeping the suggestions positive and emphasizing the progress he is making. When the student has mastered Step Two, move on to Step Three. However, revisit Step Two periodically to make sure that the student's new skills are maintained. (Note: Students usually become accustomed to being video-taped quite rapidly.)

Step Three: Practice conversational responses in videotaped, *naturally occurring situations.*

This step allows students to practice their responses in a naturalistic, small group setting. Choose a small group of students who are working at about the same level. If possible, also include a few student helpers who are at a more advanced level and train them in advance to help cue the other students to make appropriate responses when necessary. Then, set up situations that encourage conversations. For example, choose environments that are as non-distracting as possible (i.e. try to minimize background noise, foot traffic, visual distractions, etc.), and make sure the participants are well acquainted and enjoy being together. When possible, have the students plan and organize the events (with your guidance, of course). This will insure that the activity is one the students want to do, thus encouraging more enthusiastic participation on their parts.

Let the students know in advance that you will be videotaping them. During the event, prompt responses if necessary to encourage the flow of conversation, but as much as possible allow the student helpers to do the majority of the prompting. *Videotape* the students at the event, making sure to include those who do not talk much. Review the tapes later with the students, complimenting each student who participated, and giving specific praise to students who used the responses learned in this program. Keep feedback positive and specific. For example, rather than simply commenting, "Your responses were really good this session," it is more instructive and helpful to say, "I really liked it when you answered John's question about your favorite computer game with the statement, 'My favorite game is Star Wars Pit Droids; what's your favorite game?' It was a great response because you directly answered his question, and then asked a related question. That showed John that you were interested in his question." Initially, it is important to minimize corrections so as not to discourage the students. As the students become more adept in conversing, they most likely will accept a few more corrections, but remember to aim for a ratio of at least five positive comments for every correction. Repeat Step Three in different settings until the student is reasonably comfortable using the different types of responses in real life situations.

Note: It is very important for family members, teachers, and whenever possible, peers, to make a specific point of listening for and responding to attempts by the student to use these new skills in **all** *naturally-occurring situations. As mentioned in previous programs, responding to the student's spontaneous attempts to use new skills is crucial to his ability to generalize those skills to new situations.*

EXAMPLES OF CONVERSATIONAL RESPONSES

Response Type	Example
1. Answer yes/no questions.	Q: Did you find your book? A: Yes.
2. Answer simple questions with a one to two word reply.	Q: What is your favorite T.V. show? A: Nickelodeon.
3. Respond to a statement with a statement.	S: I have a dog and two cats. S: Cool. I have an iguana.
4. Answer open-ended questions.	Q: What was that Star Trek episode about? A: It was about the Enterprise getting lost in space.
5. Respond to a statement with a question.	S: I saw a great movie last night! Q: Oh, what was it?
6. Respond to a question with a brief statement and a reciprocal question.	Q: What is your favorite class? A: Science. What's yours?
7. Respond to a statement with a statement followed by a question.	S: I love horseback riding. S/Q: Me too. Do you own a horse?

Figure 7a. Examples of the seven different types of simple conversational responses covered in this program.

PROGRAM 8
RECOGNIZING and INTERPRETING NONVERBAL and CONTEXTUAL CLUES IN OTHER PEOPLE

INTRODUCTION

Most people quite readily recognize and interpret both contextual clues and the nonverbal clues found in other people's body language and facial expression. However, many individuals with AS/HFA have significant problems doing this. This contributes to their core problems with understanding other people's thoughts, intentions and emotions.[23] This program will focus on *using nonverbal and contextual clues* to help recognize other people's emotions, thoughts, and intentions. It also will introduce *sequencing* skills that will help the student more accurately predict how other people might react in different situations. It will begin with identifying emotions depicted on a stylized chart, and will progress through several steps until the final step of identifying emotions in dynamic, real life situations.

In the case of Paul, a nine-year-old boy with Asperger's Syndrome, problems with understanding nonverbal cues often caused him to misread other people's intentions. This frequently led to a great deal of confusion on the parts of both parties. For example, on several occasions Paul hit or shoved another student who had accidentally bumped into him in the hallway or on the playground. Although he was not aggressive by nature, Paul tended to assume that the other child had done

---

[23] In addition, they may assume that other people's thoughts, feelings and opinions are (or should be) always the same as their own thoughts, feelings and opinions.

this with malicious intent because he failed to correctly read the contextual and nonverbal cues that would have told him otherwise. Having been targeted by other children in the past, Paul assumed that the other child's intentions were unfriendly and lacking a better way of expressing his anger, his response was all too often to "deck" the other student. As a result, he developed a reputation as being an aggressive child, known for attacking fellow students with little or no provocation. Similarly, he had trouble reading the nonverbal and situational clues that would have helped him differentiate between friendly kidding and unfriendly teasing. He often reacted by shouting at the other person, even if the kidding had been friendly in nature.

Danielle, a thirteen-year-old girl with high functioning autism, was very good at talking. So good, in fact, that she often talked about one of her favorite subjects, birthmarks, until the other person became either quite alarmed or bored to tears! Danielle's core problem was her poor theory of mind skills (the ability to effectively understand other people's feelings, thoughts or intentions). A closely related problem was her inability to rapidly analyze the *context* of the situation for clues as to the other person's *likely* reactions, or to scan and read the other person's *face and body language* for clues to their reactions to her words or actions. Danielle's listeners sometimes had to quite abruptly extricate themselves from a particularly long monologue, and she was left wondering why they had so suddenly ended the conversation. At other times, Danielle's frank talk about birthmarks and moles (another of her favorite subjects) embarrassed her listeners, but she had no clue that the other person wasn't just as thrilled as she was about the subject. In short, she failed to recognize that when a listener turned his body away, looked away, tapped his fingers, and so forth, it probably meant that he was bored. (She also needed to differentiate between *situations* in which it would be acceptable to talk about a certain topic, and those in which it would not be acceptable. For example, talking with her sister about her birthmark might be okay if the two of them were alone, but it might embarrass her sister to talk about it in front of another person. To help her distinguish between appropriate and inappropriate social contexts, she also worked on the program "Public vs. Private" *[see program 15, page 143]*).

Both of these students frequently misperceived or failed to recognize other people's thoughts, feelings and intentions. As a consequence, they all too often found themselves stranded in the midst of an uncomfortable, or even unsafe, social situation without any real idea of how they got there or how to get out of it. This inability to "mind read" is a core deficit in people on the autism spectrum, and there currently is much debate about how, or even if, these individuals can learn this skill.[24] The ability to perceive and understand other people's states of mind is both complex and poorly understood. As such, it cannot be taught as a simple, discrete skill. However, one workable (although not foolproof) approach to helping people with AS/HFA *begin to recognize* thoughts, feelings and intentions in other people is to teach them to use 1) contextual clues and 2) external clues such as facial expression, body language and tone of voice, to make educated guesses about other people's states of mind. This program focuses on contextual, facial expression and body language clues. Tone of voice clues are addressed in the following program.

GOALS

The goals of this program are to:

1. Help the student learn to recognize body language, facial expression and contextual clues to *other people's thoughts, intentions and feelings.*

---

[24] Baron-Cohen, Simon. *Mindblindness: An Essay on Autism and Theory of Mind.* (1995). The MIT Press. Cambridge; Howlin, P., Baron-Cohen, S. and Hadwin, J. *Teaching Children with Autism to Mind-Read.* (1999). Wiley. New York.

2. Help the student use the above skills to predict *what is most likely to happen next* in a given social interaction, (i.e. to begin to teach sequencing skills in the context of social interactions.)

INSTRUCTIONS

Students should master each of the following steps before moving on to the next step. Before beginning the program, give your students a copy of the student handout *"The Secret Language." (See figure 8a, pages 81-82. Also, a student copy can be found in Appendix B.)* This handout explains the reasons for learning about nonverbal communication (and the reasons for working on this program). Discuss the handout with your students, specifically addressing the crucial roles of body language, facial expression and contextual clues in human communication. Make sure that they understand the reason for learning these skills before proceeding. Also, periodically reviewing the individual steps will help the students retain the skills they have mastered.

Step One: Teach nonverbal cues using *stylized pictures*.

Refer to the *"Emotions Picture Chart" (pages 83-84, figure 8b)*, before beginning this step. *(A student copy can be found in Appendix B.)* Teach the student to identify the emotions illustrated by the faces on the chart. Discuss the meaning of each emotion, using examples to illustrate as needed. It works best to teach only one or at most a few emotions per session. Review previously taught emotions periodically. After the student is competent at recognizing and defining the emotions on the chart, use the same chart to play the following ***role-play game***:

1) Ask the student to choose one line from the emotions chart.

2) Review the emotions on that line with the student and demonstrate both the body language and facial expression that typically accompany this emotion.

3) Take turns portraying the emotions on the chosen line. Have the other person guess which emotion their partner is demonstrating.

This game can be played by teacher and student alone, or by a small group of students. Keep the activity fun and light-hearted.

Step Two: Teach nonverbal cues using *photographs*.

Have the student cut out photographs of people in magazines whose expressions and/or body language display a variety of emotions. Then choose an emotion from the Emotions Picture Chart and ask the student to find as many photos as possible that illustrate that feeling. Alternately, the teacher can choose one or a group of photos showing a certain emotion, and ask the student to guess the emotion. Let the student quiz the teacher periodically to make it more fun and to encourage participation. Discuss with the student what specific facial changes and elements of body language are common to most of the pictures showing a particular emotion. For example, people who look worried generally have furrowed brows and mouths in a fairly straight line, whereas people who look angry often have knitted brows, a down-turned mouth and clenched fists.

Step Three: Role-play emotions: Exercise #1

Choose an item from the list of scenarios *(see figure 8c, pages 85-86)*, describe the scenario for the student, and demonstrate the corresponding emotion through your facial expression and body language. Ask the student to guess the emotion that you just demonstrated (the student may refer to the Emotions Picture Chart for help if needed). As in Step Two, discuss the elements of body language and facial changes (furrowed brows, slightly open mouth, etc.) that you used to show the emotion. Also discuss contextual clues (i.e., *why* a person *in that scenario* would feel that particular emotion). Ask the student if she has ever been in a similar situation, and if so, how she felt at the time. Then have her relate how *she* felt to how *another person* might feel in the same sort of situation. As the student gains skill in this activity, have her rank the *level* of emotion you are showing in the role-play. The student may use the emotions scales that she created in Program Three for a visual guide if desired. *(See Appendix C for a blank template.)*

Conversely, first choose an emotion and then ask the student to find a scenario on the list that would elicit this emotion. Ask her to read the scenario and demonstrate the appropriate facial expression and body language. Discuss contextual clues from the scenario.

Next, have the student tell about emotional events that have happened to her or to someone else she knows, and then have her demonstrate the corresponding facial expression and body language. Ask the student to rank the level of the emotions she has demonstrated for you. Help the student use contextual clues to make an educated guess as to why the people involved felt and reacted the way they did.

Step Four: Role-play emotions: Exercise #2

Demonstrate how varying one's body language and facial expression can completely change the meaning of *an identical set of words*. Say the identical phrase several times, using different body language and facial expressions each time to illustrate how the intended meaning changes as the nonverbal clues change. For example, using the words "We're having spaghetti again for dinner tonight," use body language and facial expression messages to portray angry, happy, disgusted, disappointed and confused. Ask the student to identify the correct emotion. Repeat the activity using different phrases and contexts. Reverse roles with the student intermittently.

Step Five: Teach emotions using *drama*.

(If you have access to a drama teacher or coach, inviting that person to help with the following drama sessions can make a wonderful addition to the program.) In a small group, have three or four students put on a simple skit. Have the students rehearse the skit, while coaching them in the use of appropriate facial expression and body language clues. Next, have the students perform the skit. Ask individual students to "freeze" at different points and then have the other students identify the emotions and corresponding facial expressions and body language clues that they see. Ask the students to rank the level of the emotions being portrayed as in Step Three. If desired, have the students reverse roles and repeat the activity. Alternatively, videotape the skits, then when reviewing the tapes, pause them at different points and ask the students to identify facial expressions, body language clues, contextual clues, and corresponding emotions.

Step Six: Teach nonverbal and contextual clues, sequencing, and recognition of thoughts and emotions using *passages from books*.

Choose a passage *from a book that is familiar to the student* and that depicts an emotion she has worked on. Have her read the passage aloud (or read the passage to her). Then ask her to:

1) Guess the feelings, thoughts, and intentions of the characters, using contextual clues.

2) Rank the intensity of the feelings identified as in the above steps.

3) Demonstrate the body language and facial features that the characters would likely be exhibiting.

4) "Predict" what happens next (the student will likely already know this since the book is familiar to her).

Repeat the above three steps using books with which the student is *not* familiar. For #4, ask the student to predict one or two things that *might* happen next. Then have her read the next passage to see how closely her predictions matched the outcome.

Step Seven: Teach nonverbal and contextual clues, sequencing, and recognition of thoughts and emotions using *video movies*.

Choose a *video movie that is familiar to the student.* If possible, choose a movie that represents one of the student's special interests. View a scene from the movie that demonstrates an emotion the student has been working on. Pause the movie and ask the student to:

1) Guess what the characters were thinking, feeling, and intending using contextual clues. Ask the student to rank the emotions portrayed.

2) Identify the facial expressions and body language clues that suggest these feelings and thoughts.

3) Tell what happens next (as this movie is familiar to the student, this task should be an easy one).

Repeat the above three steps using a movie with which the student is *not* familiar. For #3, discuss with the student what *might* happen next, and how contextual clues and the feelings and thoughts of the characters can help her to make this prediction. Then play the next part of the movie to check how closely her prediction matched the outcome.

Step Eight: Teach the student to recognize nonverbal and contextual clues in *real life situations*.

Look for situations in which the student is not directly involved. Ask her to:

1) Use contextual, body language, and facial expression clues to guess what the other people might be thinking and feeling.

2) Rank the feelings she identifies.

3) Predict what might happen next.

For example, at recess time the student and teacher see John shouting at Dave. Dave is holding a kickball behind his back. When asked to identify what John is feeling, the student might respond that John appears angry. When asked to identify the nonverbal clues, she might note that John's fists are clenched, his eyebrows are scrunched up, and he is shouting. When queried about contextual clues, an appropriate response would be that it appears that Dave might have taken John's kickball and will not give it back. The student might then predict that either John will go on to grab the ball from Dave, or that he will report the problem to the playground aide (all of these responses are acceptable because they are *reasonable* guesses).

A variation of this step is to videotape other people in various situations at home or at school. (The playground is a good starting place, but it may require consent from parents or guardians for videotaping the other children.) Then play back the video, freeze the tape at various spots, and have the student complete the above three steps. (Note: Start with simple, obvious emotions and gradually progress to more subtle ones.)

THE SECRET LANGUAGE

You probably know that people talk to other people with words. But have you ever noticed that people also "talk" with their faces (especially their eyes), their bodies, and their tone of voice? This type of talk is like a *secret language*. In this language, people give important messages with the expressions on their faces, the ways they hold or move their bodies, and the way their voices sound. Believe it or not, these messages are just as important as the words we use when we talk! In fact, we can totally change the meaning of words just by changing our tone of voice, the way we hold our body, or the expression on our face as we speak. For example, consider the following story:

> There once was a boy named Peter who had a big sister named Jane, a lazy cat named Hairball, and a fat dog named Toothpick. Peter and Jane loved to eat fish and chips. They were thrilled one day when Mom decided to prepare her delicious, homemade fish and chips for dinner. That evening, Peter and Jane were helping to put dinner on the table, when Peter accidentally stumbled over Hairball, who was lying in the middle of the kitchen floor. Unfortunately, Peter was carrying the platter of fish and chips, which went flying across the room, landing squarely in front of Toothpick. In a flash Toothpick gobbled up all of the tasty fish and chips, leaving none for the family's dinner. At this, Jane looked over at Peter and said, "Good job, Peter!"

Did Peter think that Jane was complimenting him for tripping and letting Toothpick eat the fish and chips? The answer is no! Peter knew right away that Jane was really upset, and that her words actually meant "bad job," not "good job." How did Peter know this? Well, first of all, Peter heard Jane's angry and sarcastic tone of voice and saw her clenched fists, scrunched up eyebrows, and down-turned mouth. **(continued)**

81

These were *nonverbal* clues that Jane was angry. Peter also knew that Jane loved fish and chips and therefore would be upset to lose her dinner. This was a *contextual clue* that helped Peter figure out that Jane probably was upset over losing her chance to eat Mom's fish and chips.

Some people seem to understand these types of clues easily. Other people need help to understand them. But one thing is for sure – a person needs to know how to figure out these clues in order to make sense of other people's words and actions. As a matter of fact, some people who have trouble doing this say that they feel like they live on another planet where everyone around them speaks a strange, secret language with their eyes and bodies, and that they understand only half of what these strange beings are trying to say!

If you have ever felt this way, help is on the way. This program will help you understand *how* people's facial expressions and body language can change the meaning of their words. You will get lots of practice using facial expression and body language "clues" to help figure out what other people may be feeling and thinking. This will help you learn to predict how other people might react to your words and actions, and what they are going to do next. If this sounds like it might be helpful, then it's time to get started on this program! Have fun!

Figure 8a. A copy of the Student Handout "The Secret Language." Program 8, Recognizing Nonverbal and Contextual Clues in Other People.

Student Handout

Emotions and Facial Expressions

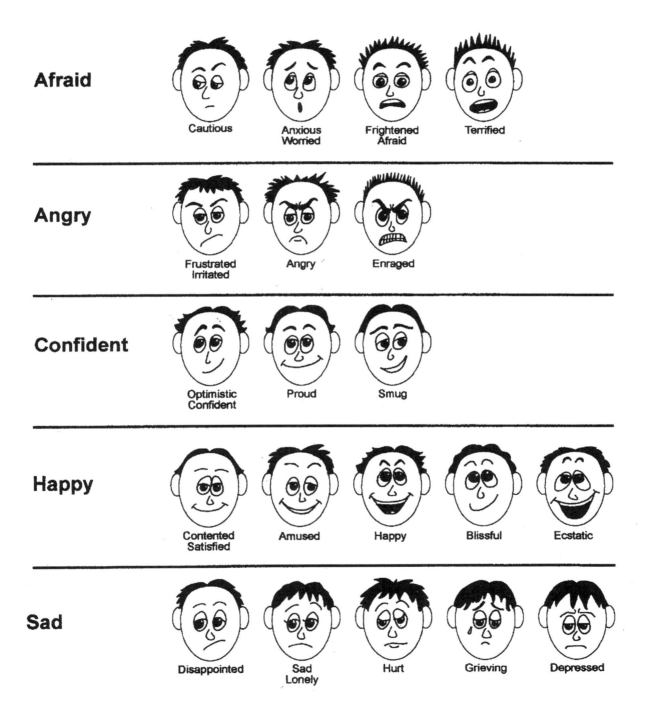

Afraid

Cautious — Anxious Worried — Frightened Afraid — Terrified

Angry

Frustrated Irritated — Angry — Enraged

Confident

Optimistic Confident — Proud — Smug

Happy

Contented Satisfied — Amused — Happy — Blissful — Ecstatic

Sad

Disappointed — Sad Lonely — Hurt — Grieving — Depressed

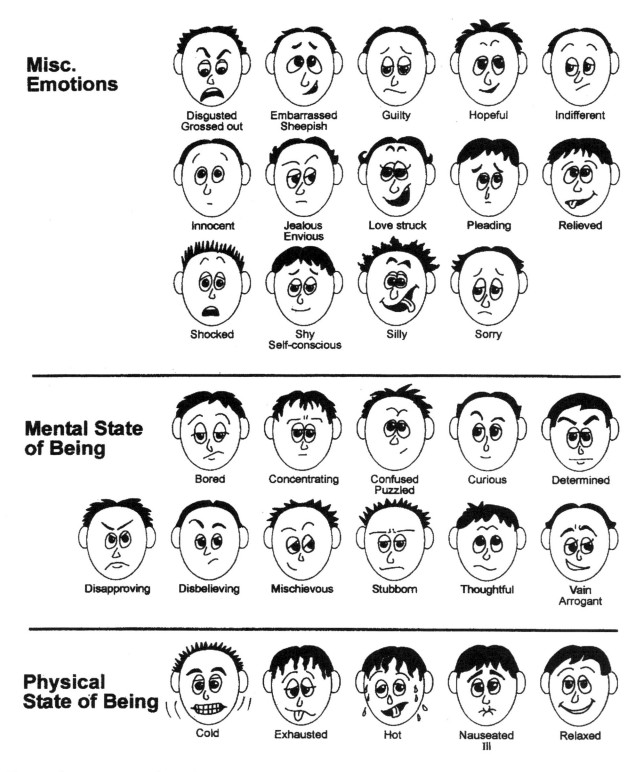

Figure 8b. Emotions and Facial Expressions

(From *Navigating the Social World*, Program 8.)
Graphics and layout by Dane Wilson. Artwork by Donna Burton.

LIST OF SCENARIOS

1. You are sitting in class one day when you notice that Sarah, one of your classmates, has just received a paper back from the teacher. Sarah looks like this: (demonstrate disappointed -- Sarah got a lower grade than she expected).

2. You are in the cafeteria having lunch when you look over at Sam and see that he is looking at Bob like this: (demonstrate angry).

3. As you pass by a second grader on the playground, you see that he is sitting on the ground looking like this: (demonstrate pain; the kid has a twisted ankle).

4. On the playground one day you see a girl approach a group of other girls. They say something to her, and then she turns and walks away. She looks like this: (demonstrate sad/rejected).

5. You are watching a baseball game at your school. As a player rounds home base, he does this: (demonstrate excitement/happiness).

6. You are explaining how to play a new computer game to a friend. When you look at him, you notice the following expression on his face: (demonstrate puzzled).

7. When playing near the woodpile with your sister, she suddenly does this: (demonstrate fear -- for example, the sister just saw a black widow spider inches from her hand).

8. Trains are Peter's favorite subject. One day he is talking about trains to the man who is repairing his parents' broken fence. After several minutes of listening, the repairman looks like this: (demonstrate bored and/or impatient).

9. While you are talking to your friend, John, you notice that Lisa has entered the room. Instead of paying attention to you, John is looking over at Lisa like this: (demonstrate lovesick or rapt attention).

10. You have something you just have to tell your mom, but she is talking with a neighbor. You walk up and start talking in the middle of your mom's sentence. Your mom looks like this: (demonstrate annoyed).

(continued)

Figure 8c. A list of scenarios to be used for role-play activities. *Program 8, Recognizing Nonverbal and Contextual Clues in Other People.*

11. Your dad has just finished talking to someone on the phone. After he hangs up, you see that he looks like this: (demonstrate worried. The father just got bad news.)

12. Your science teacher walks over to Lori, who is sitting next to you, hands her the quiz that the teacher just graded and pats her on the back. Lori looks like this: (demonstrate happy -- Lori got a good grade).

13. Your history teacher tells your study group that you all have done an outstanding job on your group project. You glance around at the kids in your group and they look like this: (demonstrate proud).

14. At the end of the semester your English teacher announces the names of the top three students in the class. When she calls out Joe's name, he looks like this: (Demonstrate surprised. Joe did not expect to be one of the top students.)

Note: This list is only a sampling of possible scenarios. Because it is often easier to understand and relate to people we know, the teacher should add scenarios to the list that include real life characters from the student's family, peers and teachers.

PROGRAM 9
GREETINGS AND GOOD-BYES

INTRODUCTION

The simple act of greeting or taking leave of another person comes naturally to most of us. Even if we are inherently shy, most of us learn *how* to do this at a very early age. In contrast, children with AS/HFA find this task more daunting than it appears at first glance. As a result, they often fail to respond to another person's greeting, or walk right past people whom they know well without saying hello. A person with AS/HFA might leave her listener struggling to catch up by starting right in talking, without first greeting the other person. She might fail to close the conversation with a form of good-bye, leaving her listener puzzled and unsure of what to do next. Likewise, she might unthinkingly use an informal greeting when a formal one is called for (or the reverse), and so on.

Bridget, for example, sometimes appeared to rebuff other children by failing to respond when they greeted her. (Once, when asked why she had done this, she replied that she had seen the other child, but had been busy thinking about something else and had trouble refocusing her attention.) On other occasions, Bridget remembered to say hello, but chose the wrong type of greeting for the situation. She left adult visitors unsure of what to reply when she greeted them with, "Hey, what are *you* doing here?" On the other hand, her peers teased her when she greeted them with a handshake and a formal, "Hello, how are you today?"

With the help of some simple rules, scripting, and role-play as presented in this program, Bridget eventually began to apply what she had learned in naturally occurring settings.

GOALS

The goals of this program are to equip the student with basic rules regarding:

1. Formal vs. informal greetings.
2. Handshakes.
3. The use of nonverbal clues during greetings and good-byes.

INSTRUCTIONS

Step One: Teach *rules* for greetings and good-byes.

Refer to the handout *"Rules for Hello and Good-bye" (see figure 9a, page 92)*. Provide the student with her own copy *(see Appendix B)*. Discuss the rules and why they are important.

Step Two: Show *examples* of greetings and good-byes in *movies*.

Choose video movies that have good examples of greetings and good-byes. If possible, choose films that pertain to the student's special interests. Preview the movie and take note of the seconds into the tape at which various greetings and good-byes occur, so that you can fast forward to those spots when showing the tape to the student. View the movie with the student, "freeze-framing" scenes to show different types of hellos and good-byes. Discuss how the actors used (or didn't use) the rules from Step One.

Step Three: Create *scripts for hellos and good-byes.*

Refer to the examples of completed "Words to use for Hello" and "Words to use for Good-bye" charts (see page 93, figure 9b.) Also, blank templates can be found in Appendix C. Help the student fill out her own charts, following the social and cultural customs of her particular environment. The teacher may wish to spend some time with the student beforehand, taking note of the words that adults and peers in the student's environment typically use to greet or take leave of one another. Discuss the differences between greeting familiar and unfamiliar adults and familiar and unfamiliar children. *(Definitions for these categories are listed on the chart.)*

Step Four: Role-play.

(Refer to figure 9a, "Rules for Hello and Good-bye", page 92.)

1. Create different scenarios in which two people meet and greet one another. (Vary the types of characters between familiar and not-familiar adults and familiar and not-familiar peers.) Using the five rules from "Rules for Hello and Good-bye" and the scripts from the student's "Hello" chart (from Step 3 above), *role-play* the scenarios with the student. Reverse roles with the student intermittently.

2. Play *"Actors and Director,"* practicing ways to say hello: Have two "actors" (the teacher and another adult or student helper) act out scenarios in which they intentionally make mistakes in their greetings. For example, they might purposefully make mistakes in their use of nonverbal clues or handshakes, choose the wrong timing to say hello, or use an informal greeting

when they should use a formal one. Include scenarios where one person fails to say hello to someone she knows well. Next, the student, assuming the role of "director," identifies which parts were done correctly, which were done incorrectly, and how to improve the "performance." The student/director then may demonstrate to the others how to do it correctly.

3. Repeat the above two steps practicing ways to say good-bye.

Step Five: Videotape the student in *practice* situations.

Videotape sessions during which the student role-plays correct and incorrect ways to say hello and good-bye in different scenarios. Review the videotape with the student. Give friendly but specific feedback, referring to the "Rules for Hello and Good-bye" handout. Ask the student to critique her own performance as well.

Step Six: Use index cards to prompt greetings and good-byes in real life situations.

Help the student choose a small number of people she frequently needs to greet, or would like to greet. Then ask her to write down simple scripts for hello and good-bye on index cards for each of those people. She may want to include boxes to check when she has greeted and said good-bye to each person. Have her choose different people and make new index cards periodically. Prompt the student to carry out the greetings and good-byes, referring to the scripts she has prepared. Reinforce her each time she makes an attempt at this task, even if the outcome is not perfect at first. Give feedback after each greeting or good-bye, keeping in mind that, although it is important to correct significant errors, the majority of your comments should be positive.

Step Seven: Videotape the student in *real life* situations.

Videotape the student greeting and saying good-bye to different people. Try to videotape a variety of settings such as classrooms, playground, home, community, etc. (Note: students usually become accustomed to being videotaped quite rapidly.) Replay the tape(s) and give feedback as above.

STUDENT HANDOUT

RULES FOR HELLO AND GOOD-BYE

1. **Always start a conversation with a greeting.**
   (This is not necessary if you have already greeted the other person.)

2. **Always end a conversation with an appropriate form of good-bye.**

3. **Choose the right *type* of hello or good-bye.**

   The words that people use to say hello or good-bye are different, depending on the type of person they are talking to. In this program, we divide people into four categories: familiar adults, not-familiar adults, familiar kids and not-familiar kids.

4. **Use good nonverbal signals:**

   - face the other person
   - stand or sit up straight
   - make eye contact
   - smile (Exception: on certain serious occasions people do not smile when saying hello or good-bye.)

5. **Use a good handshake style.**

   Sometimes when people greet or say good-bye to each other, they also shake hands. If you are not sure whether or not to shake hands, it is usually best to shake only if the other person offers his or her hand. (Men and teenage boys shake hands more often than do women and girls.)

   When you do shake hands, try to:

   - Grip the other person's hand firmly, but not too hard.
   - Give two short shakes, and then let go.
   - Make eye contact.
   - Smile. (See exception in step 4.)

Figure 9a. Copy of student handout, Rules for Hello and Good-bye. Program 9, Greetings and Good-byes.

Student: Laura C.

Words to use for *Hello*

Adults		Kids	
Familiar*	Not familiar*	Familiar*	Not familiar*
Hi!	Hello.	Hi!	Hi.
Hello.	Hello, Mrs. Foster.	Hi, Juan!	Hi, Justin.
Hi, Mom! or	Hello, Sir.	Hello.	Hello.
Hi, Belinda!	Good morning.	How's it going?	
Good morning.	Good morning, Mr. Ang.	Hi, guys!	
Hi, Mary. How are you?		Hey, dude!	
		Hey, man!	
		What's happening?	
		Hey, what's up?	

Words to use for *Good-bye*

Adults		Kids	
Familiar*	Not familiar*	Familiar*	Not familiar*
Bye!	Good-bye.	Bye!	Bye!
Good-bye.	Nice meeting you.	Bye, Heidi!	Good-bye.
Bye, Stacy.		Good-bye.	Good-bye, Tranh.
Good-bye, Mom.		Catch you later.	Nice meeting you.
See you later, Dad.		See you around.	
		Later!	
		See ya'!	
		See ya' later!	
		Gotta go.	
		Take care.	

*A "familiar" adult means a family member or a close friend of the family.
A "not familiar" adult is someone you do not know well, or someone you need to treat more formally because of his or her position (such as a teacher, doctor, store keeper, policeman, etc.).
A "familiar" kid is a kid whom you know well.
A "not familiar" kid is a kid whom you do not know well.

Figure 9b. Examples of completed charts showing ways to say hello and good-bye. Note that the appropriate words to use will vary according to the social and cultural context. *See Appendix C for templates of these charts.*

PROGRAM 10
INITIATING CONVERSATIONS

INTRODUCTION

Striking up a conversation can be a challenge for everyone at times, but for individuals with AS/HFA, the challenge may be so daunting that they simply avoid attempting it altogether. Alternatively, they may make the attempt, but since they lack the unspoken rules of how to do so, their efforts may yield a less than desirable outcome. For example, an individual with AS/HFA may fail to identify a conversational topic that will interest the other person, or he may not be able to tell whether or not the timing is good for starting a conversation. In addition, he may give the wrong nonverbal signals or use speech that is overly formal or overly casual.

Ethan very much wanted to be a part of the "action" on the playground, but did not know how to join an on-going conversation or game. As a result, he often pushed his way (both physically and verbally) into conversations without waiting for an appropriate opening, and then started right in talking about a subject of interest to himself, regardless of the on-going topic of conversation. Similarly, Ethan often tried to enter a game on the playground by stepping into the middle of it, and then made matters worse by attempting to reorganize the game according to his own set of rules. The other students, understandably feeling irritated with him, all too often responded by avoiding Ethan.

Paul, a nine-year-old boy with AS, also did not understand how to enter conversations or games. But in his case, he simply did not attempt to enter in.

When he was in preschool and early grade school, Paul seemed preoccupied with his own world. He appeared to not care about what the other children were doing and showed little interest in joining in their activities. However, when he turned eight years old, things changed for Paul. Quite abruptly, he began to notice the other children on the playground and show definite signs of wanting to join in. However, it was painfully obvious to his parents and teachers that he did not know how to accomplish this. He wandered around the perimeter of the playground with a combination of hope and anxiety, intently watching the various groups of children. Yet, he rarely ventured close enough to the others to enter into the activity.

Although the outward signs of their difficulties were very different, it was obvious that both of these children desperately needed help with the skill of *entering conversations*. Program 9 focused on how to greet another person. This program goes on to teach how to move from a greeting into a conversation (or how to start a conversation if the greeting was given at an earlier time).

GOALS

The goals of this program are to:

    1) Provide the student with a set of basic rules for initiating conversations.

    2) Help the student create scripts for starting conversations.

    3) Help the student apply these rules and scripts through the use of role modeling and videotaping.

Step One: Teach *rules* for starting conversations.

Introduce the student to the mnemonic, "*PATHS.*" This mnemonic contains five rules for starting conversations: **P**repare ahead, **A**sk yourself what you are going to talk about, **T**ime it right, (say) **H**ello, and (nonverbal) **S**ignals. *(Refer to figure 10a, page 100, for a copy of the student handout "PATHS to Starting Conversations." An additional copy for the student can be found in Appendix B.)* Discuss the PATHS rules with the student. It may be helpful for her to memorize this mnemonic and to actively recall it before starting conversations during this program and in real life situations.

Step Two: Show examples of conversation starters in *video movies*.

Choose video movies that have good examples of conversation starters. If possible, use movies that pertain to the student's special interests. View the movie with the student, "freeze-framing" various scenes to show beginnings of conversations. Discuss how the actors used (or didn't use) the rules from Step One.

Step Three: Create *scripts*.

To start out, help the student prepare *"fact files"* on index cards as described in the PATHS handout. Assist her in choosing a few people she knows fairly well (such as parents, siblings, teachers, and one or two peers, if possible.) Ask her to interview one person on her list to obtain the information she needs to complete a fact file for that person. (Role-play the interviewing process with her a few times before she sets out to do the actual interviews.) Help her collect facts about the person on one side of the index card, and interests on the other side. Repeat this activity over several sessions until she has collected several fact files on people she sees on a regular basis. (Note: it is not necessary to complete all of the fact files before continuing with the next steps.)

Next, help the student fill out a *"Conversation Starters Chart." (See figure 10b, page 101 for an example of a completed chart. Also, a blank template can be found in Appendix C.)* Have the student use information from the fact files she has created to complete the chart. (Help her to follow the social and cultural customs of her particular social group and subgroups as she fills out the chart.) It may be helpful for the teacher and student to watch the ways different people in the student's environment start conversations before completing the chart. If the student has difficulty differentiating between topics that are appropriate and inappropriate in different social settings, refer to the program "Public vs. Private" *(Program 15, page 143)* for more help.

Compliments as conversation openers*

Although the type of compliment and the words used may vary, paying someone a compliment is a great way to start a conversation with almost anyone, from a close friend to a stranger. Compliments about someone's appearance or achievements work especially well as conversation starters with strangers or acquaintances because these compliments usually do not require in-depth knowledge about the other person. Also, sincere compliments are friendly and encouraging by nature, and as such they often encourage the recipient to enter into further conversation.

(Also refer to Program 17, page 173. This program covers the subject of compliments in depth.)

Step Four: Role-play.

1. Create different scenarios in which one person starts up a conversation with another person or with a group of people. Create some characters

that are adults and others who are children of varying ages. Begin by using scenarios drawn from the student's Conversation Starters chart, and then expand the exercise in further sessions to include new scenarios. Using the PATHS rules from Step One, role-play the scenarios with the student. Begin working with students individually, reversing roles intermittently. When the students are comfortable with this activity, have them work in pairs or small groups. In the latter case the teacher acts as a facilitator, and prompts both students to use the PATHS rules as they practice starting conversations.

2. Play *"Actors and Director"*: Have two "actors" (the teacher and another adult or student helper) act out scenarios in which they intentionally make mistakes in starting conversations (for example, starting the conversation when the other person is obviously too busy to talk, failing to make eye contact, or starting a conversation about their own topic of interest while ignoring the other person's lack of interest in the subject). Next, the "director" (one of the students) identifies which parts were done correctly and which were done incorrectly, and models a better way to do it.

3. When the students are comfortable with these activities, videotape some of the sessions. When reviewing the tapes, feedback should be friendly but specific, and should address the five PATHS rules for starting conversations.

Step Five: Practice initiating conversations in *real life* situations.

Have the student choose a person from her Conversation Starters Chart with whom she can practice starting a conversation later that day. Have her think of a topic of interest to the other person and rehearse the script. Review the PATHS rules. Prompt the student to start the conversation when she feels the timing is right. (If possible, let the other person know in advance that the student will be approaching him or her to practice starting a conversation later that day.) When possible, videotape the student initiating conversations with different people in a variety of settings such as classrooms, playground, home, community, etc. Replay the tape(s) and give feedback as mentioned in Step Five. Ask the student to critique her own performance as well.

PATHS to Starting Conversations

(Remember this mnemonic when you are about to start a conversation.)

Prepare ahead: keep "fact files" with important facts about the people you know. Most people who are good at conversations keep track of facts they know about other people. They use these facts in their conversations with the other person to: 1) use as conversational topics that will interest the other person, and 2) show the other person that they care about him or her. Start by keeping fact files on index cards. Write the name and personal *facts* such as birth date, family members, favorite color and favorite school subject, on one side, and interests, such as soccer, science fiction reading and computer games on the other side. Later on, you might want to keep invisible "files" in your head.

Ask yourself what you are going to say and how you are going to say it *before you start talking.* (You will be making a list of examples of conversation starters in Step 2.) Try to choose topics that:

1. Compliment the other person (compliments on appearance and achievements often work well with people you don't know well).
2. Show that you are interested in the other person by asking about a subject that is important to him even *if it is not important to you* (check your fact file).
3. Give information that the other person needs to know *or* ask for information that you need to know.
4. Offer or ask for help (see Program 10 for more help with this topic).

Time it right. Make sure that it looks like a good time to start a conversation with the other person.

Some *not so great* times to start a conversation are when the other person is:

1. Having a private conversation with someone else (their voices are low and they are standing or sitting close together), or when he or she is in the middle of a phone conversation.
2. In a rush (walking fast, keeps his words very brief, looks at watch or tells you that he is on his way to somewhere).
3. Involved in an activity that requires his or her full attention (for example, reading, watching a movie, counting, working on a computer, etc.).

   *Exceptions: *true* emergencies or an urgent need to give or get information (such as telling Mom that she has a long-distance call waiting).

Hello. Start with a hello unless you have already greeted the other person (see Program 4 on Hellos and Good-byes).

Signals. Give good nonverbal signals:

1. smile (unless you are talking about a serious or sad subject)
2. keep your body turned toward the other person
3. use a friendly tone of voice
4. use eye contact to:
   - show the other person you are going to speak
   - show the other person you are interested and listening to him/her
   - check the other person's reaction to what you are saying
   - emphasize a point
   - close the conversation later on

Figure 10a. Copy of student handout, PATHS to Starting Conversations. Program 10, Initiating Conversations.

Student: __Chloe B.__

CONVERSATION STARTERS

	P	**A**	**T**	**H**	**S**	
Scenario	Recall info from **P**ersonal file	**A**sk yourself what you are going to say	Check **T**iming	Start with a **H**ello	Use good nonverbal **S**ignals	Start the conversation
I see Diane standing alone on the playground.	Diane is leaving in one week for a vacation in New York.	I will say, "How are plans for your vacation coming along?"	Diane is alone and appears not to be busy. Good time to talk.	"Hi, Diane."	• Smile. • Body turned toward her. • Friendly tone of voice. • Good eye contact.	"Hi, Diane. How are plans for your vacation coming along?"
I arrive at class early and see my math teacher, Mr. Cohen, sitting at his desk writing.	Yesterday, Mr. Cohen mentioned that he just bought a new computer.	I will say, "How do you like your new computer?"	Mr. Cohen is writing. I will wait until he pauses before I talk.	"Hello, Mr. Cohen."	(Same as above.)	"Hello, Mr. Cohen. How do you like your new computer?"
While leaving class, I see two friends talking together.	Everyone in the class had a test last Friday.	I will say, "What did you think of the test last Friday?"	The friends are talking. I will wait for a medium to long pause before I talk.	"Hey, guys."	(Same as above.)	"Hey, guys. What did you think of the test last Friday?"
Mom is talking on the phone.	When I get home from school, Mom likes to know how my day went. I had a good day today.	I will say, "I had a fun time playing with my friend Dan today."	Mom doesn't like to be interrupted when on the phone. I will wait until she hangs up.	"Guess what, Mom!"	(Same as above.)	"Guess what, Mom! I had a fun time playing with my friend Dan today."
I see my Uncle Bob watching TV.	Uncle Bob loves anything to do with computers.	I will say, "I am having problems typing my English assignment on the computer. Can you help me?"	Uncle Bob is watching TV. I will wait for a commercial before I talk.	"Excuse me, Uncle Bob."	(Same as above.)	"Excuse me, Uncle Bob. I am having problems typing my English assignment on the computer. Can you help me?"

Figure 10b. An example of a completed Conversation Starters chart. Give the student various scenarios & have him or her complete the chart. In addition to imaginary scenarios, use some real scenarios in which he has had trouble before. *(For Template, see Appendix C.)*

PROGRAM 11
USING NONVERBAL CONVERSATIONAL SKILLS: MAKING SENSE IN CONVERSATIONS

INTRODUCTION

"Doctor Simms, this is your next patient, Mr. Randolph," said the nurse. As Dr. Simms rose to welcome his new patient, Mr. Randolph's eyes immediately found the doctor's examination light, and there they rested. Without a word of greeting and without once glancing in the direction of the doctor, Mr. Randolph walked directly over to the examination light. With his back to Dr. Simms, Mr. Randolph began to inspect the light. Turning the object this way and that, and craning his head around in a most odd fashion to get a better look, Mr. Randolph finally spoke. "This is a Welch Allyn exam light, Risk Class Model 48830 with 3.0 amp/12 volt single light output," he said in a loud-pitched monotone. After several unsuccessful attempts to gain Mr. Randolph's attention, Dr. Simms, now nearly shouting, finally stood up and pleaded, "Mr. Randolph, if you will *please* just come here and have a seat, I will explain to you what we will be doing this morning." At this, Mr. Randolph moved to take the offered seat, keeping his eyes on the floor as he walked. As Dr. Simms began to explain the physical examination that he would be doing, Mr. Randolph stared straight ahead with his eyes seemingly fixed on some nebulous point over Dr. Simm's left shoulder. Mr. Randolph sat with hunched shoulders, so motionless that he seemed frozen in his seat. Two vertical lines like exclamation points occupied the space between Mr. Randolph's eyebrows, and his jaws were clenched together.

In this short vignette, Mr. Randolph's behavior and demeanor appear socially odd and even rude at times. Throughout the entire scene he fails to make eye contact with the puzzled Dr. Simms. He speaks with his back turned toward the doctor and is so intent on talking about his favorite subject, light fixtures, that he does not notice the doctor's increasingly desperate attempts to change the subject. When in the end he does listen to the doctor, Mr. Randolph's facial expression makes him look angry – although in reality he is not upset at all. (He simply is concentrating on the doctor's words.) Mr. Randolph does not realize that he appears irritated when his brows are furrowed and when he looks "past" Dr. Simms instead of making eye contact. Nor is he aware that his hunched shoulders and lack of gestures may mislead Dr. Simms to think that he is depressed or unhappy, when indeed he feels fine.

Understanding how to use nonverbal language is a task that greatly confounds many people with AS/HFA. They may be unaware of the messages that they give with their body language and facial expression. Even if they are aware of this unspoken language, they may not know how to go about *using* body language and facial expression in tandem with the spoken word to accurately convey their thoughts, feelings, and intentions. Program 8 helped students to recognize other people's nonverbal clues. In this program, the student with AS/HFA will have the opportunity to practice using this silent language. The nonverbal conversational skills covered will include eye contact, nodding, facial expression, and maintaining an appropriate distance from the other person. In addition, this program includes practice in asking follow-up questions and making brief comments that encourage the other person to continue talking. (Although the latter are verbal rather than nonverbal skills, they are included here because this program provides a useful format for introducing them.)

GOALS

The goals of this program are to teach the student the following conversational skills:

Space – Maintaining the right physical distance from the other person.

Eye contact – Making appropriate eye contact.

Nodding – Nodding the head to show attention, agreement and disagreement.

Statements of encouragement – Making standard, brief comments such as "hmm," "uh huh," or "really!" to show encouragement or attention.

Expressions – Using appropriate facial expression and body language.

INSTRUCTIONS

Step One: Introduce the *SENSE* skills.

Give the student a copy of the handout, *"Making SENSE in Conversations."* *(See figure 11a on page 108. Also see the student handout in Appendix B.)* Demonstrate each of the *SENSE* skills for the student, and discuss the function of each skill. It is helpful to have two people, such as a teacher and an aide or another student, demonstrate while the student observes.

Step Two: Teach the use of *SENSE* skills through video movies.

View scenes with the student from a variety of video movies, pausing the movies at various scenes to show the actor's use of the *SENSE* skills within different conversations. Choose one or two of the *SENSE* skills to work on at a time, spending as much time as needed for the student to learn one skill or pair of skills well before moving on to the next ones.

Step Three: Use *SENSE* skills in practice conversations.

Using the "Making *SENSE* of Conversations" handout *(Appendix B)*, target one or two of the *SENSE* skills to work on, and review them with the student. Point out that you will be rehearsing these skills in short practice conversations. Next, prompt the student to choose a topic that will be of interest to both you and the student and ask him to start a short conversation *(see Program 10, "Initiating Conversations," page 94 for help with starting conversations).* Start with two to three minute conversations and slowly increase to ten-minute conversations over several sessions. During the dialogue, prompt the students as needed to use the target skills, gradually decreasing (or "fading") the number of prompts over many sessions. When the student is competent using the SENSE skills during conversations with you, have two students practice with each other. Prompt as needed.

Use *trained student aides* to help teach the *SENSE* skills during conversations.

Often children and teens will learn more rapidly from peers than they will from an adult teacher. If possible, train one or more peers to be student aides. Teach the student aides how to prompt a student with AS/HFA to 1) stay engaged in a conversation and 2) use the *SENSE* skills. Teach them how to prompt in as unobtrusive a way as possible, using age-appropriate language. (In other words, student prompts should be short, friendly, and matter of fact reminders with the tone of a friend talking to a friend.) Then have a student aide work with the student with AS/HFA while the teacher stays in the background as much as possible, in the role of facilitator. Explain in advance that you will be prompting both the student with AS/HFA and the student aide if needed. However, to the extent possible, avoid prompting the student with AS/HFA directly, but rather *prompt the aide to prompt the student with AS/HFA* when needed. Remember that the more this can be done in a fun, relaxed way, the more successful will be the sessions.

When the students are comfortable using one or two of the SENSE skills, start to **videotape** *their practice conversations.* Review the videotapes with the students, focusing on the target skills on which they have been working. Help the students assess their use of the target skill(s), making sure to give roughly the same amount of feedback to student aides as you give to the students with AS/HFA. When giving feedback, attempt to keep a ratio of at least five positive comments to one correction. Again, it is important to make the review sessions fun, using friendly humor whenever possible. Work on one or two skills at a time until the student can use these skills comfortably before moving on to the next *SENSE* skill.

Continue working on the *SENSE* skills in practice conversations until the students are comfortable using all of the skills. This may require several weeks, or even several months, depending on the needs of individual students.

Step Four: Use *SENSE* skills in naturally occurring conversations. Reinforce skills through the use of videotapes.

Look for, or if need be, create situations that will encourage conversations between your students and that allow for videotaping. In general, look for situations where there are small numbers of people present, and where the students know and are comfortable with the other people present. Also, attempt to *provide an activity* that is fun, allows for conversation, and is of general interest to the group. For example, you might organize a science, computer, or art club to match the students' special interests. Likewise, you might help the students plan a community outing or a pizza party. Avoid situations that might cause sensory or other environmental stress, such as noisy or crowded settings.

Videotape the students' interactions during planning sessions and during the event itself. Review the tapes with the students at a later time, using the *SENSE* skills as guidelines for discussion.

Be sure to *notice and reinforce* students when they spontaneously use the *SENSE* skills in naturally occurring situations, whether this happens at home, school, or elsewhere. As with the other programs in this book, after finishing this program, be sure to review it with the student periodically to assure that he maintains the skills he has gained.

STUDENT HANDOUT

Making *SENSE* in Conversations

Space

Remember personal ***space.*** Stand or sit at arm's length from the other person. *Exceptions*: You may sit or stand closer if the other person is a close relation, like a mom, dad, husband, wife, etc. Also, you may need to sit or stand closer in crowded conditions, such as on a crowded bus, etc.

Eye contact

Make ***eye contact*** intermittently throughout the conversation, and especially:
- when you or the other person is beginning to speak or is ending a conversation.
- to emphasize or acknowledge an important point.
- *to check the other person's reaction to your words* (check for nonverbal clues to the other person's reaction, such as facial expression and body language clues).

Nod

People ***nod*** while listening to another person to show agreement, disagreement, understanding, or sympathy. Nodding "yes" occasionally during a conversation shows other people that you understand or agree with what they are saying, or sympathize with how they feel. Nodding "no" shows disagreement, and should be done with a gentle shake of the head, if done at all. (In most cases, it is better to express disagreement using carefully chosen words.)

Statements of encouragement

Using the following kind of ***statements*** while listening to the other person will show that you care about what he or she is saying (note: even if what the other person is talking about is not one of your favorite subjects, he will think better of you if you take the time to listen to him carefully and make encouraging statements):

Hmmm. Uh-huh. I see. Cool! That must have been funny (or scary, awful, etc.).

Expression

Check the ***expression*** on *your* face. When listening, you usually will appear friendly and sympathetic if you smile from time to time during "small talk". Alternatively, you can convey surprise, disappointment, excitement, and countless other reactions to the speaker's words by using the corresponding facial expression. Also, remember to turn your body toward the other person during a conversation.

Figure 11a. Copy of the student handout, Making Sense in Conversations. Program 11, Using Nonverbal Conversational Skills.

PROGRAM 12
RECOGNIZING AND USING TONE OF VOICE CLUES

INTRODUCTION

Just as there are specific meanings associated with various words in the English language, there also are specific meanings associated with different tones of voice. These clues conveyed by tone of voice can be so powerful that they can change, or even reverse, the meaning of a word or phrase. The average person relays tone of voice messages using subtle variations in volume, pitch, tempo, rhythm and timbre with little conscious effort. Moreover, most people rapidly recognize and interpret these sorts of messages in other people's speech and then assimilate this data with countless other pieces of spoken and unspoken information in order to understand the speaker's intended meaning. They do this instantaneously, with little conscious effort.

While the average person learns to recognize tone of voice clues by "simple osmosis," or by subconscious observation, people with AS/HFA often need step-by-step teaching and rehearsal to learn to recognize these clues. This program presents a series of small, incremental steps to help the student learn to recognize hidden voice messages. Note: for the purposes of this program, a "tone of voice message" is defined as a message whose meaning is conveyed to the listener through variations in the volume, pitch, tempo, rhythm or timbre of the speaker's voice.[25] Such messages typically are clues to the intentions, thoughts and feelings of the speaker.

Danielle, a thirteen-year-old girl with HFA, had trouble understanding the different

---

[25] The use of volume, pitch, tempo and rhythm collectively are termed the *"prosody"* of speech. In the formal study of speech, the term *"tone of voice"* is used to refer specifically to timbre or "voice quality." However, for the purposes of this program, the term "tone of voice" will refer to the elements of prosody and the timbre of the voice collectively, in keeping with a broader, popular definition.

meanings conveyed by varying tones of voice. She was a bright girl and already noticed that the way a person's voice *sounded* carried a distinct meaning that modified the person's actual words. However, her skill at guessing *what* these meanings might be was far behind that of her peers. As a consequence, she frequently became confused while talking with others, particularly her peers, who tended to make fewer accommodations than did adults to help her out during conversations. For example, she had learned about the existence of sarcasm, but then unfortunately began to assign sarcasm to the tone of voice of anyone she suspected (often erroneously) of having unkind intentions toward her. Similarly, Danielle often mistakenly heard anger in other people's tone of voice, and would react with her own anger. This, of course, did little to encourage other people to attempt further conversation with her. However, as Danielle worked through the steps in this program, she began not only to more accurately recognize tone of voice messages in others, but also to *use* them with increasing confidence.

GOALS

The goals of this program are to:
1. Teach the student to more accurately identify tone of voice messages.
2. Help the student use this information to make reasonable *guesses* about what other people are thinking, feeling and intending.
3. Help the student understand how to use tone of voice messages to help accurately convey his own emotions, thoughts and intentions.

INSTRUCTIONS

Step One: Demonstrate and role-play tone of voice messages.

Choose a sentence such as "Oh, I'd love to go to that party." Repeat the sentence using different tones of voice to convey each of the following messages:

enthusiasm

sarcasm

anxiety

disappointment (i.e., I wish I could go, but I can't.)

When starting this program, exaggerate your tone of voice in each case. This will help the student hear the differences in your use of tone of voice clues (inflection, rhythm, volume, pitch and timbre). Decrease the exaggeration as the student becomes more proficient. You may wish to *audiotape* your demonstrations and then review the tapes with the student, pausing and rewinding as needed. Alternatively, try turning your back to the student while speaking and then ask her to identify which of the four messages you demonstrated. (Both of these techniques will help the student focus on tone of voice clues, without depending on body language or facial expression clues.) Again, discuss how your tone of voice clues vary with the different messages. Reverse roles and have the student model the different messages while using identical words. In a group setting, have pairs of students practice the same activity.

Now repeat this activity using a variety of sentences and tone of voice messages (e.g., "Oh, that was brilliant," or "That dress would look great on me," or "I'm sorry," etc.).

Step Two: Use *movie videos* to teach <u>recognition</u> of tone of voice messages in

others.

Choose a few of the student's favorite movies or find movies that correspond to his special interests. Freeze and review different scenes with the student and ask him to identify the emotions and thoughts that go with different tone of voice messages, again demonstrating variations in pitch, rhythm, inflection, volume and timbre. Ask the student to mimic the actor's tone of voice. Discuss *why* the characters think and feel as they do. If the movie is new to the student, discuss with him what might happen next in the plot, and why.

Step Three: Use *audiotapes* of naturally occurring conversations to teach recognition of tone of voice messages in others.

Make an audiotape of various conversations between two or three people (obtain consent in advance, if needed). Review the tape with the student, covering a short section of the tape in each session. Ask the student to identify the speakers' tone of voice clues and the messages they give about the speakers' thoughts, emotions, and intentions. Discuss what might have happened next in the conversation. During the following session, listen to the next part of the tape to see if the student's predictions were correct. (This adds some fun and suspense to the activity!)

Step Four: Use *observations of other people in real life situations* to teach recognition of tone of voice messages.

Look for naturally occurring situations *in which the student is not directly involved*. Ask the student to identify the tone of voice clues. Start with simple, obvious messages and gradually progress to more subtle ones.

For example, at lunchtime the student and teacher see a nearby group of boys walking across the playground. One boy trips as he is walking, and a second boy says, "Wow, that was really coordinated!" Ask the student to identify the tone of voice clues and the associated meaning of the sentence (in this case the tone of voice might indicate either sarcasm with an unfriendly intention or kidding with a friendly intention).

Step Five: Use *audiotapes* to teach the student to <u>use</u> tone of voice messages.

1. *Audiotape the student(s) while he role-plays* different tones of voice for the same phrase or sentence. Repeat using several different sentences and tone of voice messages. Play the tape back and give feedback, addressing the student's use of tone of voice clues. In cases where improvement is needed, model a more appropriate tone of voice, and then have the student practice what he has learned. Also give specific help with how to achieve the desired tone of voice (such as "make your voice go up at the end" or "make each word come out slower"). Try to maintain a ratio of five positive comments to one correction. As the student becomes more adept at this activity, help him critique his own role-plays. Remember to keep the sessions fun. (Note: while students may at first act shy or silly near the tape recorder, most will forget about the recorder and go back to their usual behavior after a few taping sessions.)

2. *Audiotape* the student in different *naturally occurring situations* across environments, including if possible, classroom, playground, home, and community. Play the tapes back and ask him to identify his own tone of voice messages and related changes in pitch, volume, etc. Discuss how his tone of voice reflects his feelings and thoughts. In cases where the student's

tone of voice does not reflect what he actually was thinking or feeling, model a more accurate tone of voice for him. Ask him to practice the sentences or phrases that gave him trouble, working on his tone of voice. Give assistance with specific components such as pitch, volume, and rate when necessary.

Step Six: Correct tone of voice mismatches.

Sometimes individuals with AS/HFA will mistakenly 1) use a tone of voice that does not match their actual thoughts, feelings, or the intensity of those feelings, or 2) assign an incorrect meaning to other people's tone of voice clues. If this is the case, set aside some practice time to role-play those situations that are confusing. For situations where the tone of voice messages reflect a strong emotional component, use the emotions scales from Program 3 *(page 16)* to help the student identify both the type and the *level* of emotion conveyed by his own and the other person's tone of voice.

Sometimes it may be helpful to work on tone of voice messages in conjunction with Comic Strip Conversations.[26] If the student has misunderstood the other person's thoughts, feelings, or intentions (or vice-versa), this misperception often will show up in the Comic Strip Conversation. The teacher then can address the misunderstanding, either through discussion or by re-drawing the comic strip with her own perception of what happened. This technique can be modified to address tone of voice misperceptions: have the student read back the words he has written in his word bubbles, using the tones of voice he remembers hearing and using during the conversation. Listen for errors in using

---

[26] Comic Strip Conversations, by Carol Gray, are a series of pictures containing stick figures and thought and speech bubbles that are drawn by the student and a helper to explain in a visual format the thoughts, emotions and intentions of the participants in a conversation. See reference for Comic Strip Conversations, Appendix A

and understanding tone of voice messages. Use this information to help the student 1) correct misperceptions about the thoughts, feelings, or intentions of the other person, and 2) practice using tone of voice messages that more accurately reflect his own thoughts, feelings and intentions.

PROGRAM 13
CONVERSATIONAL MANNERS

INTRODUCTION

Many people with AS/HFA want very much to have successful social contact with other people, but they find that such contact is like a puzzle for which they do not have all the pieces. One of the many pieces to this puzzle is the ability to carry on a balanced, two-way conversation. "Conversational manners" are a set of rules that people follow to show respect and courtesy toward their conversational partners. These rules include taking turns talking, staying on the other person's topic until an appropriate time to change topics, making smooth topic transitions, waiting to interject, and using good volume control and tone of voice. Most people learn these rules during childhood and retain them into adulthood (although a temporary regression during adolescence is not uncommon). This learning occurs partly through observing other people communicate and partly through direct teaching by parents and other caregivers. Although caregivers of children with AS/HFA typically do their best to teach these manners to their children, they often find this to be a challenging task. Because these children do not easily read social cues, they often have trouble learning conversational rules through simple observation. Also, because of poor theory of mind skills they may not understand the purpose or relevance of conversational rules. Finally, these students often are already overwhelmed by other social and communication problems and may have trouble "remembering their manners," even when they do understand their importance.

In this program the student first is introduced to the concept of conversational manners and their relevance to successful communication. The conversational manners are then taught as four specific skills: 1) turn taking, 2) making interjections, 3) staying on topic and making topic transitions, and 4) controlling volume and tone of voice. The student is given as much time as he needs to practice these skills, initially working on each skill individually and then progressing to using all of the skills together in a conversational format.

Danielle, a thirteen-year-old girl with HFA, was able to speak quite fluently, making only occasional errors in syntax. However, her poor conversational etiquette sometimes left other people offended or unsure of how to carry on a conversation with her. Danielle tended to start speaking before the other person had finished, sometimes abruptly changing the topic before acknowledging or responding to what the other person had said. Sometimes it appeared as if she had not heard the other speaker at all. For example, during a period when her special interest was genealogy, she frequently interrupted people in the middle of a conversation to ask them detailed questions about their genealogy. On one such occasion her teacher asked Danielle to describe the book she was reading. Much to the teacher's surprise, Danielle's response was, "Where are your ancestors from? Do you have any royal blood in your family? I have English royal blood in my family!"

Steven, a fourteen-year-old boy with AS, floundered in a similar way during conversations. He could deliver a lengthy monologue about one of his favorite topics, using appropriate syntax and an impressive vocabulary. Because of this, other people often mistakenly assumed his conversational skills were normal. However, he lacked the ability to include the other person in a conversation. He did not understand how to ask relevant questions, make follow-up statements, or change topics gracefully. Steven annoyed peers and adults alike with his frequent interrupting, yet he did not pick up on the nonverbal clues that would have alerted him to their irritation. And, although Steven himself hated to be interrupted, he could not recognize that another person might feel the same way when Steven was the one interrupting. To make matters even worse, he had the tendency to speak too loudly, often talking "over" someone else's words. As a result, although he was a bright boy with many outstanding qualities, other people often felt that Steven was self-centered and rude. Not surprisingly, he was increasingly avoided by his peers and disliked by his teachers. This was a constant source of pain for Steven because he so desperately wanted to fit in. Consequently, he developed a significant depression requiring cognitive behavioral therapy and treatment with long-term anti-depressants.

Both Danielle and Steven clearly needed help with conversational etiquette. In response to this, their teachers guided them through the steps covered in this program. Both students responded well, although each learned at a different pace. Once they began to use these skills in actual conversations, they were naturally reinforced by the improved responses they got from others.

GOALS

The goal of this program is to teach the function and use of conversational manners, including:

1. Turn taking
2. Making interjections
3. Staying on topic and topic transitions
4. Using an appropriate tone of voice and volume control

INSTRUCTIONS

In this program, students will utilize skills they have built in the previous conversational skills programs. Therefore, they need to be reasonably proficient in these previously learned skills before beginning this program. Note that each of the four skills targeted in this program will be taught in three phases: 1) introduction of the target skill, 2) observation of other people using the target skill, and 3) practice using the target skill.

Because these are complex skills, most students will need to work on them over long periods of time. Expect this program to require repetition in regular sessions over several weeks to several months, with review sessions scheduled intermittently after the skills are mastered. As in previous programs, you will begin by introducing the skills in more static practice sessions to give the student as much time as he needs to process new information. Then the student will move on to practicing the skills in more naturalistic situations to help the generalization[27] process. As with all of the programs in this book, keeping the activities in this program light-hearted and fun will help the student to focus better and learn more.

Two handouts are included with this program, one for the average student (Handout 1) and another, more detailed one, to be used as a reference by teachers and advanced students (Handout 2). Give the student a copy of the "Conversational Manners" handout that best fits the needs of that particular student. Refer to the handout for teachers and advanced students throughout the program as you teach. Have the student review the handout as he works on each of the four steps of the program. (See figures 13a and 13b, pages 134 and 135-136 for copies of the handouts. Also, both handouts can be found in Appendix B.)

---

[27] See the glossary for a definition of "generalization."

Step One: Taking turns in conversations. (See # 1 in handouts 1 and 2.)

1. **Introduce the concept** of conversational turn taking.

   Discuss what is meant by turn taking in conversations and why it is important for people to take turns talking (i.e. everyone needs a chance to share their thoughts, feelings, and opinions, and if he does not get this chance, it can make him feel frustrated with, or not valued by the other person, etc.). Spend enough time on this step to ensure that the student understands why it is important to learn conversational manners (i.e., in concrete terms, when people do not use these rules other people may perceive them as being rude and will not want to talk with them. However, when people do use conversational manners, other people are much more apt to perceive them as being friendly and polite and to enjoy conversing with them). For those students who learn better from a more visual format, consider writing a social story[28] that explains the concept and relevance of conversational manners.

2. **Observe other people** taking turns speaking during conversations.

   In *role-plays*:

   Working with another person (a second adult or a student helper), role-play a variety of conversations in which the players use either good or poor turn-taking techniques. Stop the conversations at various points and ask the student to guess what each player is thinking and feeling in that particular scene. For example, ask the student to guess what one character may feel when she can't "get a word in edgewise" or what another character may think when his conversational partner is unresponsive and fails to carry on his part of the conversation. Cue the student to use nonverbal, tone of

---

[28] See Gray, Carol. 1994. *The Original Social Story Book*. Future Horizons. Arlington, TX

voice, and situational clues she has learned from previous programs to predict the characters' feelings and thoughts. Discuss the student's answers, keeping the activity as positive, light-hearted and fun as possible.

In *video movies:*

Preview a few video movies, marking the locations on the tapes of both good and bad examples of conversational turn taking. Then review the tapes with the student. Freeze the tapes at the scenes you have chosen and point out how the conversation passes back and forth between the characters. Use examples of poor turn taking to demonstrate what not to do. Help the student to guess what the characters may be thinking and feeling in such situations. Repeat this activity over a few sessions until the student can easily recognize appropriate vs. inappropriate turn taking in conversations.

3. *Practice* turn taking.

In *beanbag toss game:*

A fun (and visual) technique for introducing turn taking to a small group of students is to play the following beanbag game with them:

Stand with a small team of students in a circle. Have the players toss a beanbag back and forth to each other. Explain that the main rules are that the beanbag needs to stay in motion at a relaxed, even rate, and that all players must be given roughly the same number of chances to catch and throw the beanbag. This means that the students need to watch to make sure everyone gets about the same number of chances to catch the beanbag. When they see that someone has not been tossed the beanbag in a while, they should help that person by tossing the bag to him or her. If necessary, prompt the students to toss the bag to teammates who are being missed.

Start with 30-second games, increasing the length of the games in subsequent sessions.

Explain that taking turns talking during a conversation is similar to tossing the beanbag back and forth in the game. All of the players are responsible to make sure that each of them gets about the same number of chances to participate. In the same way, all of the speakers in a conversation need to make sure that each one of them gets about the same number of chances to talk.

In *practice conversations:*

In this step you again will use a beanbag, but this time as a visual cue to remind the students to pass the chance to speak back and forth as they toss the bean bag to each other. First, set the student up with a partner (another adult or a student helper) and have them agree on a topic of interest to both of them. (See Program 10, Initiating Conversations, on page 94 for more help with starting conversations.) Ask the players to talk about the chosen subject, focusing on taking turns speaking. Explain that in this game, they will toss a beanbag back and forth during the conversation. When a player catches the bag, he needs to make a comment or ask a question about the chosen topic. The teacher's job is to cue the students to stay on topic or to toss the bag when it is the other person's turn to talk. Direct the participants to make sure each player has roughly the same number of times to catch the beanbag and to speak.

If necessary, prompt the players to ask questions, give answers and ask follow-up questions, but keep the prompts as general as possible. (See Program 7, "Basic Conversational Responses," page 64, for more help with these skills.) Start with one-minute conversations and gradually work up to five-minute conversations over time. Start this activity with two conversational partners. When each student is competent at taking turns with one partner, consider adding a third partner. Videotape the sessions when the students are comfortable with the turn taking, and review the tapes with the students. When discussing the tapes, remember to keep a ratio of at least five positive comments to one negative comment, and to encourage the students to evaluate their own performance. Repeat this activity on a regular basis, using different conversational topics and different combinations of players.

In naturally occurring conversations:

Whenever possible, train student helpers, family members, and others who work with the student to encourage her to use good turn-taking skills in naturally occurring conversations. The best way to achieve this is to teach the individuals working with the student to actively watch for her use of good turn-taking skills and to reinforce her for doing so. (Reinforcement can range from verbal praise to tokens that the student can "cash in" for treats later on. Regardless of the reinforcer, the student should be given specific feedback about what she did right.) Helpers also should be taught how to briefly prompt the student in a friendly manner, if necessary, to remind her to take turns (e.g., by saying "it's my turn now," or by using a hand signal, etc.). This process of noticing, reinforcing, and occasionally prompting the target skill is very important in encouraging the generalization of the skill to new situations.

Step Two: Making Interjections. (See # 2 in handouts 1 and 2.)

1. <u>**Introduce the concept**</u> of making interjections.

   Discuss the meaning and use of interjections. In short, an interjection is a brief comment or question made by the listener during a short pause between the other person's words. Interjections can be used for many purposes, including affirming something the other person has said, clarifying a point, letting the other person know you are following along and paying attention, etc. In real life some interjections introduce a completely new topic (for example, "Excuse me, but we need to get going," or "Sorry to interrupt, but you have a phone call"). However, for the purposes of this program, direct the student to use interjections that are relevant to what the other person is talking about. When discussing interjections with the student, give examples of interjections that commonly are used in the student's daily environment. Also, go over the length and timing of interjections. In general, interjections that are short and made when the speaker pauses briefly are much more successful than those which are lengthy or cut into the speaker's words. (Note: tone and volume of voice also affect the appropriateness of an interjection, and are addressed in Step Four of this program.)

2. <u>**Observe other people**</u> making appropriate and inappropriate interjections.
   In *role-plays:*
   Working with another adult or a student helper, role-play a variety of conversations in which the participants demonstrate 1) appropriate interjections (well-timed and brief interjections that encourage the speaker to continue) and 2) inappropriate interjections (interjections that are too long, interrupt the other person's words, and/or are inappropriate in content).

Stop the conversation at various points and ask the student to guess what both players might be thinking and feeling at that moment. Ask her to give the reasons behind her answers. Help the student to use nonverbal, tone of voice, and contextual clues to answer the questions (see Programs 8 and 12 for more help with these topics). Gradually decrease the amount of help you give as the student becomes more competent at the skill.

In *video movies*:

Preview a small number of video movies, marking the locations on the tapes of examples of both appropriate and inappropriate interjections. Then review the tapes with the student. Freeze the tapes at the previously noted locations, and discuss the timing, length, and content of the interjections. Use examples in which the actors interrupt, abruptly change topics, or talk too long to demonstrate what not to do. Help the student to guess what the characters may be thinking and feeling in such situations. Cue her to use nonverbal, tone of voice, and situational clues she has learned from previous programs to predict the character's feelings and thoughts. Repeat this activity over a number of sessions until the student can recognize appropriate vs. inappropriate use of interjections within conversations.

3. Practice making interjections.

In *practice conversations*:

Set up a practice conversation between teacher and student. Ask the student to choose a conversational topic and tell her that the purpose of this conversation is to practice making interjections. Review with the student appropriate timing and words for interjections (refer to handouts 1 and 2, pages 134-137). Start by practicing a 30-60 second dialogue without interjections. Then, choose a brief interjection that the student can use during the same dialogue, and have her practice the words for the interjection. Demonstrate a hand signal that you will use to cue her when it is time to add the interjection. Next, rehearse the previous dialogue, signaling her to make the interjection at the correct time. Start with 30-second dialogues and one interjection, then gradually lengthen the dialogue and increase the number of interjections. Vary the activity by taking turns making the interjections and by periodically timing your interjections incorrectly or making them too long. When you do this, stop and ask the student to 1) tell you what you did wrong, and 2) identify her thoughts and feelings in response to the inappropriate interjection. As the student becomes more adept at using interjections, consider adding one or two more students to the conversations. Fade the hand signal gradually (i.e. make the signal less and less obvious, and then begin to use it only intermittently). When possible, discontinue the signal altogether. If the student makes interjections that are inappropriate in content, are too long, or are timed poorly, try using a humorous way to get her back on track.

Repeat this activity as needed over several sessions, using different scripts. After a few sessions, or when you feel the student is ready, start videotaping the sessions. Review the tapes with the student, using the feedback techniques discussed in previous steps.

In *naturally occurring conversations:*

As in Step One, train student helpers, family members, and others who work with the student to encourage the student to use the skills she has learned in this step in naturally occurring conversations by using positive reinforcement and, when necessary, prompting.

Step Three: Staying on topic and making topic transitions. (See handouts 1 and 2, step 3.)

Teach *staying on topic*.

1. **Introduce the concept** of staying on topic during conversations.

    Discuss the meaning of staying on topic and why it is important to do so during conversations. For example, if a person abruptly introduces a new topic before the previous topic is finished, the following problems can occur: 1) the other person may not be able to switch his attention quickly enough and may become confused by your new topic, or 2) if the other person has been talking about a topic of interest to him, abruptly changing the topic may make him feel as though you do not care about what he has to say. In contrast, when both partners stay on topic until an appropriate time to change topics, both will be much more likely to understand and enjoy the conversation.

2. **Observe other people** staying on topic vs. getting off topic.

    In *role-plays:*

    Working with a second adult or a student helper, role-play a variety of conversations in which the participants 1) stay on topic and 2) abruptly change topics. It is helpful in the beginning for the players to exaggerate their nonverbal and tone of voice clues in their responses to each other. Stop the conversation at various points and ask the student to guess what each speaker is thinking and feeling at that moment, and ask her to give the reasons behind her answers. Help the student use nonverbal, tone of voice, and contextual clues to answer the questions. Gradually decrease the amount of help you give as the student becomes more competent at the skill. Continue this activity over several sessions until the student can answer the above questions reliably.

In *video movies:*

Preview a few video movies, marking the locations on the tapes of both good and bad examples of staying on topic. Then review the tapes with the student. Freeze the tapes when needed, and discuss how well the actors do at staying on topic. Use scenes where the actors change topics at inappropriate times to demonstrate what not to do. Help the student guess what the characters may be thinking and feeling in such situations. Cue her to use nonverbal, tone of voice, and situational clues she has learned from previous programs to predict the characters' feelings and thoughts. Repeat this activity over a few sessions until the student can recognize appropriate topic maintenance within conversations.

3. **Practice** staying on topic during conversations.

In *practice conversations:*

Set up a practice conversation between the student and a helper. Ask the participants to choose a conversational topic, and tell them that the purpose of this conversation is to practice staying on topic. Have them carry on the conversation using the skills learned in previous conversational skills programs. If one participant gets off topic, prompt him or her to get back on topic. Start with explicit prompts, such as saying, "On topic, John," and gradually progress to using less explicit prompts, such as a discreet hand signal. Begin with one-minute conversations and slowly increase to three or four minute conversations. When the student is comfortable with this skill, videotape the sessions, and then review the videotapes with the student as described in Step Two. Remember to keep the activity fun and the mood light!

In *naturally occurring conversations*:

As in the previous steps, train student helpers, family members and others who work with the student to use positive reinforcement and, when necessary, prompting to encourage the student to apply the skills he has learned in this step to naturally occurring conversations.

Teach *topic transitions*.

1. **Introduce the concept** of making topic transitions.

   Review with the student the section on topic transitions in handouts 1 and 2. Briefly, a topic transition is a change from one topic to another within a conversation. In this step, the student will learn about timing a transition, and linking the new topic to the old topic with the help of transition phrases.

2. **Observe other people** making appropriate vs. inappropriate topic transitions.

   In *role-plays*:

   Working with another adult or a student aide, create and role-play different conversations that include topic transitions. Make exaggerated pauses in the conversation to show more clearly how to time the transition. Also, use transition phrases to demonstrate how to link the new topic to the previous topic. Stop the conversation within two or three sentences following the transition to allow the student to process what she observed. Ask the student to identify the transition phrase and how it linked the two topics. Discuss why you chose that point in the conversation to make the transition. Repeat this activity over a few sessions until the student is comfortable with the concept of topic transitions.

In *video movies:*

Preview a few video movies, marking the locations on the tapes of both good and bad examples of topic transitions. Then review the tapes with the student. Freeze the tapes when needed, and discuss the examples of topic transitions. Use examples of abrupt changes of topic to demonstrate what not to do. Help the student guess what the characters may be thinking and feeling in such situations. Cue her to use nonverbal, tone of voice, and situational clues she has learned from previous programs to predict the characters' feelings and thoughts. Repeat this activity over a few sessions until the student can recognize appropriate vs. inappropriate use of topic transitions.

3. **Practice** making topic transitions.

In practice conversations:

Set up practice dialogues between the student and another student or helper. Ask the participants to choose a topic that both of them would like to talk about. (If the student has not already made a "fact file" card for the other person, help her to create it now. See "Initiating Conversations," Program 10, page 94.) Ask the student to choose in advance the second topic to which she will transition, and a transition phrase to use. Have the participants start the dialogue, and then cue the student when it is time to make the transition. Stop the dialogue two or three sentences later to allow her to recall the transition. Discuss how it went. Start with very brief (e.g., thirty second) dialogues with one transition, and progress over time to longer dialogues with one or two transitions.

As the student becomes more skilled at this task, allow her to choose the new topic and transition phrase as the situation arises in the conversation (instead of choosing them beforehand). Prompt only as needed. Videotape the sessions when the student is ready for this, and use the tapes for later feedback and discussion. As mentioned in other programs in this book, keep a ratio of five or more positive comments to every correction, and encourage the student to assess her own performance.

In naturally occurring conversations:

As in previous steps, train student helpers, family members, and others who work with the student to use positive reinforcement and, when necessary, prompting to encourage the student to apply the skills he has learned in this step to naturally occurring conversations.

Step Four: Teach how to use good tone of voice and volume control. (See #4 in handouts 1 and 2. Refer also to Program 12, "Recognizing and Using Tone of Voice Clues" on page 109.)

1. *Introduce the concept*

   Demonstrate and discuss good volume control (i.e., speaking at, but not above, a volume that allows listeners to hear the words clearly). Review the use of a variety of tones of voice that are either appropriate or inappropriate for a given conversation. (For example, using a sarcastic or angry tone of voice while exchanging information, or a silly tone of voice when talking about a serious topic would be inappropriate.)

2. *Observe other people* using inappropriate vs. inappropriate volume and tone of voice.

In *role-plays:*

Working with another adult or a student aide, role-play short scenarios that demonstrate both appropriate and inappropriate volumes and tones of voice. Enact each scenario a few times, using the same script each time but varying the volume and tone of your voice. Help the student identify 1) examples of good use of volume and tone of voice, and 2) errors in the use of volume and tone of voice. Exaggerate your volume and tone of voice at first, and then gradually decrease the exaggeration as the student's skill level improves.

In *video movies:*

Look for examples of appropriate and inappropriate use of volume and tone of voice in one or two video movies. Then review and discuss them with the student. Use examples of inappropriate volume or tone of voice to demonstrate what not to do. Help the student guess what the characters may be thinking and feeling in such situations. Repeat this activity over a few sessions until the student can recognize appropriate volumes and tones of voice for various types of conversations.

3. **<u>Practice</u>** using appropriate tone of voice and volume control.

In *practice conversations:*

Set up a practice dialogue between the student and another student or helper, and describe a short scenario to them. Tell them that they will be using their acting talent to role-play the scene a few different times, using roughly the same words but a different combination of volume and tone of voice each time. Then ask them to act out the scenario, with one actor using overly loud volume, then overly quiet volume, and finally appropriate volume. (Encourage the players to exaggerate the differences when they first start this step. Then in later sessions ask them to make the differences more subtle.)

Ask the players to compare their responses when a participant uses a volume that is too loud or too soft vs. when his volume is more appropriate. Repeat this process using appropriate and inappropriate tones of voice. Continue this step over as many sessions as needed, using a variety of scenarios. When the student is comfortable with the process, videotape some of the sessions, and review the tapes with her. Give specific feedback, keeping the ratio of positive to negative comments high.

In *naturally occurring conversations:*

As in previous steps, train student helpers, family members and others who work with the student to use positive reinforcement and occasional prompting to encourage the student to use appropriate volume and tone of voice in naturally occurring conversations.

Step Five: Practice the whole kit and caboodle.

By now your student has had extensive practice with the individual skills of turn taking, interjecting, staying on topic, changing topics and using appropriate volume and tone of voice. When you feel that the student is competent in all of these skills, have her practice using them together in the same conversation. Start with practice conversations, first with the teacher, and then with peers. Review the four target skills frequently, prompting as needed. Fade the prompting as the student's performance improves. Videotape later sessions and use for discussion and self-evaluation as described in previous steps.

After the student has completed this program, hold review sessions periodically to help her retain the skills she has acquired. Also, continue to reinforce the student for spontaneously using appropriate conversational manners until these skills have generalized across settings.

STUDENT HANDOUT (Handout #1)

CONVERSATIONAL MANNERS

1. _Take turns talking._

Make sure you give the other person plenty of chances to talk.

2. _Make comments and ask questions to show the other person you are interested._

   - Use comments like: _"Cool." "Wow." "Then what happened?" "Uh huh." "Really?" "I know what that feels like."_

   - Time the comment or question well (when the speaker pauses for a moment).

3. _Topics:_

   A) _Stay on topic_ until the other person has had enough time to finish talking about his subject.

   B) _Change topics:_

   - When there is a pause in the conversation.
   - By linking the new topic to the old topic if possible. Use words like:

     "Speaking of . . ." ("Speaking of food, I had the best lunch yesterday!")
     "By the way . . ." (By the way, I saw Dave last week.")
     "That reminds me . . ." ("That reminds me. Did you finish the book yet?)

4. _Voice: Tone and Volume_

Check to make sure that your volume and tone of voice fit the situation. (See Program 12 for more help.) Lots of practice will help with this one!

* If you like to use silly sayings to remember things, try this one for conversational manners: _Tricky Micky Tickled Vicky_ (for _Take_ turns, _Make_ comments, _Topics_, and _Voice_).

Figure 13a. A copy of _Conversational Manners, Handout # 1. Program 13, Conversational Manners._ The user may choose between this handout or a more advanced version. (See handout 2, figure 13b.)

STUDENT HANDOUT-Advanced Version (Handout #2)

CONVERSATIONAL MANNERS

1. Turn-taking

A conversation is like a tennis game (only it moves slower). The chance to speak moves back and forth between the speakers in a conversation in the same way the ball moves back and forth between the players in a tennis match. If one player caught and held on to the ball, it would make for a very dull and frustrating game for the other player. Likewise, if one person does nearly all of the talking in a conversation, the other person may become bored and irritated. Each speaker in a conversation needs a chance to share his or her thoughts, feelings, or opinions. If people do not get this chance, it can make them feel frustrated with, and not valued by the other person.

2. Making Interjections

An interjection is a *brief* comment or question made by the listener during a pause in the other person's talking. If made in the right way, an interjection will show the other person that you are listening to him and that you care about what he is saying. To make a friendly interjection, do these three things: 1) time it for when the speaker pauses briefly, 2) keep it short, and 3) make sure the interjection is related to the current topic.* Here are some words that people often use as supportive interjections:

Cool; *Wow*; *Then what happened?*; *Uh-huh*; *Hmm*; *Really?*; *I know what that feels like*; and *I can't imagine how that must feel.*

*When an interjection cuts into another person's words, it is called an *interruption*. Interrupting another person's words, or making *long* interjections may cause that person to think that you do not care about what he is saying and that you are not acting in a friendly way.

3. Topics

Staying on topic

"Staying on topic" means continuing to talk about a topic until *both* speakers are finished saying what they want to say about that subject, or until a reasonable amount of time has been spent on that topic. If a person abruptly introduces a new topic before the previous topic is finished, listeners 1) may not be able to switch their attention quickly enough, and may therefore become confused by the new topic, or 2) may feel offended because they think the other person does not care about the topic that they brought up.

(continued)

Recognizing when the other person has finished what he wants to say about a given topic can be tricky. It helps to realize that sometimes people bring up *topics that are very important to them*, and other times they bring up *topics that are not as important to them*. When two people talk about something that is not of great importance to them, this is called *small talk*. In our culture, making small talk serves to help people feel more comfortable with the other person and allows for the exchange of information. If you are acquainted with the other person, check your memory for information about what is important to him. This can help you decide if this is a topic of interest to him or simply small talk. *(Refer to Initiating Conversations on page 94 for information on keeping "fact files" to help you remember facts about other people.)* Also, check the other person's nonverbal and tone of voice clues. For example, if the person has an excited, sad, or upset facial expression, the subject probably is important to him. If, however, he has a neutral or bored expression or tone of voice, the topic probably is less important to him.

In general, if the other person brings up a topic that clearly is important to him, then you will need to spend more time on that topic than if he brings up a subject that is intended simply to fill silent periods in the conversation. If the topic is being used as *small talk*, people often share only two or three comments or questions about the topic (although more is acceptable). However, if the topic is *important* to the other person (i. e. it is a special interest to him, or he is excited or upset about the topic), then he generally will feel better about the conversation if you follow-up with several questions, comments, and statements of encouragement.

Making Topic Transitions (Changing topics)

A *topic transition* is a change from one topic to another within a conversation. Here are some rules for making successful transitions:

a) *Time the transition right.*

If the other person is talking about something important to him, give him enough time to finish talking about it. When possible, let him be the one to change the topic. If, for some reason, you need to change the subject sooner, wait for a pause in the talking before you change topics. Likewise, if the other person is making small talk (see #2), you may change the topic during a pause, but first respond with at least one or two related comments or questions.

b) *Link the new topic to the previous topic if possible.*

Look for a way to relate the new topic to the old one. For example, if the first topic is about your friend's dog, you might choose to bring up the *related topic* of the dog show you just attended.

c) Use transition phrases.

These are phrases that let the other person know that you are about to introduce a new topic. A transition phrase can help link a new but *related* topic to the previous topic. For instance, in the above example, you might use the phrase *"speaking of dogs . . . "* ("I went to a dog show the other day," or "I am looking for a new dog," etc.).

Another type of transition phrase lets the other person know that you are going to change to an *unrelated* topic. An example of this type of transition phrase is to use the words *"to change the subject". . . (for example: "To change the subject, I started classes yesterday," or "To change the subject, how is your mother doing?").*

Using Good Volume Control and Tone of Voice

Using the right volume in a conversation can make a big difference in how the other person accepts your words. When people speak too quietly, other people may not be able to hear what they are saying. On the other hand, speaking too loudly is likely to unnerve or irritate the listener. Good volume control means speaking at, but not above, a volume that allows listeners to hear the words clearly. You will have plenty of chances to practice the skill of volume control in this program.

Program 12 talks about how a simple change in tone of voice can completely change the meaning of the words spoken. In the same way that you interpret other people's words according to their tone of voice, other people will interpret *your* words according to *your* tone of voice. For example, when you are having a friendly or interesting chat, it usually works well to use a "neutral" or "friendly" tone of voice. In contrast, if you are upset about something, using an overly intense tone of voice can cause listeners to react negatively, or to stop listening to you altogether. (For more help with dealing with conflicts, see *Program 18, "Resolving Conflicts"* on page 182.)

PROGRAM 14
MAKING INTRODUCTIONS

INTRODUCTION

In this program, the student will be taught a set of rules that he can use in making introductions, and he will be helped to develop a variety of scripts for introductions that he can use in differing social situations. The student will learn to apply this information initially during role-playing and subsequently in naturally occurring situations.

GOALS

The goals of this program are to teach the student to use the following skills when making an introduction:

1. Choose good timing for the introduction.
2. Choose the right words for the particular social situation.
3. Use good nonverbal clues.
4. Use handshakes appropriately.

INSTRUCTIONS

Step One: Teach *rules* for making introductions.

Refer to figure 14a, "Rules for Making Introductions" on page 141. Provide the student with his own copy *(see copy in Appendix B)*. Discuss the rules and *why they are important.* Briefly, introductions are important because they make it easier for people to meet new people. The rules used in this program help people know what to do and say when meeting someone new.

Step Two: Show *examples* of making introductions in *movies*.

Choose video movies that have good examples of people making introductions. If possible, select movies that pertain to the student's special interests. Preview the movie and take note of the seconds into the tape at which different introductions occur, to allow you to fast forward to those spots when sharing the tape with the student. View the movie with the student, freeze-framing the scenes that show introductions. Discuss how the actors used (or didn't use) the rules from the student handout.

Step Three: Create *scripts*.

In this step, the student will create scripts for different types of introductions. *Refer to figure 14b on page 142 for an example of a completed "Scripts for Making Introductions" chart.* Review the chart with the student. Help the student fill out his own chart following the social and cultural customs of his particular environment. *(See template, Appendix C.)* The teacher and student may wish to spend some time beforehand noting the phrases that adults and peers in the student's environment typically use to make and respond to introductions. Discuss the differences between formal and less formal introductions.

Step Four: Role-play.

1. Create different scenarios in which one person:
    a) Introduces himself to another person or to a group of people.

b) Introduces two other people to each other.

c) Introduces another person to a group of people.

2. Using the "Rules for Making Introductions" handout and the student's scripts from Step Three, role-play the above scenarios with the student. Reverse roles with the student intermittently.

3. As in previous programs, play *"Actors and Director"*: have two "actors" (the teacher and another adult or student) act out scenarios where they intentionally make mistakes in their introductions. For example, they may make mistakes in their use of nonverbal clues or handshakes, choose the wrong time to make the introduction, or use the wrong type of introduction. Ask the "director" (the student) to identify which parts were done correctly and which were done incorrectly. Then have him demonstrate a better way to make the introduction.

Step Five: Videotape the student in *practice* situations.

Videotape sessions during which the student role-plays correct and incorrect ways of making and responding to introductions in different scenarios. Give specific feedback, referring to the four rules for making introductions listed on the student handout. Ask the student to critique his own performance. Keep the atmosphere as light and fun as possible.

Step Six: Reinforce spontaneous use of introduction skills.

Be sure to notice and reinforce the student for any spontaneous attempts to use the skills he has learned through this program. This is critical in helping the student make the transition from using these skills in training sessions to employing them in naturally occurring situations.

STUDENT HANDOUT

RULES FOR MAKING INTRODUCTIONS

Have you ever felt like you did not know what to say when meeting someone new or when introducing other people? If you have, this program is for you. It will help you learn how to make great introductions!

Rule one: **Check your timing**.

If a person is already talking to someone else, wait for a pause in the conversation or for the end of the conversation before speaking.

Rule two: **Choose the right type of words for the introduction.**

The words used in an introduction are different for different types of people. For instance, you would use one set of words for introducing your teacher to your mom, and another set of words for introducing your friend to your little brother. When introducing your teacher to your mother, you might say: "Mom, I'd like you to meet my teacher, Mrs. Wagner. Mrs. Wagner, this is my mother, Mrs. Jensen." This is formal compared to the words you might use when introducing your friend to your younger brother: "Jim, this is my little brother, Dave. Dave, this is Jim."

Rule three: **Give good nonverbal signals.**

- face the other person
- stand or sit up straight
- make eye contact
- smile

Rule four: **Use a good handshake style.**

- Grip the other person's hand firmly, but do not overpower him or her.
- Shake hands for two shakes. (Avoid handshakes if you are not certain that the other person is a safe person to be physically close to. *See Program 15, Public vs. Private, page 143 for more help with this topic.*)
- In general, men and teenage boys shake hands during introductions. This is optional for women and girls.

Figure 14a. A copy of the student handout *Rules for Making Introductions: Program 14, Making Introductions.*

SCRIPTS FOR MAKING INTRODUCTIONS

Student: _Juan Mendoza_

People being introduced	Examples of phrases to use	Possible responses
Introducing self to another person or to a group	1. Hello, my name is Juan Mendoza. (more formal) 2. Hi, I'm Juan. (less formal)	1. Hello, Juan. I am Dana Larkin. 2. Hi, Juan. I'm Dana.
Introducing two other people to each other	1. Mr. Kaji, this is Heidi Smith. Heidi, this is Mr. Kaji. (more formal) 2. Mom, this is Kim. Kim, this is my mom. (less formal)	1. Hello, Heidi. Hello, Mr. Kaji. 2. Hi, Kim. Hello, Mrs. Mendez.
Introducing someone to a group	Everyone, I'd like you to meet Rachel Butler. Rachel, this is X and X and X and . . . (say the name of each person in the group)	Hello, Rachel. (each person in the group responds)

Figure 14b. An example of a completed scripts chart for making introductions.
Note: For more advanced students, consider having them give a single relevant detail about a person when introducing that person to someone else. For example, "Mom, this is Rebecca. Rebecca is in my class at school." or "Blair, this is Rachel. Rachel just moved here from New York."

PROGRAM 15
PUBLIC VS. PRIVATE

INTRODUCTION

People with AS/HFA can have quite severe problems in distinguishing socially appropriate from inappropriate conversational topics and activities. The consequences of this range from the individual being perceived as odd and eccentric to being labeled as rude and unfriendly. For example, a student with AS/HFA may genuinely not understand what is wrong with telling a rather large store clerk that he is fat, or telling her teacher that she has a bad memory because she constantly gets her history dates wrong. Another student may announce to a store clerk that her parents just bounced several checks the day before. To the student with AS/HFA these are simply honest facts, and indeed she may even feel that she is being helpful by pointing out these facts to the other person.

Even more problematic is that the socially inappropriate behavior of people with AS/HFA can lead to situations that are dangerous or unlawful. A young woman with AS/HFA who has the habit of hiking up her dress to scratch an itch or adjust her underclothes in public may become the victim of unwanted sexual advances. Likewise, a young man with AS/HFA may join up with the wrong sort of peers in an attempt to be accepted. It is not uncommon for this to lead to trouble with the law when his supposed "friends" leave him holding the bag of illegal drugs or the knife they used to slash car tires. Because people with AS/HFA often have no idea how dangerous or inappropriate their behavior is, they become prime targets for being set up or victimized.

Paul, a nine-year-old boy with AS, would quite innocently inform peers that they were terrible in math or that they looked funny, and then be perplexed as to why these comments, which to Paul were simply honest statements of the truth, would cause such a negative reaction in the other student. Similarly, Steven, a bright fourteen-year-old student with AS, routinely angered both fellow students and teachers when he insisted on correcting them for an endless list of minor infractions in the classroom and on the playground. A teacher caught talking in the library (where "no talking" signs were posted) was informed that she was breaking the "no talking rule" and peers were corrected for getting out of their seats without permission or for using "bad language."

Neither Paul nor Steven intentionally set out to alienate or insult other people. Instead, they both were exhibiting one of the core deficits in people with an autism spectrum disorder—poor theory of mind skills.[29] This difficulty made it very hard for them to predict what reaction their words would elicit from the listener. To compound the problem, once having said the offending words, both boys often missed the nonverbal clues that would have alerted them that all was not well with their conversational partner. Instead, they would continue blithely on with even more damaging comments.

Over several sessions, both Paul and Steven were introduced to the concept of "Privacy Circles" through the use of individualized privacy circles charts. *(See figures 15e and 15f, pages 156 and 157 for two examples of completed privacy circles charts.)* These charts were used to help the boys identify different categories of people with whom they could safely and appropriately share different types of comments and

---

[29] The term "theory of mind" refers to the ability to understand other people's thoughts, beliefs, emotions and intentions. For more information on the subject of theory of mind, see: Baron-Cohen, S. 1995. *Mindblindness: An Essay on Autism and Theory of Mind.* The MIT Press. Cambridge, Massachusetts.

activities. In Paul's case, he initially was helped to create his own privacy circles chart and then was taught how to use the chart in multiple practice sessions with his tutor. For example, he was taught that comments about someone's bad breath or funny looking hair belonged in the "Paul" circle; in other words, he could make the comment silently to himself, but not to anyone else. On the other hand, comments about the weather or his favorite T.V. show belonged in the "Other Friends" circle and the circles inward from that, and so forth. (Note: initially the privacy circles were defined in a fairly rigid fashion to avoid confusing Paul. As he became more adept at their use, the circles were defined less rigidly, and exceptions and overlapping of the circles were discussed with him.) Once Paul was able to correctly place a variety of conversational topics in an appropriate circle during one-on-one sessions with his aide, he moved on to using the privacy circles in role-play with his aide and in a small group setting. Next, his teacher and parents identified situations in which Paul was likely to make inappropriate comments. Just before these events, the teacher or parent briefly reviewed with Paul the "suspect" conversational topics and their appropriate place on his privacy circles chart. They monitored Paul inconspicuously during the event and reinforced him later on for keeping his comments in the correct privacy circle. Finally, they slowly dropped the review sessions, but continued to reinforce him for correctly using his privacy circles. Over time, Paul's inappropriate comments began to decrease, and both parents and staff were quite pleased when he began to ask which circle a certain comment belonged in *before* he made a questionable comment.

Likewise, Steven was taught that comments about other people breaking small rules belonged in the "Steven" circle. Comic Strip Conversations[30] were used in addition to Steven's privacy circle chart as a visual format to show Steven how the other students were apt to react to his comments about rule breaking. However, in this

---

[30] Gray, C. *Comic Strip Conversations*. For further information, see Appendix A.

case, although Steven stopped correcting adult staff members, he continued to correct other students for small infringements of the rules. Although he had become adept at placing different types of conversational topics in the appropriate categories on his privacy circle chart, he was unable to use this information to stop making inappropriate comments to peers. After further work with Steven, it became apparent that although he had learned that making such comments to other students was apt to cause them to dislike him, his need for consistency and adherence to rules and schedules was so strong that he was unable to keep his comments to himself. At this point, the instruction was modified to encourage him to make the damaging comment privately to a "safe" third party, such as his aide or parent. This small modification resulted in Steven making significantly fewer detrimental comments to peers.

Bridget, a fifteen-year-old girl with HFA, shocked and worried both parents and school staff when on more than one occasion she walked out of the bathroom or bedroom with her top or bottom half completely unclothed, heedless of who else might be in the room. (This behavior, while not as worrisome at age four, had become both socially unacceptable and potentially dangerous by the time she was fifteen.) Through the use of a privacy circles chart, Bridget was taught that she could appear undressed only in front of her mother, sisters, other girls in her P.E. class, or doctor and nurse, and only in a limited number of places (the locker room, her bedroom, the bathroom at home, or in an exam room at the clinic.) Discussion and Comic Strip Conversations were used to help Bridget understand the most likely reactions of other people to her appearing partly unclothed in public. After a few sessions, Bridget demonstrated a much-improved understanding of the potential problems that might occur if she appeared unclothed in front of the wrong people, and her behavior changed accordingly.

GOALS

The goals of this program are to teach the student to:

1. Distinguish what types of *topics* are safe and appropriate in various settings and with different categories of people (e.g., strangers vs. acquaintances vs. family members, etc).

2. Discern what types of *activities* are safe and appropriate in various settings and with different categories of people.

3. Recognize in what types of *places* it is safe and appropriate to be with different categories of people.

INSTRUCTIONS

Step One: Complete the Privacy Circles Chart.

Using the "Privacy Circles" template in Appendix C, work with the student and her caregivers to create a *Privacy Circles Chart* that is individualized to the student *(see figures 15e and 15f, pages 156-157 for examples of completed Privacy Circles Charts)*. The innermost circle always is labeled with the student's name. Subsequent circles, however, will vary according to the makeup of the student's family and other social contacts. For example, the second circle for one student may contain "Mom and Dad," whereas for another student in a single parent family it may contain only "Mom."

Note: The social, religious, and cultural belief systems of the student's parents or guardians will affect what types of activities and conversational topics fit in which privacy circles. Therefore, it is crucial to consult with the student's parents or guardians regarding their viewpoints before working on this program. For example, in one family it may be considered acceptable to discuss family finances with close friends, while in another family this may be taboo. Likewise, a family from one culture may find it acceptable for a girl to be partially undressed during a chaperoned medical examination by a male physician, while this may be taboo in a family from a different culture.

Discuss with the student any terms that may be ambiguous to her. For example, you probably will need to spend some time discussing what constitutes "good friends" versus "other friends" versus "acquaintances," and most likely, you will need to periodically review this with the student.

Step Two: Match conversational topics with appropriate Privacy Circles.

Using the *List of Conversational Topics (see figure 15a, pages 151-152),* choose a topic and ask the student to identify where that topic belongs on her Privacy Circles Chart. For example, if you choose the item "your address," the student might choose the "Other Friends" circle. This answer indicates that the student feels that it is acceptable for her to share her address with people in the "Other Friends" circle and with people in all circles inward from that one. Discuss the student's response, giving examples and detailed feedback. Redirect her to a more acceptable answer, if necessary. Repeat this step over as many sessions as needed, covering a variety of conversational topics. Rotate Step Two with Steps Three and Four to keep the activity more interesting.

Step Three: Match places with appropriate Privacy Circles.

Using the *List of Places (see figure 15b, page 153),* choose a place and ask the student where that place belongs on the Privacy Circles Chart. For example, if you choose "bedroom, with door closed," a female student probably would be safe in choosing the "Sisters" circle on the Privacy Circles Chart. This means that it would be okay for that student to be in a bedroom with the doors closed with her sisters or with the individuals listed in the circles inward from that. (As noted in Step One, the correct answer may vary with the particular belief systems of the student's family.) Discuss the student's response, giving specific feedback. Redirect her to a more appropriate circle, if necessary. Repeat this activity over several sessions, covering different types of places. It works well to rotate this step with Steps Two and Four to keep the activity more interesting.

Step Four: Match activities with appropriate Privacy Circles.

Using the *List of Activities (see figure 15c, page 154),* choose an activity and ask the student to identify where that activity belongs on the Privacy Circles Chart. For example, if you choose "sitting close to the other person," the student might choose the "Other Friends" circle. This response shows that the student feels that it is okay to sit close to people who are in the "Other Friends" circle and the circles inward from that. As above, carefully discuss the student's answer, redirecting her to a different response, if necessary. Repeat this step over subsequent sessions, rotating it with Steps Two and Three.

Notes:

1. *If a particular topic or activity could lead to a personal safety problem, it is important to (calmly) point this out in clear and specific terms to the student (e.g., the topic of underclothing could lead to embarrassment or even unwanted sexual advances if brought up with the wrong person).*

2. The Lists of Places, Activities and Conversational Topics presented in this program should be modified to meet the needs of the individual student.

Note that items can be added as needed during the program (and after the program is finished) as new issues arise.

3. Certain individuals, such as police officers, counselors, pastors, and physicians form a special category of people who may, at times, be privy to very personal information that would not otherwise be shared with someone they do not know well. Therefore, this category has been purposefully omitted from the Privacy Circles Chart. Instead, one or more *Social Stories* can be used to help the student understand what to expect when interacting with people in this category. (*See figure 15d, page 155 for an example of a Social Story written for this purpose.*)

LIST OF CONVERSATIONAL TOPICS

1.   the weather

2.   clothes (outer)

3.   underclothes

4.   your health

5.   the other person's health

6.   your teacher

7.   space and planets

8.   people you like

9.   people you don't especially like

10.   your religion

11.   the other person's religion

12.   restaurants

13.   food

14.   pets

15.   anyone's private parts

16.   the other person looks tired

17.   brothers and sisters--what they are like, things that they do

18.   vacations

19.   your or someone else's skin rash

20.   music

21.   the cost of your family car

22.   the value of the other person's car

23.   computer games

24.   your or someone else's menstrual period

(continued on next page)

Figure 15a. A list of conversational topics to be used with Program 15. The reader is encouraged to modify this list to address the needs of the individual student.

25. movies

26. your address

27. books

28. your phone number

29. your family's income, or the other person's income

30. your allowance or how much money you currently have

31. sports

32. the other person's bad habits (smoking, overeating, etc.)

33. a third person's bad habits

34. your bad habits

35. family arguments

36. the other person's zipper is unzipped

37. the other person has something on his/her face (food, ink, dirt, etc.)

38. the other person looks nice

39. your friend's address

40. homework/schoolwork

41. a secret that someone else has shared with you

42. using bad language while talking

LIST OF PLACES

1. your kitchen

2. your bedroom with the door open

2. your bedroom with the door closed

3. the playground at school with a supervising adult present

4. the playground at school with no supervising adult present

5. a public street

6. a public park

7. your living room

8. your parents' bedroom

9. the public library

10. a bathroom in someone else's home

11. your bathroom at home

12. a public bathroom

13. the back room of a store

Figure 15b. A list of places to be used with Program 15. Note that the reader may modify this list to address the needs of the individual student.

LIST OF ACTIVITIES

1. going for a walk

2. sitting close to the other person

3. sitting in the other person's lap

4. holding hands

5. kissing (short kiss on the lips)

6. kissing (short kiss on the cheek)

7. giving or receiving a back rub

8. dancing with the other person

9. dancing in front of the other person

10. tickling the other person

11. being tickled

12. getting dressed or undressed

13. letting your underclothes show

14. sharing the bathroom

15. inviting the other person over to your house

16. accepting an invitation to go somewhere with the other person

17. standing very close to the other person

18. smiling at the other person

19. hugging or being hugged

20. starting a conversation

21. answering questions

22. a handshake

Figure 15c. A list of activities to be used with Program 15. Note that the reader may modify this list to address the needs of the individual student.

VISITING THE DOCTOR
A Social Story

My mom or dad takes me to the doctor for different reasons. Sometimes I visit the doctor to get a checkup to make sure that my body is growing well, and that I am staying healthy. Once in a while, when I go to the doctor's office they give me a shot, called a vaccination, to keep me healthy. Most people don't like getting shots. However, shots usually go quicker when I try to hold as still as possible. My parents also take me to see the doctor when I am sick. The doctor tells my parents and me what we need to do so that I will get better.

Sometimes my doctor needs to talk to me about private things that I normally would not discuss with anyone other than my mom or dad. My doctor needs to ask private questions at times in order to help me stay healthy or get better when I am sick. For example, she may need to ask me if I have pain when I urinate (when I pee), or what my stools look like. Although these are private subjects and I normally would not talk about them to anyone but Mom or Dad, it is OK to talk about them with my doctor because she needs this information in order to help keep me healthy.

There also are times when the doctor needs to see or touch parts of my body that I keep private the rest of the time. For example, she may need to feel my stomach, or even look at my private parts. This is OK because she is a doctor and needs to do this in order to take good care of me. However, it is still very important to remember that it is not OK for someone other than a doctor or nurse to touch me in places that are private or to touch me in a way that makes me feel uncomfortable. If this happens, the best thing I can do is to move away from that person right away and go tell my mom, dad, teacher, or another adult whom I trust.

Figure 15d. An example of a Social Story to help a child with AS/HFA understand how and why the normal rules of privacy may differ when the child visits the doctor.

Privacy Circles Chart

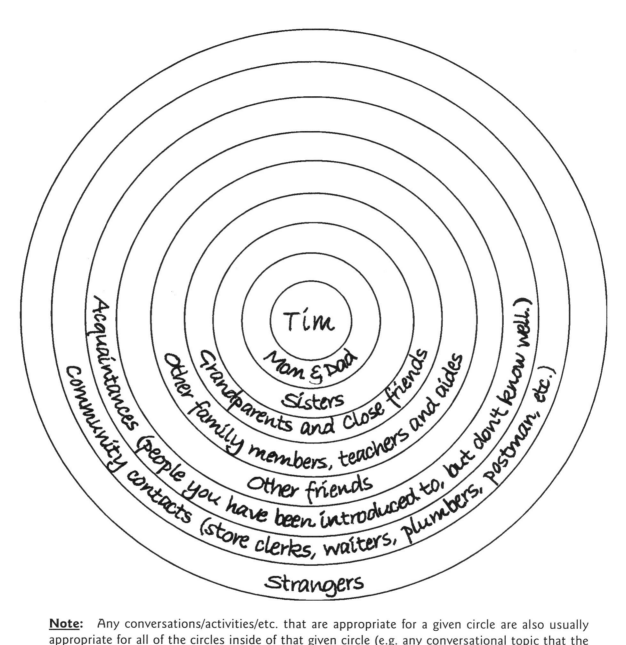

Note: Any conversations/activities/etc. that are appropriate for a given circle are also usually appropriate for all of the circles inside of that given circle (e.g. any conversational topic that the student can share with grandparents/close friends could also be shared with siblings and mom/dad).

Figure 15e. An example of a completed Privacy Circles Chart.

Privacy Circles Chart

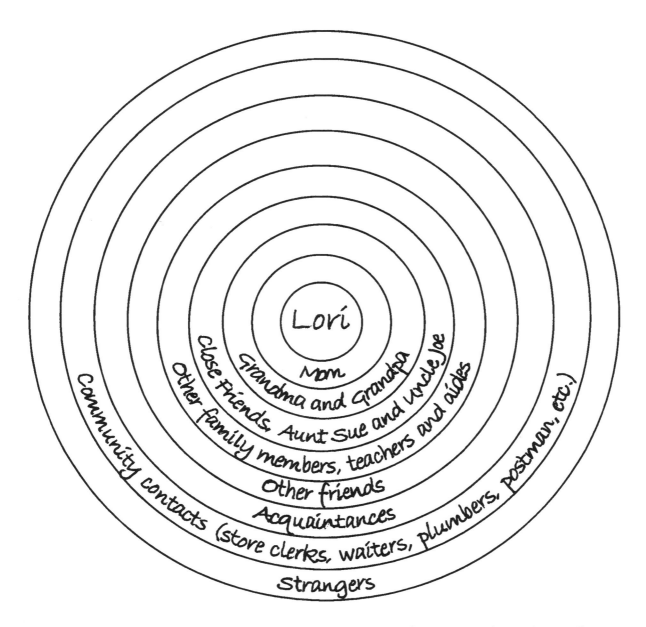

Grandma and Grandpa
Mom
Lori
Close friends, Aunt Sue and Uncle Joe
Other family members, teachers and aides
Other friends
Acquaintances
Community contacts (store clerks, waiters, plumbers, postman, etc.)
Strangers

Note: Any conversations/activities/etc. that are appropriate for a given circle are also usually appropriate for all of the circles inside of that given circle (e.g. any conversational topic that the student can share with grandparents could also be shared with siblings and mom.

Figure 15f. An example of a completed Privacy Circles Chart.

PROGRAM 16
OFFERING AND ASKING FOR HELP

INTRODUCTION

Many individuals with AS/HFA have trouble asking for or offering help. The autism literature is full of accounts of both children and adults who have endured on-going frustration over an assignment at school or even physical pain simply because they did not know how to ask for help. One speech and language pathologist described the case of a child with Asperger's Syndrome who died from burns after failing to call out for help during a fire.[32] More commonly, many of these children sit in silent confusion or display undesirable behaviors when faced with a task they do not understand.

In contrast, other individuals with AS/HFA have the persistent belief that they are right, no matter what the situation and in spite of how little they actually know about the subject at hand. This may be due in part to the fact that many people with AS/HFA have spent the majority of their time in solitary pursuits and thus have learned to rely solely on their own judgment when solving problems. In addition, rigidity in thinking and difficulty understanding another's point of view, both hallmarks of AS/HFA, often make it even more difficult for them to understand that the other person may have a better approach to solving a particular problem.

---

[32] Garcia Winner, Michelle. Lecture material from *Inside Out: What Makes the Person with High Functioning Autism or Asperger's Tick?* March, 1999.

As with asking for help, offering help can be quite challenging to people with AS/HFA. It is not uncommon for a student with AS/HFA to walk right by another student who is injured, or ignore the classmate sitting next to him who could use his help with a math problem. In cases like this, the student is missing both the opportunity to make a friend and the inherent pleasure of helping another person. Other individuals with AS/HFA may "barge into" a task someone else is working on, without first asking if they can help. This can become a rather annoying habit, even when the intention was simply to be helpful. For all of these reasons, it is imperative to ascertain the individual's skill level in offering and asking for help, and to teach these skills if necessary.

Steven, a fourteen-year-old boy with AS, was intrigued with anything mechanical. He prided himself on his knowledge in this area, and enjoyed helping people fix things or put things together. He actually could be quite helpful because of his mechanical know-how. The problem was that he did not understand how to offer help and then wait for a response before doing so. Instead, the minute he spotted someone having trouble, for instance, with a piece of camera equipment or a broken bicycle, he would walk right over, elbow the unsuspecting person out of the way, grab the nearest tool and go to work without a "by your leave." As one might imagine, Steven's honest efforts to help often earned him an angry rebuff, instead of the appreciation he was seeking. This was unfortunate because in spite of his mechanical ability, Steven was missing many opportunities to experience the joy of helping and the boost to his self-esteem that this would have provided.

Bridget, a fifteen-year-old girl with HFA, very rarely offered to help others, although she was quite talented in many of her academic courses. In fact, she sometimes seemed to be indifferent to other people's struggles and pain. Her mother relates one episode when Bridget's younger brother cut himself quite badly and was bleeding heavily from his wound. As the mother struggled to remain calm and stop the bleeding, Bridget came up and, without pausing, asked if her mother would go buy her some potato chips right away because she was hungry. Although in cases like this Bridget *seemed* oblivious to the other person's problems, she sometimes brought up the subject at a later time, (perhaps after she had had a chance to process what had happened), indicating that at least part of the time she *had* noticed the other person's suffering after all.

In the same way that Bridget had problems offering help, she also had problems asking for help. Her parents report that sometimes she went for days with a painful ear infection without saying a word about it. At school, when teased unmercifully by a group of bullies, she did not report this to the school staff. Instead, she took to hiding in the bathroom every recess and lunchtime to avoid her tormentors. This was only discovered when a playground aide mentioned to Bridget's mother that for several weeks her daughter had been hiding in the bathroom during break times. Likewise, when her central auditory processing deficit made it difficult to understand her teacher's words, instead of asking for help, she sat in silence, not comprehending a word that was said. Consequently, unless directions were given in short, clear segments or were written down, Bridget was unable to understand her class assignments. Because she did not communicate her problem to the teacher, she repeatedly failed to turn in assignments and then was reprimanded for not getting her class work done.

GOALS

The goals of this program are to:

1. Teach the student how to offer help in various situations.
2. Teach the student how to ask for help in a variety of situations.

INSTRUCTIONS

Step One: Teach how and when to *offer* help.

1. ***Introduce the concept*** of offering help.

   Give the student a copy of the student handouts *"Offering Help"* and *"News Brief: Offering Help a Big Success."* *(See figures 16a and 16b on pages 167— 168. Also, student copies can be found in Appendix B.)* Discuss the information in the handout with the student, adding any additional information or examples that you feel will help the individual student.

2. ***Identify types of situations*** in which to offer help. ***Create scripts*** for offering help.

   Help the student fill out an *"Offering Help Worksheet."* *(See figure 16e, page 171 for an example of a completed work sheet, and Appendix C for a blank template.)* Assist him in choosing examples of times when he could offer help during a typical day. Try to choose examples from a range of settings and a variety of people who might need help. Help the student choose a one-to-two sentence phrase for offering assistance that matches both the person and the situation he has chosen (e.g., he will need to choose more formal words if he is offering aid to an adult, versus less formal words in offering to help a peer). As the other person is apt to thank the student for his help, have the student include a response to the thanks, such as "you're welcome," "my pleasure," or "glad to help." Again, help the student choose words that fit the situation and the person with whom he is speaking.

3. ***Practice*** offering help in ***role-plays.*** Use ***videotapes*** as teaching tools in later sessions.

Ask the student to choose a scenario to role-play from the Offering Help Worksheet. Role-play the situation with the student. Have the student play the role of the person offering help, using the script from the worksheet. Practice the role-play a few times, varying the outcome each time. Include outcomes where the person offered help does and does not want help. Repeat both outcomes using different words and nonverbal clues in each repetition of the role-play. Reverse roles with the student, allowing him to play the role of the person being offered help. When the student becomes more comfortable with the role-plays, *videotape* the sessions, play the tapes back and discuss the student's and your own performance. (Discussing the performance of the teacher as well as that of the student helps the student feel less "singled-out," and also gives the teacher an opportunity to model positive ways of self-correction and acceptance of feedback.)

4. **Practice** offering help in naturally occurring situations. Use **videotapes** as teaching tools in later sessions.

Ask the student to choose a situation in which he can offer help later that day. (It works well to choose a situation that occurs daily or almost daily.) For example, he might choose to offer to help the student ball monitor carry ball bags to the playing field at recess time. If he has not already practiced this scenario in Step Four, role-play the scenario a few times, rehearsing different possible outcomes. When the targeted opportunity arises during the day, cue the student to offer help as rehearsed earlier. When first starting this step, if possible speak in advance with the person who will be offered help, and ask him or her to accept the help in a friendly way. On later occasions, ask the person being offered help to vary his or her response by using different words, or by saying he or she does not need help this time. Reinforce the student for all attempts to offer help, whether they are pre-planned or not. Give *specific* feedback and suggestions (e.g., "I liked the way you made eye contact with Mike before you said 'would you like some help carrying the balls?' You also did a great job of smiling when you offered to help. That showed Mike that you were happy to help him.") *Videotape* some of the times that the student offers help, and use the tapes to provide more structured and specific feedback. Ask the student to evaluate his own performance as well. Remember to keep a ratio of at least five positive comments for every correction.

Step Two: Teach how and when to *ask* for help.

1. ***Introduce the concept*** of asking for help.

    Give the student copies of the student handouts *"Asking for Help" and "News Brief: Asking for Help Makes Life Easier." (See figures 16c and 16d, pages 169 and 170. Also, student copies can be found in Appendix B.)* Discuss the information in the handout with the student, adding any additional information or examples that will help the individual student.

    *Note: Probably because of theory of mind deficits, *some students with AS/ HFA have significant problems recognizing those occasions when another person may know more than they do* about a particular subject. Teaching these students how to ask for help may be particularly challenging. However, it may be effective to discuss with the student specific examples from his past experiences when he either 1) did ask for assistance and the situation consequently turned out better, or 2) he did not ask for help and the outcome was disappointing as a result. If the student does well with visual props, consider using two contrasting Comic Strip Conversations[33]: one

---

[33] For more information on Comic Strip Conversations, see pages 114 & 145.

comic strip illustrating the outcome if the student's approach was followed, and the other showing the outcome if the other person's approach was followed. An alternate visual strategy is to help the student map out the two different outcomes using an algorithm format. Also, as these students often place a great deal of value on intelligence and logic, it may help to point out that frequently the most logical, intelligent, and mature thing to do is to ask for help.

2. ***Identify types of situations*** in which to ask for help. *Create scripts* for asking for help.

   Help the student fill out the *"Asking for Help Worksheet"*. *(See figure 16f, page 172 for an example of a completed work sheet, and Appendix C for a blank template.)* Help him identify times when he could use assistance during a typical day. Encourage him to pick examples from a range of settings and a variety of people who might be able to help him. As in Step One, help the student choose one-to-two sentence phrases for asking for help that match both the situation and the helper he has chosen. (e.g., "Excuse me, Mr. Phillips; can you help me with this math problem?" when addressing a teacher, or "Joe, I don't get this problem; can you help me out?" when addressing a peer.) Also have the student write down one or two ways of thanking the other person for his or her help. Assist the student to choose words for thank you that match the situation and the person whom he is thanking. For example, saying "thank you very much" would be appropriate to say to the librarian after she helps the student find a book, but might sound overly-formal to a peer who lends the student a pencil.

3. ***Practice*** asking for help in ***role-plays***.

Ask the student to choose an item from the Asking for Help Worksheet and role-play the scenario with the student. Have the student play the role of the person asking for help, using the script from the worksheet. Practice the role-play a few times, including outcomes when the person asked for help responds that she can help and outcomes when she cannot help, or delays the help. Repeat both outcomes using different words and nonverbal clues each time. Reverse roles with the student, allowing him to play the role of the person being asked for help. When the student becomes more comfortable with the role-plays, *videotape* the sessions, play the tapes back and discuss the student's (and your own) performance.

4. ***Practice*** asking for help in ***naturally occurring situations.***

Ask the student to choose a situation in which he frequently needs help. For example, a student who struggles with written language might choose to ask for help with paragraph writing during English class. If he has not already practiced this scenario in Step Three, rehearse the scenario a few times, using different outcomes each time. When the targeted opportunity arises during the day, cue the student to ask for help as rehearsed earlier. When first starting this step, if possible speak in advance with the person that will be asked for help, and ask him or her to give the desired help in a friendly way. On later occasions, ask the person being asked for help to vary his or her response by using different words, or by saying he or she cannot help at that time. Reinforce the student for all attempts to ask for help, whether they are pre-planned or not. As above, give *specific* feedback and suggestions (e.g., "You chose a good time to ask for help. You waited until Mrs. Foster finished helping Joseph before you raised your hand. You also waited until she called on you to ask for help. Strong work!"). If possible, *videotape* some of the occasions when the student asks for help, and use the tapes to provide more structured and specific feedback. Ask the student to evaluate his own performance as well. Remember to keep a ratio of at least five positive comments for every correction.

STUDENT HANDOUT

OFFERING HELP

Offering to help someone can be a great thing to do. Many people like to offer to help others when they need it. People usually feel good about themselves when they help someone else. The person who is helped usually feels friendly toward the helper, too. Helping someone is good for both people. Here are some hints about how to offer help:

1) *Look for chances to help.*

People usually are most helpful when they *look for chances to help*. For example, John was very good at using computers. He knew that Sam often had problems with computer assignments. John glanced over at Sam during computer class from time to time to see if he could use some help. One time he saw Sam looking frustrated and confused. John knew this would be a good time to offer help.

2) *Ask first.*

Most people like to be *asked* if they could use some help before being helped. This is because sometimes people *don't* want help. They want to do it by themselves. In these cases, the other person normally will tell you that he doesn't want help. If this happens, it usually works well to say "okay" in a pleasant tone of voice, and let him finish the activity by himself. For example, Ken saw his sister trying to replace a tire on her bike. He asked her if she could use some help. When she said, "No thanks, not right now," Ken said, "Okay," and walked away. Ken's sister felt friendly toward him because he respected her wishes and let her work on the bike by herself.

3) *Wait for a pause in the conversation to offer help.*

The other person usually appreciates it when the helper *waits for a pause in the conversation* before offering to help. For example, Helen (who knew a lot about science) noticed that Sarah and Kim were having trouble with their science project. Helen waited for a pause in their conversation, and then said, "Can I help you with your project?" Because Helen waited for a good time to speak, Sarah and Kim were able to listen to, and appreciate her offer of help.

4) *Use a friendly and respectful tone of voice.*

People appreciate offers of help that are made in a *friendly and respectful tone of voice*. (Ask your teacher or a friend to help you with good vs. not-so-good tones of voice when offering help.)

Figure 16a. A copy of the student handout, *Offering Help, Program 16: Offering and Asking for Help.* This handout is designed to be used in conjunction with the handout *News Brief: Offering Help a Big Success.*

STUDENT HANDOUT

NEWS BRIEF:

OFFERING HELP A BIG SUCCESS

A recent survey by a prominent polling firm indicates that offering to help another person benefits both the person *offering* help and the person *who is offered* help. Most people who received offers of help reported having friendly thoughts toward the person who had offered them aid. Likewise, individuals who had offered to help someone reported feeling both happier with themselves, and more friendly toward the person they had helped. The surveyors also found that offers of aid improved existing friendships, and sometimes even helped to start new friendships.

Further questioning of the respondents revealed some helpful ideas on how and when to offer help:

1. In most cases, it is best to <u>ask if the other person could use some help before starting to help</u>. One interviewee stated, "If you start right in helping, without asking first, the other person may be alarmed if your help was unexpected, or resent your assistance if he or she does not want your help at that moment."

However, another respondent gave this exception: *"In emergencies where the other person could get badly hurt or is so ill that he or she cannot communicate, and there is no one else already helping that person, you do not need to ask if you can help before giving aid."*

2. <u>Watch for opportunities</u> to help. One interviewee said, "If a person does not look for these opportunities he or she will rarely find them."

3. <u>Check your timing.</u> If it is not an emergency, it is usually best to offer help when there is a pause in the conversation or activity. Also, there are times when it is best to offer help in private. Check with a helper if you are not sure whether it is one of these times.

4. When you offer help, it is best to do so <u>willingly</u>. Both the helper and the one offered help usually end up feeling good about each other when the help is given freely and willingly. The respondents unanimously agreed that the knowledge that they were needed, and the warm feelings they experienced after helping someone usually made the experience a very positive one.

Figure 16b. A copy of the student handout *Newsbrief: Offering Help a Big Success*. From *Program 16, Offering and Asking for Help*. The pointers for offering help are written in an advanced social story format in the form of a news article.

STUDENT HANDOUT

ASKING FOR HELP

Asking for help when you need it is a wise thing to do. First of all, if you don't ask for help, other people might not know that you *need* help. Also, people usually are glad to help if you ask them to. As a matter of fact, being asked for help often makes the other person feel good about himself and good *about you, too!* People often feel closer to someone they have helped and may admire that person for having enough confidence and intelligence to ask for help. Lastly, when you get the help you need, you will finish the job more easily and a whole lot sooner! Here are some ideas about *how* to ask for help.

1. First, try to figure out the answer for yourself.

When possible, spend a little time trying to find the answer on your own. For example, Justin was having trouble doing a math problem. Before he asked for help, he went back and reread the explanation in his math book, and was able to solve the problem without help. Another student, Keith, was not sure how to make an outline for his history report. After fifteen minutes he still had no idea how to start and wisely decided to ask his teacher for help. After she helped him, Keith was able to finish the outline in twenty minutes. Brad, on the other hand, did not understand his English assignment but sat through almost the entire class before asking his teacher for help. By this time, he was so frustrated and upset that he could not focus on what the teacher was saying and left class without understanding the assignment.

2. Decide who and when to ask for help.

Before asking for help, it is best to spend a minute or two deciding who is the best person to ask, and then wait for a good time to ask your question. If possible, make a list *in advance* of the people you can ask for help in different situations. It is usually best to choose someone you trust and who knows about the subject you need help with. Usually you will be okay asking a trusted friend, family member, teacher, or aide for help. In other cases, someone like a counselor, police officer, doctor, nurse, or clerk may be the best person to ask for help. Check with a parent or mentor to decide which people to ask for help in different situations. For example, Jim sometimes did not ask for help when he needed it because he did not know *whom* to ask. So with his counselor's help, Jim made up a list of different people he could ask for help in different situations. He decided that he would ask one of his classmates, Ted or Rick, for help in math class. If they were unable to help, then he would ask the teacher. He also listed Mrs. Hardy, the playground aide, and Mr. Simpson, the vice principal, to ask for help during lunch period, and so on. Then Jim reminded himself to wait for a pause in the conversation or activity before asking for help. (The exception to this rule was that if someone was in danger, it was okay to interrupt to ask for help!)

3. Practice how you will ask for help before you do it.

Spend a minute silently practicing the words and tone of voice you will use when you ask for help. For example, Jennifer had trouble getting the words out right when she needed to ask for help. Then her mom suggested saying the words to herself beforehand. Jennifer tried this and found (to her relief!) that asking for help went a lot smoother from then on.

Figure 16c. A copy of the student handout *Asking for Help, Program 16: Offering and Asking for Help.* This handout is designed to be used in conjunction with the handout, *News Brief: Asking for Help Makes Life Easier* (*see p. 170*).

STUDENT HANDOUT

NEWS BRIEF:
ASKING FOR HELP MAKES LIFE EASIER

In a study released late yesterday, researchers on the campuses of U. Noaskitt and U. Nogetitt found that people who asked for help at appropriate times tended to suffer less anxiety and confusion than those who did not. Of the people studied, those who asked for help when they needed it rated their lives as being significantly easier than those who rarely or never asked for help. When asked why some people avoid asking for help, Dr. Sol Eution stated that sometimes people do not know what words to use, or when and whom to ask for help. He added that sometimes people are afraid that others might think they are less intelligent if they ask for help. Nothing could be further from the truth, however, according to Dr. Eution. In his words, "Our study shows that people admire individuals who ask for help when necessary."

The study also revealed some ideas to help people determine how and when to ask for help. 943 participants judged by an independent panel to have the best help-seeking skills were asked for their advice on requesting help. Here are the results:

1. Before asking for help, it is a good idea to spend a few minutes trying to figure out the answer for yourself. This may entail looking for the answer in a book, for example. However, study participants advised the reader to not wait to request help until he or she is stressed or desperate. Participants unanimously agreed that when they waited to request help until they were stressed, they were often too frustrated to understand the response. (They also advised the reader to not wait to ask for help in emergencies when someone could get badly hurt or become seriously ill.)

2. Decide whom to ask for help. Participants recommended spending a few minutes deciding who is the best person to ask for help. Their recommendation: try to pick someone who you know is knowledgeable about the subject, and be sure that he or she is someone that you can trust (for example, a trusted friend, family member, teacher or aide, or in some cases a police officer, shop keeper, etc.) Check with a family member, teacher, or aide for help determining people you can ask for help in different types of situations.

3. Check the timing. Participants suggested that if the person you plan to ask for help is busy, wait until there is a pause in the conversation or activity. (Exception: do not wait to request help in cases where someone could get harmed or become seriously ill!)

4. Practice the words you will use before asking for help. Study participants said that they found asking for help to be much easier when they had practiced the words that they would use before requesting help. Dr. Eution added, "don't forget to use good eye contact and tone of voice."

Figure 16d. A copy of the student handout, *News Brief: Asking for Help Makes Life Easier.* This handout is designed to be used in conjunction with the handout *Asking for Help.* (See page 169.)

Offering to Help Worksheet

Situations in which to offer help	Timing	Script (what to say)
Another student is having trouble with a math problem he just started.	Wait 2-3 minutes. If he does not figure it out, then offer to help.	"Do you need help with your math?"
The kitchen needs to be cleaned up after dinner.	As soon as you are done with dinner.	"What can I do to help?"
John is having trouble with a computer program and asks another student to help him.	Wait to see if the other student is able to help.	If the other student is not able to help John, then say, "I think I know how to do that. Do you want my help?"
Your brother has been trying for 20 minutes but can't figure out how to operate the new stereo equipment.	You have waited enough time (20 minutes) to give him a chance to figure it out on his own.	"Can I help?"
Your teacher Mrs. Johnson has to carry a bunch of heavy books somewhere.	As soon as you see her trying to carry them.	"Mrs. Johnson, can I help you carry the books?"
Your mom is by herself and is crying.	When you see her crying.	"Mom, do you need a hug?"
Your sister spills milk at the table.	As soon as the milk is spilled.	"Do you need my help?"
Someone gets hurt on the playing field.	Offer help right away.	"Are you okay? Do you need some help?"

Figure 16e. An example of a completed *Offering Help Worksheet.* Note that the timing and the scripts will vary according to the circumstances. It is important to include situations in which the student should wait before offering to help or should not help at all. Note also that it is helpful (whenever possible) to give approximate lengths of time that the student should wait before offering help.

Asking for Help Worksheet

Situations in which to ask for help	Whom to ask	When to ask	Script (what to say)
You are getting picked on during recess.	Yard monitor or teacher.	Right away.	"Can you help me? Those kids are picking on me."
You are not sure what stop is yours on the bus.	Bus driver.	When getting on the bus or as soon as you realize you need help.	"Can you tell me when my bus stop comes?"
You don't understand the classroom assignment.	Teacher or aide.	Raise your hand when the teacher pauses during her instructions.	"I don't understand the assignment."
You are having trouble in the morning getting your shoes on for school.	Mom or Dad.	After trying for one or two minutes.	"Can you help me? I am having trouble with my shoes."
You don't understand what the other kids are saying on the playground.	The other kids.	During a short pause in their conversation.	"I don't understand. Can you explain that to me?"
You don't understand a math problem in math class.	Teacher or aide.	After working on the problem for 5 minutes.	"Can you help me? I don't understand this math problem."
You need to go to the bathroom.	Whichever adult is in charge.	As soon as you feel the need to go to the bathroom.	"May I go to the bathroom?"
You see something on fire.	Anyone you can find.	Immediately.	"Something is on fire!"
You are in class. You are worried about what you might have for dinner tonight.		Don't ask about dinner. Class time is not the time to worry about dinner.	

Figure 16f. An example of a completed *Asking for Help* Worksheet. Note that the timing and the scripts will vary according to needs of the individual student. It is important to include situations in which the student should wait before asking for help or should not ask at all. Note also that it is helpful (whenever possible) to give approximate lengths of time that the student should wait before asking for help.

PROGRAM 17
GIVING AND RECEIVING COMPLIMENTS

INTRODUCTION

Giving and receiving compliments is often unfamiliar territory for individuals with AS/HFA. For example, they may give compliments so infrequently that family members, friends, and others may not feel valued or loved. Conversely, they may give so many compliments that the recipient begins to feel that the praise is insincere. When they are recipients of compliments they may fail to acknowledge the praise, either giving an inappropriate response or ignoring the compliment entirely.

Because of their dependence on facts and "logic" and their compromised ability to read other people's minds, individuals with AS/HFA may not understand that people sometimes need to hear the obvious. For example, Sam never tells his mother or father that he loves them because he assumes his parents already know that he loves them! Similarly, Kim misses an opportunity to praise Dana for her performance at a soccer match because she figures that Dana already knows she did well and does not need to be told something she already knows. What both Sam and Kim are missing is the understanding that other people need to be *told* that they are cared for and that they have done well, in order to feel affirmed and valued.

Most neurotypical people learn very early in life that complimenting another person can bring both people closer together. Also, over time most people observe that the right compliment at the right time may even lead a person to change some aspect of his/her life for the better. This understanding of the power and importance of praise often is missing in individuals with AS/HFA. Furthermore, they may not fully comprehend how to fit a compliment into a conversation. They may miss opportunities to use a compliment to start a conversation, to insert a compliment in the middle of a conversation, or to give a compliment without further dialogue.

This program uses Carol Gray's definitions of three types of compliments, and defines a fourth type of compliment called a secondary compliment. The student receives guidelines for how, when, and why to give compliments as well as practice in the skills of giving and receiving compliments.

GOALS

The goals of this program are to help the student to:
1. Understand and appropriately use four types of compliments.
2. Identify whom, when, and how often to compliment.
3. Respond to compliments appropriately.

INSTRUCTIONS

Step One: Identify four types of compliments. Discuss helpful hints about giving and receiving compliments.

Give the student copies of the handouts *"Four Types of Compliments"* and *"Helpful Hints About Compliments."* (See figures 17a and 17b, pages 178 and 179-180. Also, copies of these handouts are included in Appendix B.) Discuss the information in the handouts with the student, giving additional examples that relate to the student's own social situation.

Step Two: Create scripts for giving compliments.

Help the student complete the chart "Scripts for Compliments." (See figure 17c, page 181 for an example of a completed chart, and Appendix C for a blank template.) As the student fills out the chart, help him choose people he sees often, and scenarios that occur frequently, as he will be using the people and scenarios from his chart to practice complimenting in later steps. Note that the type of compliment and the formality of the words used will depend on whether the recipient is a family member, close friend, teacher, acquaintance, etc. (Refer to figure 17a, page 178, "Four Types of Compliments," for guidelines.)

Step Three: Practice giving and receiving compliments using role-play.

Before beginning, review the handout *"Helpful Hints about Compliments"* (page 179) with the student. Using scenarios from Step Two, role-play giving and accepting compliments. Exchange roles to allow the student to play the roles of both giver and recipient of the compliment. Identify problem areas for the student and intentionally make similar errors during some of the role-plays. Ask the student to point out what went well and what went wrong, and how to improve the compliment or response. Repeat the role-play incorporating the improvements. Another option is for the student to watch while the teacher and a helper perform two role-plays: once incorporating intentional errors, and once in an appropriate way. Then ask the student to critique them and choose the one he feels is more appropriate. Repeat this activity over several sessions. As the student becomes more comfortable doing the role-plays, *videotape* the sessions, and use them for later discussion. Give feedback, aiming for a ratio of five positive comments to one correction. Note: if more practice is needed, the student may complete and use as many copies of the script charts as necessary.

Step Four: Practice giving and receiving compliments in contrived situations.

Help the student choose one of the people and scenarios from his script chart. Review the scenario and script, and have the student rehearse the compliment (unless this has already been done in Step Three). Then ask the student to compliment the recipient the next time he sees him or her. (Try to arrange this for later that day, if possible.) When first starting out, enlist the recipient's support in advance, so that he or she will be sure to take notice of the compliment and respond to it in a positive way, even if the student's delivery is not quite perfect. If necessary, cue the student to give the compliment at the appropriate time. After the compliment, discuss with the student how things went. At times, it may be helpful to bring the recipient into this discussion in order to obtain feedback on what he or she thought and felt in response to the compliment. Encourage the student to critique his own actions. Feedback should be as positive and specific as possible. Repeat this step until the pupil is proficient at giving and receiving compliments with little to no prompting.

To help the student practice receiving compliments (it won't hurt his self-esteem, either), enlist various people to compliment him during the day. Praise him for responding appropriately, prompting only if necessary. Briefly, the simplest way to respond to a compliment is to say "thank you." Although usually not absolutely necessary, the student may want to add another sentence or two about the subject of the compliment. This sometimes creates an opening to further conversation. (For example, in response to the compliment "That is a beautiful dog you have!" the recipient might answer, "Thank you. I am going to be showing him this weekend." This opens up the possibility of further dialogue about the dog or the show if the other person wishes to pursue the conversation. *(Refer to "A Word about Responding to Compliments" at the end of the "Helpful Hints . . ." handout, fig. 17b, page 180.)*

Step Five: Aid generalization through reinforcement of skills in naturally occurring situations.

Be sure to actively notice and reinforce the student for giving and receiving compliments appropriately in naturally occurring situations. This will help the student generalize these skills to a variety of people and settings.

STUDENT HANDOUT

FOUR TYPES OF COMPLIMENTS*

1. Personality or Character Compliments

Personality and character compliments are positive statements about a person's general personality or character traits. (For example, "You are such a helpful person!") Because they require in-depth knowledge of the recipient, these compliments usually are reserved for family members or friends.

2. Skills, Talents, and Achievements Compliments

This type of compliment is a positive statement about a person's skills, talents, achievements, or hard work. For example, "Wow, you got a really high score on that Play Station game!" These compliments can be paid to family members and friends. Also, they sometimes work with people with whom one is not acquainted, but in such cases one must be sure to state how he or she knows this information about the other person. For example, *"I saw you play soccer at the match.* You are a great goalie!"

3. Appearance Compliments

Appearance compliments are positive statements about the way someone looks, or about their clothes or accessories. For example, "Your new haircut looks good!" Because they do not require detailed knowledge of the recipient, these compliments often are appropriate for acquaintances as well for family members and friends.

4. Secondary Compliments

Secondary compliments make a positive statement about a person, place, or thing connected to the person being complimented. For example, "Your golden retriever is beautiful," or "You have great kids!" or "Your garden is lovely." This type of compliment requires the least amount of familiarity with the recipient, and therefore works well with most categories of people, including those whom you have not previously met.

*With the exception of *secondary compliments,* the items on this list were adapted with permission from: *Gray's Guide to Compliments: A Social Workbook.* Gray, Carol. Jenison Public Schools, MI. 1999

Figure 17a. A copy of the student handout *Four Types of Compliments, Program 17: Giving and Receiving Compliments.*

STUDENT HANDOUT

HELPFUL HINTS ABOUT COMPLIMENTS*

1. While people usually pay compliments with their words, people also can give *silent compliments* by using facial expressions such as a special smile, or body signals such as a "thumbs up."

2. Compliments can be so powerful that they can change the way the other person thinks of himself, or change the way he does things. For example, a person who has been complimented for his or her smile may feel friendlier, and respond by smiling at others more frequently.

3. Some compliments give information that is already known. In these cases, the person giving the compliment tells the recipient something good about himself that he already knows. For example, John might say to Steve, "Steve, you are so talented on the computer!" Even though Steve already knows that his computer skills are good, he still likes to know that *John* notices how good he is on the computer. John's positive comment about Steve's computer skills makes Steve feel valued and recognized by John. As a result, Steve feels friendlier toward John.

4. True compliments are sincere. Carol Gray states, "sincerity . . . means that what a person is thinking and saying is the same thing." In other words, if a person says something nice about another person, but doesn't mean what he says, this is not a true compliment. More often than not, the other person will know that the words are not sincere, and may feel angry, hurt, or distrusting as a result. [People often know when someone is not sincere from the context of the situation, or from the nonverbal signals (tone of voice, body language, and facial expression) given by the person making the compliment.]

* This list has been adapted with permission from: Gray's Guide to Compliments: A Social Workbook. Gray, Carol. Jenison Public Schools. Michigan. 1999

Figure 17b. A copy of the student handout *Helpful Hints About Compliments*, Program 17, Giving and Receiving Compliments.

5. How often one should compliment depends on the category of person being complimented. Complimenting *too often* can lead the other person to feel that the compliments are insincere. Complimenting a loved one or close friend *too infrequently* may cause the person to feel that he or she is unimportant to that person. Carol Gray suggests that it is good to compliment a loved one or *close* friend 1 – 5 times a day, a co-worker who is a friend 1 – 2 times a week, a co-worker who is not a friend 0 – 1 times/week, and a friend 1 – 3 times /week.

6. A compliment and the recipient's response can constitute the entire exchange between two people. Compliments also can open a conversation or start a new topic within a conversation. Appearance and secondary compliments can work especially well as conversation starters because they do not require in-depth knowledge about the other person. For example, a person could open a conversation with someone he or she has never met by saying, "Your dog is beautiful. How old is she?" or "That's a great hat. Where did you get it?"

A WORD ABOUT RESPONDING TO COMPLIMENTS

Always remember to acknowledge a compliment paid to you. This usually can be done with a smile and a thank you. This lets the other person know that you heard him, and that you appreciate the compliment. Sometimes, it works well to add an extra sentence to the "thank you." For example, in response to "Wow, you scored really high on that Play Station game," you might say "Thanks. I've been working really hard on this game!" Sometimes an additional comment like this can start a further conversation. For example, the other person might respond to this last comment with "I can tell you have put a lot of work into your game. Have you played for long?" As you can see, the two people now have something more to talk about, and they can choose to continue with a much longer conversation if they want to.

Date: 2/3/01	COMPLIMENTS SCRIPTS		Student: Alice Andrews
Person to be complimented	**Type of compliment** **Skills/Effort/ Achievement Appearance Personality Secondary**	**When & Where**	**Script**
Sister	Appearance	–At home –Before church	Rosie, you look very pretty in that dress.
Mother	Skills/Effort/ Achievement	–In the kitchen –During dinner	Thanks Mom, this is a great meal!
Teacher	Skills/Effort/ Achievement And Personality	–In the classroom –After class	Mrs. Sanchez, thank you for helping me with math today. You are very nice, and you are smart, too.
Friend	Secondary	–In the bike parking area –After arriving at school	I really like your new bike. Where did you get it?
Father	Personality	–At home –In the evening, after finishing homework	Dad, you are a very patient person, and you are good at helping with homework!
Friend	Skills/Effort/ Achievement	–In the gym –During PE	Sue, you are great at volleyball!

Figure 17c. An example of a completed Compliment Scripts chart. *(A blank template can be found in Appendix C.)*

PROGRAM 18
RESOLVING CONFLICTS
Sharing Negative Feelings And Opinions

INTRODUCTION

Note: Effectively communicating opinions and feelings is a highly complicated process and any program designed to teach this skill is likely to be subject to oversimplification. Since this is an advanced program that incorporates several skills taught in earlier parts of this book, parts or all of Program 18 may not be appropriate or achievable for every student. In such cases, one option is to put this program aside for a while and revisit it at a later time, after the student's skill level has matured.

Knowing how to share feelings and opinions during a conflict, in a way that is both honest and respectful of the other person, is a skill that can take an average person an entire lifetime to learn and perfect. It is a complex skill that requires a person to identify her own and the other person's emotions, determine their causes, and assign some sort of rank or degree to them. In the midst of this, she must pull together as much information as possible about the other person's past history and current emotional state, and use this information both to ascertain the other person's intent and to predict how that person will respond to her words. She must keep her emotions under control while discussing them with the other party. To make matters even more complicated, as the exchange proceeds, *new* emotions inevitably arise that need to be analyzed, understood and responded to as they come up.

Considering the fact that simple social exchanges of information *without* additional emotional content can be very challenging for people with AS/HFA, it is not surprising that effectively exchanging information *with* a strong emotional overlay can be extremely difficult for them to accomplish unless they are given sufficient help. This process can be slowed down and made considerably easier by communicating in writing; this technique should be encouraged and used whenever possible. However, it is not always feasible. Therefore, this program will cover both written and verbal conflict resolution skills. It is divided into six sections that start with teaching the value of working toward a positive outcome and end with making restitution.

GOALS

The goals of this program are to help the student:

1. Learn the value of working toward positive outcomes that are fair to both parties in a conflict.

2. Learn to express emotions in written form such as journals, letters, and notes.

3. Learn to talk problems over with a trusted third person.

4. Use good discussion techniques.

5. Recognize when an apology is necessary and then apologize appropriately.

6. Make restitution for mistakes.

INSTRUCTIONS

Each of the following steps corresponds to a separate section in the student handout *"Guidelines for Dealing with Conflict." (A copy of this handout can be found at the end of this program, on pages 197-212, figure 18a, and in Appendix B.)* As you work through each step of the program, read and review with the student the corresponding section of the handout. As this is a long and complex program, plan on taking anywhere from several weeks to several months to complete it.

Step One: Teach the advantages of *working toward a positive outcome* versus *arguing to win* in a conflict.

Before beginning this step, read Step One in the student handout *"Guidelines for Dealing with Conflict" (page 197)* with the student. Discuss the pros and cons of arguing to win versus working toward a positive outcome.

1. ***Demonstrate* through role-play.**

Working with another adult or a student aide, *demonstrate* for the student examples of arguing versus working toward a positive outcome. For example, two of Phoebe's teachers made up the following role-play in which they played two students, Bob and Dave. Bob and Dave are walking towards each other in a hallway at school when Bob accidentally bumps into Dave, causing him to drop all of his books.

In the <u>first</u> scenario, Bob apologizes but Dave responds by yelling at him, calling him names, and accusing Bob of running into him on purpose. When Bob replies that it was an accident, Dave insists that Bob is a careless slob and that he (Dave) has done nothing to deserve such treatment. *At this point, the teacher(s) stop the role-play, and through the use of nonverbal, tone of voice, and situational clues, help Phoebe identify: 1) what both Bob and Dave may be feeling, and 2) what is likely to happen next.* Then the players finish the role-play, carrying it to a logical conclusion. (For example, both students leave angry, but later on Bob wonders why Dave is acting so distant.) *The teacher(s) again discusses the role-play with Phoebe and compare its conclusion with the one Phoebe predicted.*

In the <u>second</u> scenario, the teachers again play the roles of Bob and Dave. This time however, after Bob apologizes Dave takes a moment to collect his thoughts and notices that Bob's tone of voice and facial expression indicate that he appears honestly sorry. *At this point, the teacher(s) stops the action and asks Phoebe to 1) evaluate the message given by Bob's tone of voice, body language, and facial expression (i.e. is this a sincere apology?), 2) suggest what Dave should do next, and 3) predict what the outcome will be.* The teachers continue the role-play, again carrying it to a natural conclusion. *At the end of the session, the teachers ask Phoebe to compare the two ways of dealing with the conflict, focusing on the long-term outcomes.*

2. Provide *practice* through role-play.

Create scenes in which the student participates, role-playing both approaches to dealing with conflict (i.e., arguing to win versus working toward a positive outcome). Freeze the action at key points during the role-play and ask the student what she is feeling and thinking, what the *other* person might be feeling and thinking, and what is likely to occur next. As above, use situational, nonverbal, and tone of voice clues to help with this task. Alternate roles periodically.

Step Two: Teach the student to express negative emotions and to problem solve through writing, using journals, letters, notes and Comic Strip Conversations.

Prior to starting this step, read and discuss with the student Step Two in the student handout *"Guidelines for Dealing with Conflict."*

A. Journals.

If the student enjoys writing, provide her with a journal (some students may enjoy decorating the cover). Ask the student to think of a recent time when she was upset or angry with someone. Have her write down what the major problem was, how she felt, and what she was thinking. Next, ask her to *briefly* list two to four ways that she could have handled the problem and the likely outcomes of each of them. Then have her circle the approach she likes best. *Note: if the student does not enjoy writing, consider having her dictate her thoughts to the teacher, or type the journal entries using a word processing program.*

If journaling proves helpful to the student, prompt her to continue journaling when new conflicts occur. The above technique can be very helpful in teaching problem solving in a structured way, and also can be used as a mental problem-solving framework when writing is not possible.

B. Letters or notes.

During a break in a conflict, help the student draft a short letter or note to the other person expressing 1) her feelings, 2) her thoughts, 3) an apology if appropriate, and 4) her proposed solution(s). As above, this can be handwritten, dictated by the student, or typed on a word processor. Next, have her show the note or letter to a third party (either the teacher or another trusted mentor) for feedback. (See Step Three below.) Lastly, help the student edit the note or letter to arrive at a final copy. It can either be sent to the other party, or used to help the student prepare for a conversation with that person.

C. Comic Strip Conversations.[35]

Comic Strip Conversations are very helpful tools to visually illustrate the actions, feelings, thoughts, and intentions of the parties involved in a conflict, and to help the student to think of possible solutions. A Comic Strip Conversation uses stick figures to represent the people involved in a conflict. Word bubbles show the words that were said during the interchange, and thought bubbles show the *drawer's perception* of what the participants were thinking. The drawer also may write the words and thoughts in different colors to represent different feelings. The student takes the lead in creating the drawings whenever possible, with the teacher or mentor assisting as needed. A series of "frames" can be used to show both the sequence of events that already occurred, and the sequence of events that are likely to happen with different solutions. *(See figures 18b and 18c, pages 211 and 212 for two examples of Comic Strip Conversations used for this purpose.)*

One of the strengths of Comic Strip Conversations is that other people's feelings and thoughts, which can be such a mystery to people with AS/HFA, are written down in a visual format. This capitalizes on the visual strengths of many of these individuals and gives them as much time as they need to think through what happened during the conflict. Also, Comic Strip Conversations frequently reveal misinterpretations or misunderstandings that otherwise might not come to light. This can be of great help to the teacher or mentor in understanding the student and in aiding the student to understand the perspective and intentions of the other person involved. Also, the

---

[35] *Comic Strip Conversations* by Carol Gray. (See reference in Appendix B.) I highly recommend this book for anyone who works with individuals with AS/HFA. It is short, easy to understand, and very useful in helping students understand the emotions, thoughts, and intentions of other people. Likewise, Comic Strip Conversations also can give the teacher much insight into the emotions, thoughts, and intentions of the student with AS/HFA.

student with AS/HFA may be much more able to show her own feelings and thoughts in this simple written format than by using other, more traditional techniques.

Danielle, a thirteen-year-old girl with HFA, had the unsettling habit of interrupting guests at her parents' home by staring at them intently, then asking in a loud voice, "Who are *you*?" Repeated attempts to verbally explain the inappropriateness of this behavior failed to have any effect on Danielle's behavior. Finally, after one such occasion, her mother initiated a Comic Strip Conversation with Danielle. When asked to fill in the thought bubbles for the guests, Danielle wrote that the guests were thinking, "My, what a friendly girl!" In her own thought bubble Danielle wrote, "It is polite to introduce myself." The mother then showed what the guests were more likely thinking ("Wow, that was impolite."), and feeling (uncomfortable, as shown by writing the words in orange color). With her mother's help, Danielle then used another comic strip to illustrate an alternative way of greeting guests and the likely outcome of this new approach (*see Figure 18b, page 211, for an illustration of this Comic Strip Conversation*). Seeing a "slowed-down" version of the conversation in this very explicit and visual format was of great help to Danielle in understanding how she came across to guests. Subsequently, her approach to greeting new people improved significantly.

Step Three: Teach the student to *talk over problems* with a trusted third person.

Before starting this step, read and discuss with the student Step Three in the handout *"Guidelines for Dealing with Conflict," page 197.*

Verbally discussing problems is a skill that can be quite foreign to a person with AS/HFA. The idea of discussing problems with another person, even a close relation, may not have occurred to the student. And if it has, she may not know *how* to do so. The student's ability to talk things over will be improved if she has learned, at least to some extent, to identify and grade her own feelings. *(For more help with this topic, see Programs 2 and 3, pages 8 and 16, respectively.)*

Here are **three steps** to follow that can help a person with AS/HFA learn to seek out help and advice from a mentor:

1) Choose a *mentor* or set of mentors.

Help the student identify *in advance* a few mentors, or people to whom she can go for help with conflicts and other problems. It is best to try to find at least one person for each setting where she spends a significant portion of her day. For example, the student might choose a parent, aunt, or uncle who lives nearby to turn to at home, and an aide, student aide, or teacher at school. Once the student chooses a group of potential mentors, the mentors should be approached for their consent, and given information about what would be required of them, how much time this might entail, etc. If they agree to be a mentor, it would be a good idea to give them a copy of this program and the student handout so that they have a clear picture of the goals of the program and the skills that the student is working on. It is also very helpful for the mentors to give the student specific information about when, where, and how they can be reached (e.g., phone numbers, where they can be found, hours available, etc.). In addition, making a contingency plan that provides for an alternate person the student can contact if necessary can ward off future problems. Writing this information down in a daily organizer, which the student keeps with her throughout the day, will ensure that the information will be available when she needs it.

2) *Provide practice* **in discussing problems with a mentor using past or fictitious scenarios.**

Ask the student to think of a past conflict she had with someone, or create a fictitious conflict. Help the student choose one of her mentors and arrange a session with him or her to practice *how* to discuss problems with a trusted third party. The purpose of this practice session is to help the student feel more comfortable discussing real problems that may occur in the future, and to give her an idea of what types of topics might come up in such a discussion.

In general, guide the student through the following steps:

1. State the problem or conflict.

2. Discuss her feelings and thoughts about the conflict. (Also go over any journal entries or letters to the other person that the student may have written. *See Step Two, page 185.*)

3. Ask for, and listen to input from the mentor.

4. Develop a plan for how to communicate with the other person in the conflict.

5. Use her stress management techniques as needed.

Repeat these practice sessions with the student until she understands and is comfortable with the above steps.

3) *Prompt* **the student to discuss problems/conflicts with a mentor** *in naturally occurring situations.*

When conflicts or other problems arise that cannot be solved easily, prompt the student to contact one of her mentors to talk things over, preferably before having a discussion of any length with the other person involved in the conflict. Over time, she may be more able to work things out on her own and thus need to turn to mentors for help less frequently.

Step Four: Teach the student to use *good discussion techniques*.

Before starting this program, read and discuss with the student Step Four in the student handout *"Guidelines for Dealing with Conflict," page 197.* Also, refer to the handout before and during practice sessions.

This step focuses on the following eight discussion techniques:

1. *Calm down before speaking.*

2. *Organize your thoughts before you speak: Ask yourself these three questions:*
   - "What emotions am I feeling?"
   - "What level of that emotion am I feeling? Do my facial expression, body language, and tone of voice match that level?"
   - "What is the other person feeling?"
     - Check nonverbal clues.
     - Compare how you have felt in similar situations.

3. *Listen to the other person.*
   - Stop thinking about your feelings for a moment.
   - Focus on what the other person is saying.
   - To understand what the other person is feeling, picture yourself in the same situation. The other person often is feeling the same thing you would be feeling in that situation.

4. *Find <u>something</u> (anything!) to agree with in what the other person is saying.*

5. *Avoid bringing up past gripes.*

6. *Avoid the words "always" and "never" when talking about the other person's faults.*

7. *Avoid accusations. Instead:*

   ▪ Ask for clarification.

   ▪ Talk about how the other person's actions make you feel.

8. *Avoid calling names.*

Referring to the above list and the student handout, use the following teaching sequence:

1) Demonstrate.

Working with another adult or student helper, role-play for the student both desirable and undesirable ways of carrying on a discussion during a conflict. Work on one item at a time from the above list, performing at least two or three different role-plays for each item.

2) Provide practice.

After demonstrating desirable and undesirable discussion techniques in the previous step, have the student participate in the role-plays. Allow her to practice both good and not-so-good techniques over a sufficient period of time for her to firmly establish in her own mind the difference between desirable and undesirable discussion techniques. Start with simple, short role-plays and gradually make them longer and more complex as the student progresses. Continue this step and the previous step until the student has mastered using positive discussion techniques during role-plays (i.e., she can differentiate and use positive techniques during role-plays 90% of the time).

3) *Help the student use good discussion techniques during naturally occurring situations.* *Reinforce spontaneous use of good discussion techniques.* Arrange in advance for the student to contact a mentor to mediate when a dispute occurs. It will work best if there is at least one person available to mediate in each environment where she spends a significant amount of time.

Mentors should screen disputes to determine whether it would be best to start with writing down the problem or talking it over with the mentor before discussing it with the other person. (See Steps Two and Three.)

Mentors need to be comfortable with the eight techniques listed on *pages 191-192* before coaching the student during real conflicts. It is a good idea to briefly review the eight discussion techniques covered here with *both* parties before the conversation begins so that, hopefully, both individuals will be playing by the same rules.

- Try to keep conversations brief and to the point.
- Prompt both parties to use the eight positive discussion techniques as needed. Gradually fade the amount of prompting over time.
- Reinforce both parties for attempts to use the positive techniques, making your praise as specific as possible. Also, strongly reinforce the student when you notice her using any of the eight techniques without prompting at *other* times in the course of the day.

Step Five: Teach the student when and how to *apologize.*

Refer to Step Five in the student handout *"Guidelines for Dealing with Conflict,"* *page 208.* Over several sessions, present the student with several different scenarios involving *imaginary* conflicts in which both your student and another person make various mistakes.

For each scenario, follow these steps:

1) *Help the student identify one or two things in each scenario for which she could apologize.*

Many students will need some help figuring out what *they* may have done to contribute to a conflict. During both practice sessions and real life conflicts, the student may need guidance from a mentor to identify those things for which she can or should apologize. Comic Strip Conversations can be a very useful tool to help the student understand the motivations, thoughts and feelings of the other person. This knowledge about the other person will help her better understand her own misconceptions and shortcomings, making it much easier for her to make a sincere apology. (Sometimes the student will find only something small for which to apologize. This is still a good start and she should be strongly reinforced for doing so.)

2) *Help the student write apology scripts for each scenario.*

Help the student write down one or two ways to apologize for each of the items she identified in Step 1, above. Note that sometimes a short "I'm sorry" is all that is needed, while other times it is better to add a short explanation. Avoid apologies that start: "I'm sorry, BUT . . ." (followed by an excuse). Explain why this is not a sincere apology.

3) *Role-play the scenarios with the student. Coach the student to be the first to apologize whenever possible.*

Act out the scenarios with the student over several sessions. Ask the student to role-play apologizing, using a script from Step 2. Remind her to be *the first to apologize* when possible. Coach the student to use appropriate facial expression, body language, and tone of voice to convey *sincerity. (Refer to Programs 8 and 12, on pages 71 and 109, respectively, for more help with using nonverbal and tone of voice clues.)* Make sure that you include a reciprocal apology from the other character in the role-play, if applicable. When the individual student is comfortable with this activity, consider introducing the role-plays in a small group setting.

Step Six: Teach the student to make restitution for mistakes when needed.

Both during practice sessions and while helping the student with real life conflict resolution, the mentor should teach the student to recognize situations in which it is appropriate to offer to make restitution. Although it is fairly straightforward to teach someone that if they break or lose something they should offer to repair or replace the item, there are also other situations in which it is helpful to make restitution. For example, when Ethan badly lost his temper with someone, his mentor encouraged him to send an apology note. Not only did this help the other person forgive him, but it also had the effect of helping Ethan forgive himself. As Ethan tended to obsess over even small things that he had done wrong, giving him a chance to "make it right" allowed him to drop the obsession, and consequently improved his self-image.

GUIDELINES for

DEALING WITH CONFLICT

Some Simple Rules For Handling Conflict

In a More Positive Way

Figure 18a. A copy of the student handout *Guidelines for Dealing with Conflict*, *Program 18: Resolving Conflicts.*

Step One: Can Arguments Be Good?

Everyone has arguments and disagreements with other people from time to time. Sometimes we argue because one of us has made a mistake that hurt someone else. Other times we disagree because we have different opinions about what is right and wrong. And sometimes we simply misunderstand the facts, or we misinterpret the other person's actions, words, or intentions. One thing is for sure, though— disagreements and arguments are a fact of life. We all have them.

However, arguments and disagreements are not always bad. Believe it or not, there is such a thing as a good argument. It is an argument where the people involved try really hard not to worry too much about proving that they are right. Instead, they try to better understand each other's actions and words so that afterward their relationship will be as strong, or even a little stronger than it was before. This handout explains some things that people can do to understand each other better when they disagree and to make their arguments good arguments.

Step Two: Write It Down.

A. Journals

People sometimes find it helpful to take time out from a conflict to write about their feelings in a journal, before continuing to talk with the other person (both computer and book journals work well). This gives them time to "cool off" and figure out *what* their feelings are, *how strong* those feelings are, and *what events might have led* to the emotions. Also, it allows them time to use what they know about the other person to help figure out his intentions. Furthermore, by first writing his thoughts and feelings down in a journal, a person can practice what to say to the other person. Also, after writing in the journal, it can be very helpful to share the information in the journal with a trusted friend or family member to get their feedback and suggestions *before* talking to the other person in the conflict.

B. Notes or Letters

Next time you have an argument with someone, consider taking time out from the argument to write down your feelings and thoughts in a letter or note to the other person. Whenever possible, show the letter to a helper or a mentor to get feedback before sending it. (A mentor often can understand both sides of an argument more clearly than can the people directly involved in the disagreement, and may be able to offer invaluable advice about how best to approach the other person.) Also, reading about your thoughts and feelings in your note or letter gives the other person time to think about his own feelings and thoughts and how best to reply. When people have enough time to consider these things in advance, they often are able to calm down and think more clearly about how to talk with each other. They are less apt to say something that they might regret in the future. To make sure that you have not said something that you later will be sorry for, it is often a good idea to wait a while (a few hours or a day or two) before sending the letter or note. After you have shared your thoughts and emotions in writing, it can be a lot easier to talk things over in person later on.

C. Comic Strip Conversations

Another excellent way to express your thoughts and feelings in writing is to use a technique called Comic Strip Conversations. You can use a Comic Strip Conversation to show what happened during an event that upset or confused you. First, draw stick figures to represent all of the people involved, and then add word and thought bubbles to show everyone's words and thoughts. You also can show what you think everyone was feeling by coloring their words and thoughts different colors for different feelings. You can do this activity with the person or people involved in the event, or you can draw the comic strips with a mentor who can help you figure out what went wrong and what to do next. This is a great way to "slow things down" and give you time to think about everyone's thoughts, feelings and intentions. It is also an excellent way to try out some possible solutions on paper to help you decide the best way to work things out.

For example, Mark loved to help people but he could not understand why he often got in trouble for helping. His mom had always taught him that it is important to help others. One time, Mark saw his brother trying to fix his broken bicycle. Mark, who was good at fixing things, went over to his brother, grabbed the wrench out of his hand and said, "Here, let me do it. You're doing it all wrong." Mark was surprised and hurt when his brother, instead of thanking him, yelled at him. Mark's mom suggested that Mark and his brother draw a Comic Strip Conversation with her help. In the drawing, Mark and his brother drew stick figures of themselves to show what had happened. Then, they added word bubbles to show what words each boy had said. Each boy wrote the words in different colors to show how he felt during the episode. (Mark chose red for angry, orange for confused, and so on.) Finally, both boys added thought bubbles to show what they were thinking during the episode. Mark was very surprised when his brother wrote down "I wish Mark wouldn't barge in on me every time I try to fix something. I want to do it myself!" This helped Mark understand that instead of always appreciating his help, sometimes his brother wanted to do things on his own. After this, with the help of his mom and brother, Mark was able to draw a new Comic Strip Conversation that showed how he might handle the situation the next time someone looked like they needed help. In this comic strip, Mark drew himself standing a little distance away from this brother and asking, "Can I help you?" His brother wrote in the response, "Thanks for asking, but I want to try it myself." His thought bubble said, "I'm glad that Mark asked me first before trying to help me!" Since Mark learned better by seeing pictures and words, instead of listening to long explanations, he was able to see what had gone wrong and figure out a better way of doing it next time. *(See the illustrations of both of these Comic Strip Conversations on pages 211-212.)*

Step Three: Talk It Over With a Third Person.

It can be a great help to take time out of an argument to discuss the problem with a mentor who is not involved with the conflict (for example, a trusted family member or close friend). Many people find that this gives them a chance to figure out how they feel and how the other person may feel, and to plan what they want to say to the other person. Talking things over with a mentor often helps a person work things out more smoothly when it comes time to resume talking with the other person.

Here are five things to do when you discuss a conflict with an outside mentor:

1) Tell the mentor about the problem or conflict.

2) Discuss your feelings and thoughts about the conflict. (This is a good time to go over with your mentor any journal entries or letters you have written to the other person.)

3) Ask for and listen to your mentor's input.

4) Develop a plan for how to communicate with the other person.

5) Use your stress management techniques if you are stressed.

Step Four: Use Good Discussion Techniques.

Using good discussion techniques usually leads to a much better outcome in a dispute.

Here are **eight tips** that many people have found helpful when discussing feelings and opinions with another person.

1. Take time to calm down before speaking.

If you find yourself very angry with or hurt by another person, take a moment to use a relaxation technique to calm down before you speak, *whether this occurs at the beginning or in the middle of* the conversation. For example, some people count to ten before talking. Others briefly close their eyes and take three deep breaths, or picture themselves in a favorite place before they speak. It is helpful to practice these techniques regularly when you are *not* upset, as this will make it easier to use the techniques when you *are* upset. (Review the skills you learned in Program 5, page 33, for more help.)

2. Organize your thoughts before you speak.

If you need extra time to think things over, it often works to let the other person know this before trying to discuss the problem. (The time you need to think things over may vary from a few minutes to a week or more, depending on the circumstances.) *While you think it over, ask yourself these three questions:*

1) "What am I thinking and feeling?"
2) "What level of that emotion am I feeling and does it match what I am showing with my facial expression, body language and tone of voice?"

203

3) "What is the other person thinking and feeling?"

- *Check non-verbal, contextual and tone of voice clues.*
- *Compare how <u>you</u> have felt in similar situations.*

Take a moment to check the other person's non-verbal clues—does she look angry, sad, worried, afraid, etc.? What does her tone of voice tell you about what she is feeling? Are there contextual clues, such as she is irritated because you just bumped into her? Or she is worried because her school assignment is late? *(See Programs 8 and 12, on pages 71 and 109, respectively, for further help with recognizing nonverbal and tone of voice clues.)*

Compare how you have felt in similar situations. Ask yourself if you have ever been in a similar situation – if so, how did you feel? Often the other person is feeling the same way you felt when you were in that situation. Thinking how you have felt in similar circumstances can give you more *empathy* (the ability to actually feel what the other person is feeling) for the other person. The more empathy people have for one another, the easier it is to forgive each other's mistakes and find a solution that is good for both people.

3. Listen to the other person.

Most conflicts work out best if both people take turns listening to each other's words. Although it can be very difficult to really listen to the other person when you are upset with him, it is important to try your best to do so. Here are *three things* that people often remind themselves to do when they need *to listen* to the other person:

1) For a few minutes try to stop thinking about your own feelings and what you want to say next.

2) Focus on what the other person is saying.

3) As mentioned above, try to understand what the other person is feeling by imagining how *you* might feel if you were the other person.

4. Try your hardest to find something that the other person is saying, that you can agree with, even if it is something little.

(Most people need a lot of practice doing this before they learn to do it well.)

5.   Avoid bringing up past gripes.

It usually is much better to try to solve only the current conflict rather than trying to solve past problems at the same time. Bringing up old grudges can lead other people to feel that you will never forgive them for past misdeeds, or that you think they are a bad person and that nothing they can do will change your opinion. So, for example, instead of saying, "Last month you ruined my best sweater, and now you've ripped my shirt!" consider simply saying, "I'm angry because you ripped my shirt."

6.   Avoid the words "always" and "never" when talking about the other person's faults.

It is important to avoid the words "always" and "never" for a couple of reasons. First, most people don't *always* do the same thing wrong or *never* do a certain thing right, so the "never" or "always" statement probably is incorrect and the other person therefore is likely to feel unjustly accused. Second, being accused of *always* doing something wrong can make the other person feel that he or she will *never* be able to meet your expectations, so why try to improve?

In one example, Carla was upset because even though she was sure Jeff had heard her ask him a question, he failed to reply. She knew that if she said, "You *always* ignore me!" or "You *never* listen to me!" Jeff would quite logically think that he often *did* listen to her, and he might therefore become defensive and angry. So, instead she said, "Sometimes you don't answer me and it makes me feel like you aren't listening." Jeff responded to this comment by explaining that sometimes he did not hear her because he was preoccupied with another thought. He asked Carla to make sure she got his attention before asking a question. Both Carla and Jeff understood each other better after this discussion, and the result was that their relationship actually improved after the argument.

7. Avoid accusations whenever you can.

The end result of a conflict almost always will be better if the participants avoid making accusations, and instead ask for clarification and talk about how the other person's actions make them feel.

Ask for clarification.

It is all too easy to accuse another person of something before we know *if* he actually did it, and if so, what his *intentions* were. For example, it is better to ask, "Did you spill juice on my report?" and "Did you do that on purpose?" in a calm tone of voice rather than to shout, "You spilled juice on my report on purpose!" Asking questions instead of accusing will help clarify whether the other person actually did spill the juice and whether it was intentional or an accident. This, in turn, will help you decide what to say next.

Talk about how the other person's actions make you feel.

Instead of accusing, tell the other person how you feel about their actions. Start sentences with phrases like "That makes me feel like . . ." or "I feel bad about . . . " For example, say, "It makes me feel like you don't care about me when you don't return my phone calls," instead of "You are not much of a friend. You never even return my calls!" Or, say, "I'm really upset about my ruined report. I worked so hard on it," instead of "Look what you did to my report! You always ruin everything!" Or "I feel hurt and angry when you yell at me like that," rather than yelling back, "All you do is yell! You just want everything your way!"

8. Avoid calling names.

As much as you might want to call the other person a "jerk" or an "idiot" (or some other unpleasant name), don't. Even though it might make you feel better momentarily to call the other person names, in the long run it will hurt your relationship with him or her.

Step Five: Admit your mistakes and apologize for them.

A. *Actively* **look for what you could have done better,** *admit it* **and then** *apologize.*

When you are feeling angry or hurt with someone, it can be very hard to stop and think about what *you* may have done to contribute to the problem.   However, admitting what you did wrong almost always helps to resolve the problem, and it is a true sign of maturity to be able to do so. Although in some conflicts one person is completely wrong and the other blameless, it is *much* more common that both people "messed up" in one way or another. When you are having an argument, try to think of at least one thing that you could have done better and admit it to the other person.   Then apologize.   This can help him admit that he could have done things better, too.   And, believe it or not, the other person is almost guaranteed to think more highly of you if you can admit to wrongdoing than if you act as if you are blameless.

B. Keep a list of ways to apologize in your head. (You never know when you may need them!)

Here are some examples of apologies that have worked well for many people. Notice that they are *short* and *to the point*. Also notice that sometimes a simple "I'm sorry" works well, and other times it is good to add a sentence or two admitting what you did wrong.

    1) "I'm sorry."

    2) "I'm sorry. I really blew it."

    3) "I sure have been grouchy. Please forgive me."

    4) "I was being careless when I broke your tape player. I'm really sorry."

Note: Avoid saying, "I'm sorry, but . . ." (and then adding an excuse or an accusation.) This is probably the most common cause of unsuccessful apologies!

C. Whenever possible, be the *first* to admit you did something wrong and the first to apologize.

Try being the *first* to admit making a mistake and the *first* to apologize. This is not to say that you should apologize without cause, but if you did do something wrong, admit it. You might be surprised at how refreshing this can be. In addition, *someone* has to be the first to apologize. After all, if no one is willing to take the first turn, chances are that the conflict will never be resolved, which obviously is not good for the relationship.

Note: It is also possible to apologize <u>too much</u>. If you find yourself apologizing for the same thing over and over, or saying, "I'm sorry," multiple times during the day, be sure and discuss this with a trusted mentor or counselor.

D. Show *sincerity* through your facial expression and tone of voice.

Apologies are *much* more successful when they are sincere. If you feel that you cannot apologize sincerely, it probably is better to tell the other person that you need to think things over before talking with her about it. Then take a break (anywhere from a few minutes to a few days) to calm down and consider the situation. If you wait to calm down, chances are that it will be much easier to see what you might have done better and to apologize. When you do apologize, make sure that your words, facial expression, body language, and tone of voice convey sincerity. Some people find it helpful to practice these with a helper or in front of a mirror before making the apology. *(Review Programs 11 and 12, pages 102 and 109, for more help using facial expression and tone of voice to communicate effectively.)*

Step Six: Make Up for Mistakes.

Ask yourself if you need to make *restitution* (do something for the other person to make up for a mistake you made). For example, if you have damaged something belonging to another person, it is important to offer to fix or replace it (and then follow through with this unless he or she *insists* that you do not need to). Another example is to write a short apology note (or send an apology card) when you have made a mistake. Sometimes adults even send flowers to the other person along with an apology note. All of these actions can help the other person forgive the mistake more easily, and can help you feel better about yourself, too.

Figure 18b. An example of two Comic Strip Conversations used to clarify the thoughts and intentions of the student and the other people involved in this brief interchange. *The upper right frame* shows the student's perception of what her parents' guests were thinking in response to her question "Who are you?" The mother has re-written the words in large, bold print to show that the words were spoken loudly. The mother also has indicated her perception of what the four adults were thinking in response to the girl's words. *The lower frame* illustrates the solution that Danielle came up with for managing a similar situation in the future.

Figure18c. An example of how to use a Comic Strip Conversation to help both people in an argument to better understand each other's thoughts, feelings and intentions. *The top two frames* show what two brothers, Mark and Jim, were thinking and what they said during an argument over fixing Jim's bike. After each of them saw what their brother had been thinking, it helped them to calm down and figure out a better way to do things next time. *The lower frames* show the solution they came up with.

SECTION THREE

ABSTRACT THINKING SKILLS

INTRODUCTION
Abstract Thinking Skills

Individuals with AS/HFA often are very concrete thinkers and can have significant problems with abstract thinking. This tendency can have many ramifications for both their academic and social skills. In the higher grade-levels in elementary school and beyond, academic tasks become less concrete and more abstract, a process that is designed to match the cognitive development of neurotypical children. As a consequence, while they may have started out doing well at academic tasks in the earlier school years, some of these children run into difficulties as they enter higher grade levels and more abstract mental processing is required of them. For example, a student with AS/HFA may have few problems with the math facts and computation skills that dominate lower grade mathematics, but he may start to experience difficulties when he reaches algebra, which requires more conceptual thinking. Likewise, a student who did well in social studies and written language in grade school might begin to struggle in those same subjects in middle school when he runs into questions requiring him to "compare and contrast" two events, extract the main theme of a story, or infer the meaning of a metaphor.

Problems with concrete thinking also contribute to the communication and social skills deficits that are hallmarks of AS/HFA. One common manifestation of this tendency is a literal interpretation of symbolic language during social exchanges. This short section focuses on teaching abstract thinking skills through the interpretation of symbolic language. Hopefully, more programs to address this area of need will become available as more research is done on theory of mind, executive functioning, and abstract thinking in individuals with higher functioning autism.

PROGRAM 19
FIGURATIVE SPEECH

INTRODUCTION

To understand how frequently most of us use figurative (or non-literal) speech, all one has to do is to observe how often such speech is used in casual conversations over the coffee machine at work or by a group of children talking on the playground. However, for individuals with AS/HFA, interpreting non-literal speech such as sarcasm, irony, similes, and metaphors can be an enormously difficult challenge. It is not uncommon for them to mistakenly interpret a figure of speech literally. This sometimes leads to humorous situations and sometimes to more serious problems. For example, one child with HFA responded to his mother's off-hand comment that it was *"raining cats and dogs"* by peering anxiously upward, waiting for large numbers of small, furry pets to fall from the sky. In another case, a child who had overheard that there was "bad blood" between his grandfather and his uncle went for several months thinking that they had a blood disease and worrying that he might develop the same illness.

In addressing this difficulty, one approach is for other people to avoid using any form of symbolic speech when speaking with the individual with AS/HFA. This approach may be necessary in certain situations. However, it also may be possible to teach more able individuals with AS/HFA the skills to interpret idiomatic speech on their own. One study by Francesca Happé showed that the ability of autistic people to understand figurative language is linked to their performance on theory of mind tasks.[36] Happé reported that even the participants with autism who failed at all theory of mind tests were as able to understand *similes*[37] as were controls matched for age and IQ level. Those who understood first-order theory of mind tasks[38] were able to interpret certain *metaphors*.[39] A much smaller number of autistic participants who understood second order theory of mind tasks did correspondingly well at interpreting both metaphors and *irony*.[40] Clearly, for AS/ HFA individuals who *can* learn to understand symbolic speech at some level, it is a more practical solution and encourages more independence to help them to do so, rather than to attempt to eliminate the use of non-literal speech in their environment.

Thus it makes sense, whenever possible, to teach individuals with AS/HFA a *method* for interpreting figurative speech. The method presented here includes teaching the individual to 1) *become aware of the existence* of certain phrases used in everyday speech that have meanings very different from what the words mean literally; 2) *recognize* these phrases when they occur in conversations or in written form; and 3) *interpret the intended meaning* of the phrase by using *contextual, tone of voice and nonverbal clues* and, in the case of similes and some metaphors, by *finding similarities* between the literal meaning and the abstract meaning of the

---

[36] Happé, Francesca. 1995. *Understanding Minds and Metaphors: Insights from the Study of Figurative Language in Autism.* Metaphor and Symbolic Activity 10(4), 275-295.

[37] Def. *simile:* a statement that one thing is like another. Similes compare two things using the words *like* or *as*. (Barnhart, Robert. 1995. World Book Dictionary. World Book, Inc. Chicago.) For example: *That meal was like a symphony.*

[38] For definitions of first and second order theory of mind tasks, see the glossary, Appendix E. Also, refer to Happé, F. 1993. *Communicative competence and theory of mind in autism: A test of relevance theory.* Cognition. 48:101-119.

[39] Def. *metaphor:* a figure of speech in which a word or phrase that ordinarily means one thing is applied to another thing in order to suggest a likeness between the two. World Book Dictionary, 1995. For example: *That meal was a symphony of flavors.*

[40] Def. *irony:* a way of speaking . . . in which the ordinary meaning of the words is the opposite of the thought in the speaker's mind. World Book Dictionary. 1995. For example: the exclamation *"That was a brilliant move!"* said after someone makes a mistake.

phrase. The following program provides a simple way to introduce students to these three steps while simultaneously teaching them the intended meanings of figurative speech common to their culture and subculture.

Danielle, a thirteen-year-old girl with HFA, was well known for taking figures of speech quite literally, a situation that caused more than a few confusing moments during conversations. During a car trip at age six, Danielle repeatedly (and quite seriously) asked her father if her face was *green*. It took several minutes before he recalled a scene from a movie the family had recently viewed in which a character said she was so nauseated her face must be "green." Danielle's father correctly deduced that she was trying to tell him that she was sick to her stomach. He luckily was able to pull over in time to avoid an unpleasant accident in the car.

On another occasion, Steven, a teenager with AS, was quite puzzled and dismayed when he was told, *"Bite your tongue!"* by his mother, who was trying to prevent him from making a socially inappropriate comment. On another occasion, the same student was disciplined at school because he lifted his chair *up onto* the table instead of bringing it *to* the table after being told, "Pull your chair *up*." (The teacher felt that the student was being a "smart-aleck" and mistakenly interpreted his actions as deliberate disobedience.)

Both of these students clearly needed help recognizing and interpreting non-literal language. The initial work with both students centered on discussing the fact that not everything that is spoken or written is meant to be taken literally. The teacher explained that some non-literal phrases have a symbolic meaning that is very different than their literal meaning, as in the case of similes and metaphors, and that other phrases actually mean the opposite of their literal meaning, as in the case of sarcasm or irony.

Next, to help the students learn to recognize non-literal speech, the teacher taught them to use a simple test: if the literal meaning of the words does not make logical sense in a given context, then the words may have a non-literal meaning.[41]   The instructor used obvious and, whenever possible, humorous examples to illustrate this fact. For example, using the idiom "It's raining cats and dogs," she asked the students to imagine small pets falling from the sky, and then asked if these words made logical sense when taken literally within the context of normal everyday experience.   As the students gained skill in identifying non-literal speech, she introduced more subtle and difficult idioms.

Finally, she taught the students to use situational, nonverbal, and tone of voice clues to help interpret the meaning of the phrase. In addition, whenever possible she helped the student find parallels between the two subjects being compared in a simile or metaphor. In Danielle's case, with assistance she was able to learn to interpret most similes and some metaphors using a combination of these two techniques. For example, with directed questioning she was able to derive the abstract meaning of the idiom "Doing it that way is a *dead end street*" by 1) guessing from the speaker's tone of voice and nonverbal clues that the speaker did not favor "doing it that way," and 2) comparing what happened the last time she accidentally went the wrong way and got stuck on a real dead end street (she could not get where she wanted to go) and what happened the last time she tried the wrong way to do something (she did not achieve her goal). In contrast to Danielle, although Steven was able to *recognize* non-literal phrases

---

[41] Another situation in which words mean something other than their literal meaning is when the speaker is lying (or otherwise intentionally misrepresenting the truth) or when the speaker thinks he is telling the truth but is mistaken. Teaching a student with AS/HFA to recognize and differentiate between intentional and unintentional misrepresentations of the truth is a subject that is critical to address because of its obvious implications for the safety and welfare of the student. For that reason, these types of scenarios need to be addressed. However, this is a huge subject in and of itself, and, while it is appropriate to introduce it in the context of this program, a full discussion of this subject is beyond the scope of this book.

the majority of the time, the ability to accurately *interpret* these phrases proved difficult for him at his current developmental level. It was agreed to put this step aside until a later date when it could be re-attempted.

GOALS

The goals of this program are to:

1. Teach the student to *be aware of the existence of* phrases used in everyday speech that have very different meanings from what the words mean literally.

2. Teach the student to *recognize* three types of non-literal speech (similes, metaphors and irony/sarcasm).

3. Teach the student a method for deriving *intended meanings* of non-literal speech by:

    • *using contextual, tone of voice and nonverbal clues* to approximate the speaker's intentions.

    • *finding similarities* between the literal meaning and the abstract meaning of the phrase (when possible).

INSTRUCTIONS:

Step One: Introduce the information that non-literal meanings are common in both written and spoken language. Introduce three types of non-literal speech: simile, metaphor, and irony/sarcasm.

Note: Before beginning this step, you may wish to review *Programs 8 and 12 (pages 71 and 109, respectively)* on nonverbal and tone of voice clues.

Some students with AS/HFA already will be painfully aware of the abundance of non-literal speech in everyday conversation, and they may have begun to try to find a way to understand it on their own. Other students may be only vaguely aware of this odd language of disparities and opposites. The purpose of this step is to make sure that the student is aware that some words and phrases have 1) symbolic meanings that are *significantly different* from their literal meanings or 2) meanings that actually are the *opposite* of their literal meanings. Discuss the student's experiences with interpreting non-literal speech. Has he noticed that other people sometimes say things that mean something different from the literal meaning of the words? If so, how common does he think this is? What difficulties has this caused him in understanding other people's intended meanings?

Give the student a copy of the handout, *Words that don't mean what they are supposed to mean. (See figure 19a, pages 225-226, and the student copy in Appendix B.)* Discuss the three types of non-literal speech, giving examples of each that will be familiar to the student. Be sure to include some humorous examples. (Refer to Appendix A for books and web sites that offer examples of idioms.) Also ask the student to think of his own examples of each of the three types of non-literal speech. Create a list of the examples that you have collected. (Feel free to add to the list at any time.)

Step 2: Teach how to *recognize* similes, metaphors, and irony/sarcasm.

1. Give the student a copy of the student handout "*What to do when words don't mean what they are supposed to mean.*" *(See figure 19b, pages 227-228. Also, a student copy is located in Appendix B.)* Discuss the process for recognizing each of the three types of figurative speech using the methods and examples described in the handout.

2. Using the processes outlined in the student handout *(figure 19b)*, have the student label the examples he listed in Step One as similes, metaphors, or irony/sarcasm.

Step Three: Teach how to *interpret* similes, metaphors, and irony/sarcasm.

1. As above, refer to the student handout *"What to do when words don't mean what they are supposed to mean" (figure 19b)*. Discuss the process for interpreting or "figuring out" each of the three types of figurative speech, using the methods and examples described in the handout.

2. Help the student apply this process to his own examples from Step One. Discuss contextual clues. Take turns with the student using role-play to demonstrate tone of voice, body language, and facial expression clues, and discuss how these clues help guide the listener toward the intended meaning of the words. When working on similes or metaphors, whenever possible use situations that the student has experienced in the past to help illustrate any parallels between the literal and intended meanings of the words. (Obviously this will work only when there is a discernable link between the two meanings. Unfortunately, this is not always the case.)

   For example, if the student has problems understanding the idiom "I am going to *flip my lid*," start out by asking him if he has ever seen a covered pot boil over, and, if so, what happened to the lid. Then repeat the idiom to him using a tone of voice, facial expression, and body language that convey anger. If he still has problems interpreting the idiom, help him out with contextual clues by telling him about a time when you were so angry that you lost control. Then role-play the scenario, repeating the words, "I am going to flip my lid!" again giving the appropriate nonverbal and tone of voice clues. Better yet, role-play an actual occasion when the student himself got angry and lost control. *Be careful not to give the answer away too easily. The whole point of this exercise is to help the student go through this type of thinking process to arrive at the abstract meaning of the idiom.* Finally, discuss the parallel between the literal meaning and the abstract meaning. For example, point out how steam can create so much pressure inside a pot of boiling water that the steam has to escape by pushing the pot lid off. In the same way, anger can create so much pressure inside a person that he cannot keep the anger inside. His control (the "lid") is lost, and the anger comes out.

Note: this step may be too difficult for some students with AS/HFA. If this becomes apparent, omit this step and try it again at a later date.

3. Repeat Step Three using more examples. Start with easier examples and progress to more difficult ones as the student's skills improve.

Step Four: Encourage recognition and interpretation of simile, metaphor and irony/sarcasm in *naturally occurring situations.*

1. *In everyday speech:*
    - Whenever possible, introduce figures of speech that the student has studied into your daily conversations with him. Prompt the student to recognize and interpret these familiar figures of speech.
    - When feasible, help the student to recognize and interpret *unfamiliar* figures of speech and sarcasm when it is used in everyday speech, using the method outlined in the student handout.

2. *In literature:*

- Help the student identify and interpret both unfamiliar and familiar similes, metaphors, and irony/sarcasm in literature, using the method outlined in the student handouts.

Note:

If *you* are having trouble with a particular idiom or metaphor, one that makes you eat humble pie, don't sweat it. Cool your jets and get a grip on yourself. If you play your cards right, you might find out that this program is right up your alley. So, stop running around like a chicken with its head cut off and quit spinning your wheels. If you need to, just catch some z's. If you don't get up on the wrong side of the bed, you might be able to wing it, find a meaning that fits the bill, and have a blast while you're at it. But hold the phone! I think I'm getting carried away here and am about to lose my marbles . . .

Words That Don't Mean What They Are Supposed To Mean

People use words in different ways. Sometimes words mean just what you would expect. Other times words mean something very different from their usual meaning. When people use words to mean something different from their usual, or "literal" meaning, this is called *non-literal speech*. There are different types of non-literal speech—here are three that people often use.

1. Similes

These are phrases that often use the word "like" or "as" to show that one thing is similar to another. It usually is fairly easy to see how the two things are similar. For example, "her hair is *like* spun gold" is a simile that means that the lady in question has hair that is a golden color and is shiny like gold. ("*Spun* gold" means long strands of gold.)

2. Metaphors

Metaphors are words or phrases that have two very different meanings. One meaning is the expected, or "*literal,*" meaning of the individual words. The other, *non-literal* meaning is something completely different from the expected meaning of the words. In some metaphors there is a hidden similarity between the literal meaning and the non-literal meaning, but a person has to search for that similarity. In other metaphors, there is no similarity at all between the two meanings. Here are two examples.

"I have a frog in my throat."

- The ***expected, literal meaning*** of these words would be that the speaker has a small, four-legged creature (that hops and croaks) in her throat. Imagine your aunt Martha announcing, "I have a frog in my throat!" and then picture a frog popping out of her mouth! This should be quite a startling image (unless, of course, your aunt Martha likes to eat frogs). When you are surprised or puzzled by the literal meaning of someone's words, and the literal meaning simply does not *fit* the situation, this often is a *clue* that those words are being used as a metaphor. In other words, they are being used in an **unexpected, non-literal way**.

- The ***unexpected, non-literal meaning*** of these words is that the speaker is hoarse. When someone is hoarse, his or her voice sounds "croaky." A frog sounds croaky, too, and so in this case there is a connection between the literal meaning and the non-literal meaning of the metaphor. (Unfortunately, this is not always the case. Sometimes there is *no* similarity or connection between the literal and non-literal meanings of a metaphor. These metaphors tend to be more difficult to interpret.)

(continued)

Figure 19a. A copy of the student handout: *Words that don't mean what they are supposed to mean.*

"I'm in a pickle."

- The **expected, literal meaning** of these words is that the speaker is *inside* of a small, long, green vegetable that has been soaked in vinegar, garlic, and salt. But, whoa—wait a minute, how could this be? That would have to be one very small person or one extremely long pickle! Besides, how many people do you know who could survive being soaked in vinegar, salt, and garlic? (Well, okay, I admit there is my great uncle George, but he is an exception . . .)

- The **unexpected, non-literal meaning** of these words is that the speaker is in a difficult or awkward situation. For example, your mom says, "I'm in a real pickle— I have to be at the dentist's office and the bank at the same time." She certainly cannot mean that she is stuck inside a salty cucumber! This gives you a *clue* that the literal meaning can't be the right one! Now, if you look, you might see a look of worry on your mom's face. *(See Program 8, page 71 for more help with recognizing facial expressions.)* This gives you another *clue*—she might be telling you that she is worried. You know from the context (she has to be two places at once) that she is in a difficult situation, so you might guess that she really means that she is worried because she is in a difficult situation. If this is what you guessed, you are right! (By the way, you *can* find a similarity between the literal meaning and the non-literal one here if you really look for it. After all, being stuck inside a pickle would be a difficult situation!)

3. Ironic or sarcastic phrases

These are phrases that mean the *opposite* of the normal meaning of the words. For example, consider the following scene: Mary is a girl who loves chocolate. One evening, the family is having chocolate cake for dessert, but unfortunately Mary's brother drops the chocolate cake on the floor. Mary glares at him and says, *"That was really good!"* What Mary *really* means is the opposite of what she said. In other words, what she really means is "That was really bad!" Mary has used sarcasm to show her brother that she is not happy with him for dropping her cake on the floor.

- The **expected, literal meaning** of the phrase "That was really good!" is that the other person did something well and is to be complimented.

- The **unexpected, non-literal meaning** of the phrase "That was really good!" is exactly the opposite. What Mary really means is "That was really bad!" We know from the context that Mary loves chocolate cake, and therefore probably was *not* happy to have the cake land on the floor! This is a *clue* that the literal meaning does not fit the situation. If we could look at Mary's face we would see that she is frowning. This is another *clue*—one that tells us that probably what Mary *really* means is that she is angry.

What To Do When Words Don't Mean What They Are Supposed To Mean

1. Similes*

How to recognize one:
- Ask: Does the phrase compare two things, using the words "like" or "as"? If so, chances are it is a simile.

Example:
- That old dog is *as slow as molasses in winter.*

How to figure it out:
- *Look for similarities* between the two things being compared. For example, winter is the coldest time of the year. Molasses flows very slowly when it is cold, so slowly, in fact, that we sometimes get impatient and wish it would flow faster. So if an old dog is as slow as molasses in winter, this means that the dog moves so slowly that sometimes people wish he would move faster.

2. Metaphors*

How to recognize one:
- Ask: Does the usual (or literal) meaning of the phrase make sense *in that situation?* If the answer is no, then this may be a metaphor.

Example:
- A man named John just tried his new skis and he likes them a lot. Afterward, John says, "I'm *hooked* on my new skis!"

How to figure it out:
- **Use *contextual clues:***
  For example: John just tried out his new skis for the first time. Afterward he exclaimed, "I'm hooked on these new skis!" The context is that John just used his new skis for the first time. His clothes are not "hooked" on his skis and as a matter of fact, there are no hooks anywhere on or near him. Therefore, the context tells you that he is not *literally* hooked on anything.

(continued)

(*When many different people use the same similes or metaphors to mean the same thing over a long period of time, these are called **idioms**. Idioms also are called *figures of speech*.)

Figure 19b. A copy of the student handout: *What to do when words don't mean what they are supposed to mean.*

- **Use *nonverbal* and *tone of voice clues*:**
  Check John's facial expression and body language. He is standing up tall, and he makes a "victory" fist as he talks. His mouth is turned up in a big smile, he looks right at you as he talks, and his eyes are crinkled up. His tone of voice sounds excited and happy. All of these clues tell you that he is happy. He is talking about his skis, so it is reasonable to assume that he is happy about his skis.

- **Check the usual (or literal) meaning of the word or phrase for hints to the "hidden" meaning:**
  (Note: This works sometimes, but not always.)
  For example, the word to "hook" literally means to "firmly attach to" or to "fasten together" so that whatever is fastened won't separate. So, if John is *hooked* on his new skis, then this *could* mean that he won't separate from his skis.

- **Put it all together:**
  So, here is what you know so far:
  1. John is not physically hooked on or caught on his skis, so this must be an idiom about the subject of his new skis.
  2. He is happy and excited about something—most likely his skis.
  3. *Hooked on* means "firmly attached to."

  Therefore, a reasonable interpretation of this idiom is that he is happy with, and very attached to, his new skis.

3. Ironic or Sarcastic Words

How to recognize them:
- Ask: Does the literal or usual meaning of the words fit in that situation? If not, and if the *opposite* meaning would fit better, then this probably is sarcasm or irony.

Example:
- Sue burns her finger on a hot burner. She exclaims, "Ouch! That sure was clever of me!"

How to figure it out:
- **Use *contextual, nonverbal* and *tone of voice clues*.** If the situation and the speaker's facial expression, body language, or tone of voice make you think that she must mean the <u>opposite</u> of what her words normally would mean, then you probably are right. In this example, what the speaker really means is that it was <u>not</u> very clever of her to touch the hot burner on the stove.

SECTION FOUR

BEHAVIORAL ISSUES

INTRODUCTION
Behavioral Issues

Some individuals with AS/HFA develop problem behaviors that are not fully addressed by the previous programs in this book. One of these is the issue of non-compliance. Not infrequently, students with AS/HFA develop problems following through on school assignments and other responsibilities, such as chores and personal hygiene. There probably are several reasons for this—reasons that truly contribute to an inability to complete the task. However, for those students who understand what is expected of them, are capable of doing it at that point in time and are not particularly stressed, but still fail to follow through with reasonable requests, compliance may be the issue that needs addressing. While it is critical to be certain that this is, indeed, a non-compliance issue and not some other problem, it is necessary to the student's success in school and his ability to achieve some degree of independent living, that he learn to carry out tasks that may not appeal to him. Although treating compliance problems is a difficult task at best, significant improvement often can be achieved by using an organized, incremental, behavioral approach. An added benefit to addressing compliance issues is that as compliance problems decrease, there often will be a parallel decrease in other behavioral problems as well.

In addition to Program 20, which addresses compliance problems, this section also includes a list of common behavioral terms, a brief look at reinforcement techniques, and a short segment on hidden causes of problem behaviors.

BEHAVIORAL TERMS USED IN THIS BOOK

To following are definitions for some basic behavioral terms that have been used in this book. They have intentionally been written in layman's terms. For readers interested in a more detailed treatment of the terminology and techniques used in applied behavioral therapy, please refer to the resources listed in Appendix A.

Delayed gratification: The ability to put off receiving a reward for doing a task until a later time.

Extrinsic reinforcement: The use of a reward to encourage the recipient to perform a target task. This can take the form of praise, a desired object, participation in a favored activity, or a token that later can be traded for a desired object or activity.

Fade: To gradually withdraw either prompts or reinforcers to encourage the student to do a task without outside influence.

Generalization: The transference of skills learned in one environment to different environments, including the ability to use those skills in different locations with varying stimuli, with different people, and at different times.

Graded approach: To teach a skill by starting with small, easily achievable tasks, and gradually increasing the difficulty of the tasks until the skill is mastered. Also known as "shaping."

Intrinsic reinforcement: An inner sense of achievement or pride in having completed a task. Alternatively, a feeling of pleasure or happiness associated with doing an activity.

Mastery (of a skill): The point at which the student can accomplish a task correctly nine out of ten times. (It is generally accepted that this is the point at which the student will be able to *retain* the ability to independently accomplish the skill at future times.) An alternate definition sometimes used in this book is the point at which a student can do a task correctly three times in a row.

Negative stimulus: A situation or task which a person strongly dislikes, and which she will avoid if possible.

Non-preferred activity: An activity that a person does not enjoy doing.

Preferred activity: An activity that a person enjoys doing.

Prompt: To encourage, remind or "cue" someone to do something. Prompts can take several forms, ranging from physically guiding the student through a task (e.g., placing one's hand over the student's hand to guide the student to pick up a pencil), to a verbal reminder or a slight gesture (such as pointing or nodding one's head) that reminds the student to start or continue a task. In general, it is best to use the least intrusive and least noticeable prompt that works for the particular situation. Also, it is important to fade prompting by slowly decreasing the number of prompts and by moving from more intrusive and noticeable prompts to those that are subtler, until the student requires only that amount and type of prompting that is appropriate for his peer group.

Reinforcement menu: A list of extrinsic reinforcers from which the student may choose a reinforcer after successfully completing an assigned task.

Reinforcer: A *positive* reinforcer is anything that follows a behavior that increases that behavior. Types of positive reinforcers include social praise, preferred activities, edible reinforcers, and tangible reinforcers (e.g., stickers, toys, tokens, etc). A *negative reinforcer* is an aversive situation that a person can stop or avoid by changing his behavior. For example, after Jim became ill every time he drank milk, he changed his habit of drinking milk and thus avoided repeated nausea. In this case, nausea is the negative reinforcer. In another example, a student with learning disabilities becomes exceedingly frustrated and tense every time he tries to work on an English assignment. In this case, the boy's mental and emotional discomfort is the negative reinforcer. In order to avoid this aversive situation, he changes his behavior by refusing to attempt the work, and acting out instead. As a result he is sent to the principal's office, which allows him to escape the negative reinforcer, stress.

Target task: An isolated task that the teacher or student designates for the student to accomplish.

Token economy: A system of reinforcement in which the student earns different numbers of tokens, or tokens of differing value for doing various types or numbers of tasks. The student then "cashes in" the tokens (either immediately or at a later time) for a reward of corresponding value.

A BRIEF LOOK AT REINFORCEMENT

Choosing the right reinforcers for the individual student

(See examples of reinforcers on page 239.)   When choosing reinforcers for an individual student, it is best for the student, teaching staff, and parents to work together as a team to create the list of reinforcers. The list should contain only reinforcers that have value for that particular child (i.e., they must be attractive enough to the child to motivate him to work for them).   It is important to establish that a reinforcer actually works for the particular child before attempting to use it during a program. In addition, in order for the reinforcers to retain their value to the student, it is important that they are available to him only during program time and not at any other time. For the same reason, it is a good idea to rotate use of different reinforcers so that the student does not always have access to each reinforcer.

General notes on reinforcement

- **Extrinsic vs. intrinsic reinforcement**

   Reinforcement systems usually start out using *extrinsic* rewards, and then gradually withdraw these rewards while simultaneously fostering the student's self motivation and the ability to rely on *intrinsic* rewards. In the ideal case, by the end of a program the student will perform the target task simply for the inner satisfaction he derives from accomplishing it. In cases where this is not possible, the extrinsic reinforcers used should be kept as close to a naturally occurring outcome as possible.

- **Immediate vs. delayed reinforcement:**

In normal development, children gradually progress from needing immediate reinforcement (or immediate gratification) as infants and toddlers to accepting delayed reinforcement (or delayed gratification) as they move through childhood and adolescence. Most well written reinforcement programs follow the same pattern, starting with immediate reinforcement if necessary, but progressing toward delayed reinforcement. For students who start with little ability to delay gratification, giving the child a reinforcer as soon as he completes the task may work best initially, with the expectation that he later will graduate to a system that requires him to wait longer for his reinforcers. For example, in order to hold nine-year-old Paul's attention, he initially needed to be reinforced *immediately* with an item or activity from his list of reinforcers. (Because his favorite interests were Thomas the Tank Engine and trucks of all sorts, his parents and teachers created a list that varied from five minutes of playtime with a favorite truck to a choice of Thomas the Tank Engine stickers.) However, over time Paul was taught to accept delayed reinforcement. Gradually, his reinforcers were given at increasingly longer intervals, starting with doing two tasks before receiving his treat, then increasing to three tasks, etc. Eventually he was introduced to two different levels of reinforcers: "B" reinforcers – small treats that he could earn after doing a small number of tasks, and "A" reinforcers – larger treats which he could receive only after accomplishing a larger number of tasks.

In working with a more advanced student, it may work well to create a ***token economy***. In simple terms, this means that the child earns tokens that he later exchanges for reinforcers of corresponding value. Depending on the needs of the individual student, you may choose to give only one type of token that the student later exchanges for a choice of reinforcers of roughly equivalent value.

Alternatively, there may be two or three levels of tokens that can be exchanged for reinforcers of different values (one way to do this is to use different colored poker chips as tokens). For a higher-level token, the child needs to do either more difficult tasks or a greater number of tasks. A variation of this is to allow the student to exchange x number of lower level tokens for a higher-level token, which he then can exchange for a more significant reinforcer. When introducing a token economy to the student, it initially may be necessary to give the token to the student right after he completes the required task. Also, you may need to allow him to immediately exchange the token for a reinforcer. This will help the student to understand the token system. After this, gradually increase the amount of time the student must wait to 1) receive a token and 2) exchange the token for a reinforcer.

- **Brag Books** [42]

A brag book is a small journal or diary in which the student writes down his achievements, big and small, in his own words. (For those students who have problems with writing, it works well to have the student dictate the words to an adult, who then writes down the information in the brag book.) The teacher first praises the student, making the praise as specific as possible, and then asks the student to talk about his achievement in *his* words. Next, the student (or the teacher, if the student does not write) writes the information down in the brag book. If possible, both school staff and parents should contribute to the brag book, with all parties reviewing new items with the student.

For students who have self-esteem problems, this method of recording positive things about themselves can be enormously helpful. It teaches students to

---

[42] The concept of brag books as it is used here was introduced by Tony Attwood, and is included in this book with his permission. (Attwood, Tony. 2000. Unpublished communication. Brisbane.)

actively look for things they have done right, and replaces negative self-talk with positive self-talk. In addition, recording praise in this format is an excellent way to reinforce *spontaneous* achievements which otherwise might go unnoticed. The act of *vocalizing* self-praise can be very helpful in cementing the praise in the student's mind. Also, collecting a number of these confidence boosters in written form allows the student to look back at all the things he has done right. Finally, brag books are both inexpensive and easy to implement.

The use of a brag book proved to be very successful in the case of Danielle, a thirteen-year-old girl with HFA who had significant problems with self-esteem. As a young child, she did not notice other children, and had few concerns about "fitting in." However, at around age nine the social interactions required of her became more complex. As she began to struggle with this, her peers began to target her, teasing her and setting her up to lose control in front of her teachers. (Unfortunately, the other students were rarely caught in the act, and Danielle most often was blamed for the outbursts.) At the same time, as Danielle matured she began to want very much to make friends, but was unable to do so. She could not make sense of the intricate and subtle exchanges that somehow allowed the other children to communicate with one another so easily. As a result, she became increasingly depressed and her self-esteem plummeted. She was put on antidepressant medication, which helped significantly. Later she received cognitive behavioral therapy, which was of great benefit as well. As part of the cognitive behavioral therapy, she started keeping track of her achievements in a brag book. The results were remarkable. Her mood improved, her self-talk became more positive, and she was able to focus better on both her social skills and academic programs. Brag books may not produce this degree of improvement in all individuals with AS/HFA, but they certainly will be of benefit in the majority of cases.

LIST OF REINFORCERS *(List #1)*   **For:** Ethan T.   **Date:** 3/01

    1. 5 minutes of listening to selection from a favorite book
    2. 5 minutes to play computer game
    3. 2 pieces of Star Wars Lego set
    4. 1 Pokemon card

LIST OF REINFORCERS *(List #2)*   **For:** Ethan T.   **Date:** 6/01

"B" Reinforcers: (10 white tokens = 1 blue token = 1 reinforcer from following list)

    1. Brief trip to doughnut store to buy doughnut
    2. Brief trip to bakery to buy cookie
    3. 15 minutes to play computer game
    4. 15 minutes to listen to selection from a favorite book
    5. 15 minutes swim time (weather permitting)

"A" Reinforcers: (50 white tokens = 1 red token = 1 reinforcer from following list)

    1. 1 Star Wars computer game
    2. 1 pair riding boots
    3. 1 pair riding pants
    4. 1 set riding helmet/gloves
    5. 1 day trip to theme park
    6. 1 Star Wars Lego set, small-medium size

An example of two different reinforcement lists for a thirteen-year-old boy with HFA. This student was particularly interested in Star Wars, computer games, and horses. When he started, he immediately was given his choice of reinforcers from the first list (see list #1). Next, he was introduced to a simple token system, in which he received one white token for each task completed, and "cashed it in" immediately. Soon after this he learned to wait for progressively longer time periods to trade in a few tokens at a time for the corresponding number of reinforcers from list #1. In the next part of the program, a new token economy was introduced (see list #2). With this system, he could trade ten white tokens for a blue one, with which he could "purchase" a medium-value reinforcer. Alternatively he could choose to wait and trade fifty white tokens for a red token, which he could then trade in for a "large-value" reinforcer.

HIDDEN CAUSES OF PROBLEM BEHAVIORS

Problem behaviors are a common occurrence in students with AS/HFA. Non-compliance, in particular, is a behavior that occurs frequently in this population and will be addressed in the following program. However, before starting a program to treat problem behaviors, it is critical to look for the causes of the behavior. In individuals with AS/HFA, *high levels of stress, undiagnosed learning disabilities, undiagnosed illness, neurologically based problems with attention,* and *poor organizational skills* are common but often overlooked causes of problem behaviors. When one or more of these conditions is missed, it is common for the student's difficulties to be attributed erroneously to deliberate disobedience, defiance or a "bad attitude" on the student's part. In addressing problem behaviors it is critical to actively look for and initiate treatment of underlying causes such as those listed above, and then to apply behavioral management techniques as adjunct therapy, if necessary. While behavioral management programs (such as the following program on compliance) can be invaluable in treating behavioral problems, they at best will treat only the surface of the problem if underlying causes of the behavior are not adequately addressed.

Some of the causes of problem behaviors are noted below.

Learning Disabilities

Many students with higher functioning autism have one or more learning disabilities. Because these students are bright and can appear *on the surface* to be fairly "normal," it can be easy to miss very real problems with learning. As with any child in this situation, if a student with AS/HFA has learning disabilities that go unrecognized, he undoubtedly will face the daily frustration of not understanding how to go about the tasks required of him. As he watches other students moving ahead of him in the classroom, and as his failure continues day after day, his self-esteem is almost certain to plummet.

Unfortunately, it is not uncommon in such cases for the child himself to be blamed for his failure to complete his work. Both teachers and parents may recognize that the child lacks interest in certain subjects and may arrive at the mistaken conclusion that the child "could do it if only he wanted to." The student may be viewed as being lazy or defiant. In such cases it is not uncommon for the student to face on-going disapproval which, of course, further compromises his self–esteem. Many a student like this reaches a point where he simply gives up and stops trying. Exposed day after day to a situation in which he cannot succeed, such a student is apt to develop *secondary* avoidance behaviors and non-compliance to escape this no-win situation. The student may indeed end up with compliance problems, but they are problems that have resulted from inappropriate treatment of his learning disability. If this situation continues for a significant amount of time, the avoidance and non-compliance behaviors become firmly entrenched and it becomes increasingly difficult to remediate either the academic problems or the non-compliance.

Stress

Sometimes, failure to attempt or complete a task is due to stress, which results in an inability to focus. If the people working with the AS/HFA student have not learned the subtle stress signals that the student may show at lower stress levels, they may mistakenly conclude that the student is purposefully not cooperating when he fails to carry out a task. This can lead the person in charge to use the wrong tactic with the student. If the problem is treated as non-compliance when it actually is stress-related, the student's problem behavior is very likely to escalate. As the student becomes more stressed, he may become increasingly unable to focus and, in some cases, may completely lose control. When a student loses control, it obviously makes everyone's task more difficult. After a blow up, it invariably takes much more time to bring the child back down to where he can focus than it would have had the stress been recognized and treated early on. In addition, repeated blow-ups often cause tension between student and teacher and are apt to damage the student's self-esteem when he realizes that he has once again failed to stay in control. Therefore, it becomes very important for teachers and parents to try to recognize and treat stress as early in the process as possible. (*Section One, "Recognizing and Coping with One's Own Emotions,"* contains several programs that address the recognition and treatment of stress.) When, as sometimes happens, there is a compliance problem in *addition* to the problem of stress, the teacher will be much more successful in working on the compliance issue after the student is helped to calm down.

Problems with attention and organizational skills

Difficulties with focusing attention and with organizational skills are very common, if not universal, in individuals with AS/HFA. It is important to understand that these are "hard wiring" deficits that originate in the person's central nervous system. In fact, the student may try as hard as he can to stay organized and focused, but if those parts of his brain that mediate attention and organizational skills do not function normally, then his *ability* to do so will be impaired. Particularly when the student is obviously bright, this lack of organization and attention can masquerade as non-compliance or laziness. Thus, when the student works diligently on an assignment and then leaves it at home or loses it en route, the student is called irresponsible. Likewise, the student who quietly stares out the classroom window for an hour because he cannot figure out how to organize and start his writing assignment is labeled as a poor or lazy student when he fails to turn in the assignment at the end of class. In cases such as these, it is obvious that behavioral programs alone will not solve the problems. To succeed, they also must be provided with thoughtfully planned programs to help them specifically with their organizational and attentional problems. [43]

---

[43] The best programs for organizational and attentional problems rely on input from the child's physician, parents or other caregivers, teachers, and sometimes a psychologist. A well-designed program will include 1) medical evaluation (and possibly treatment with medication), 2) environmental adjustments (such as providing a quiet, non-stimulating environment and preferential seating), 3) organizational supports such as daily planners, visual clues and sometimes provision of an aide to monitor assignments and organization of the student's work environment and 4) an effective reinforcement system.

Undiagnosed illness

Children with AS/HFA are notorious for not speaking up when they are in pain or when they are not feeling well. Their discomfort may instead show up in the form of problem behaviors. Therefore, particularly when the child displays unusual or unexpected behaviors, it is always wise to check to make sure that he is feeling well and is not in pain. For example, one student with HFA was having a particularly bad day at school. She was tearful, grumpy, and unable to focus. It was not until two days later that she mentioned, in passing, that one of the wires from her dental braces had broken. Her mother discovered a large, painful sore on the inside of her mouth. Once this was taken care of, her behavior returned to normal.

A case study

Ethan, a thirteen-year-old boy, was diagnosed with HFA at age twelve. Starting at age two and a half, he attended an early intervention program followed by a preschool program for severe speech and language delays. When he entered regular school at age six, his speech and language had improved considerably, but still were not at grade level. Upon Ethan's entry to grade school, his mother gave the school the records from his previous treatment programs, but unfortunately they were never read. Although he functioned poorly in language, social-emotional, and academic skills, he received no specialized treatment in these areas for the first eighteen months of school. When he failed to complete assignments, it was felt that Ethan was being merely non-compliant, and he was disciplined accordingly. Ethan's daily stress level began to rise and his inability to understand the assigned work, coupled with stress related to changes in his environment or schedule, caused several "blow-ups" in the classroom. Finally, his behavior escalated to the point where he was suspended from school for threatening to kick a teacher. After his return to school, the school staff referred him to his physician for possible attention deficit and obsessive-compulsive disorders. Ultimately he was diagnosed as having ADD, OCD, and learning disabilities in the areas of math, reading, and written language.

Ethan subsequently received intervention for some of his problems, but it varied considerably from year to year. Some of his teachers made efforts to work with his learning disabilities and other problems. Others made very few attempts to learn about or treat his disabilities, believing instead that Ethan was simply being non-cooperative and obstinate. The more he was treated this way, the worse his behavior became, thereby validating the teachers' opinions that he was simply a "bad apple." This created a vicious circle of social and academic failure that resulted in stress, followed by problem behaviors, which led to punishment (including multiple suspensions) and further failure and so on. This cycle continued throughout his primary school years, and was accompanied by worsening self-esteem. Finally his parents, dismayed by the regression they were seeing in their son's social, emotional, and academic functioning, took him to a well-respected child psychiatry unit where he finally was given the diagnosis of High Functioning Autism. Unfortunately, by this time Ethan had developed a set of well-entrenched avoidance and "acting out" behaviors that were negatively reinforced each time he successfully managed to be suspended or sent home or to the principal's office. By this point he had developed such severe problems with compliance that he refused to attempt even simple academic tasks that were far below his ability level. This was true even when consistent efforts eventually were made to understand and address his learning disabilities.

Before beginning to address Ethan's academic needs, it was necessary to first teach him to comply with reasonable requests. Without the ability to comply with tasks that were *below* his skill level, there was little hope that he could be taught new information. It was no small task to teach Ethan to comply; his non-compliance and avoidance behaviors had been intermittently reinforced over a period of several years. He had become very good at mimicking a high level of stress as a way of avoiding a non-favored task, and at times it was very difficult to differentiate between true stress and avoidance/non-compliance. However, after working with him over a period of time, his teachers began to find it easier to differentiate between the two and became skilled in using stress reduction techniques when he was stressed and non-compliance techniques when he was non-compliant. The following program presents the basic technique Ethan's teachers used to teach him how to comply. The same program can be used for students whose non-compliance stems from simple lack of initiative.

PROGRAM 20
COMPLIANCE[44]

INTRODUCTION

Non-compliance with academic, self-help, or other tasks is a common occurrence in students with AS/HFA. When non-compliance interferes with the student's acquisition of necessary skills, it can compromise her potential for achieving independence later on. Why do some individuals oftentimes find it so frustratingly difficult to follow through with requests, especially when their teachers know that they *need* to do these tasks for their own good? In answering this question, it is helpful to divide non-compliance into two categories: 1) *primary non-compliance*, and 2) *secondary non-compliance*. As used here, primary non-compliance is due to a lack of interest in the task at hand, whereas secondary non-compliance is a *chronic, learned response* to repeated failure. (To put it another way, repeated failure is a strong negative stimulus and non-compliance is a behavior that allows the student to escape or avoid the negative stimulus.)

In the case of *primary* non-compliance, the person with AS/HFA may simply lack the initiative to complete tasks that she views as having little intrinsic value.[45] Because people with AS/HFA tend to focus their energy on their special areas of interest, sometimes there just is not much energy left over for other interests or activities.

---

[44] Parts of this program were adapted with permission from unpublished work by Autism Partnership, Long Beach, CA.
[45] See Howlin, P. *Autism – Preparing for Adulthood* for further discussion of this topic.

For example, Bridget, a bright, fifteen-year-old girl with HFA, refused to brush her hair or check the mirror to make sure her appearance was at least minimally presentable. She would routinely appear in public with her hair matted and tangled, and with toothpaste or the remains of lunch on her face. The other students at school immediately noticed this, and teased her unrelentingly. In spite of this, when asked why she did not carry out these relatively simple grooming tasks, she replied that she did not *care* how she looked, as her appearance simply was "not important."

In another case, a bright young high school student with AS, who had proven to have excellent writing skills, consistently failed to work on his history assignments, despite much effort on the part of his teacher and parents to provide him with extra help in understanding and organizing the work. When asked why he was not doing the assignments, his reply was "It's a waste of time to do history assignments. I'm much better off spending that time on computer programming." (His main topic of interest was computer programming, a skill at which he was quite talented.)

Secondary non-compliance, on the other hand, is a learned trait and has a much more complicated cause. If a student is repeatedly *unable* to complete certain tasks due to untreated learning disabilities, stress, or other reasons, this chronic failure can become a powerful negative stimulus. Habitual failure can become so discouraging to the student that he develops avoidance behaviors to escape the negative situation, resulting in secondary non-compliance. Therefore, it is very important to clearly establish that the student is *capable* of doing the assigned task before concluding that he is being non-compliant. Ironically, mistakenly treating a child who has an impediment to learning as if he is non-compliant can lead to the very non-compliance that the teacher was trying to stop.

An important caveat in teaching a child to comply is to also teach him when not to comply. The literature is full of anecdotal cases of individuals with autism spectrum disorders being unwittingly manipulated into unsafe, illicit, or otherwise risky situations.[46] The burden is on those who work with and care for these individuals to help them, from as early an age as possible, to differentiate between safe and appropriate activities and those that are potentially risky. When defining what is risky, the teacher needs to address behaviors that may not be unsafe at the time but may become unsafe later in the child's life. For example, it may seem amusing when a three-year-old removes her clothes in public, but this behavior will hardly be humorous or safe at age sixteen. Also, individuals with AS/HFA can be very naïve and unable to see the subtle clues which may signal that they are being manipulated. In addition, they often lack the experience and ability to predict the likely outcome of their actions. (Program 15, *"Public vs. Private"* (page 143) presents one way to teach students to differentiate between activities and conversational topics that are appropriate and safe, and those that are not. One advantage of this program is that it allows the teacher to tailor the agenda to match the needs of the individual student.)

The program that follows is designed to help the student with either primary or secondary non-compliance learn to comply with requests to do reasonable academic or self-help tasks. It uses a *graded approach,* in which the student gradually progresses from complying with *low-demand* tasks (preferred tasks that are easy for him to accomplish) to *high-demand* tasks (non-preferred tasks that are at or slightly above his ability level). The success of this approach depends on first setting up an effective reinforcement system designed specifically for the individual student. [*Refer to "A Brief Look at Reinforcement"* (page 235) *that precedes this program for more*

---

[46] For example, refer to Donna Williams' autobiography, *Nobody Nowhere.* (Williams, Donna. 1992. Avon Books. New York.)

information about reinforcement.]   In most cases, it will require more time to make progress in cases of long-standing secondary non-compliance than it will in cases of primary non-compliance.

GOALS

The ultimate goal of this program is to teach students with either primary or secondary non-compliance to learn to comply with academic or self-help tasks at their level of ability. The rationale for teaching compliance is to help these students learn the academic and self-help skills that they will need in order to meet their potentials for independence and personal fulfillment.

INSTRUCTIONS

Step One: Set up an individualized reinforcement system.

Referring to the preceding section on reinforcement,[47] make a list of personalized reinforcers for the student. Remember that in order for this program to succeed, *it is critical to use reinforcers that are of value to the student and for which he will be willing to work.*

Because the student with a true non-compliance problem, by definition, does not find *intrinsic* value in the target tasks, this program relies initially on *extrinsic* reinforcers. (See definitions on *page 232*.)   However, whenever possible the ultimate goal is to help the student gain enough sense of accomplishment in doing the target tasks that the extrinsic reinforcers can be gradually eliminated.

---

[47] Note: If you are not comfortable with setting up a reinforcement system, an applied behavior therapist can help you to do so.

Step Two: Make a compliance hierarchy list. (See figures 20a and 20b on pages 255 and 256 for examples of completed compliance hierarchy lists.)

Preferably using input from both teachers and parents, create a list of academic and/or self-help activities with which the student typically has problems complying. It is important that the student is already familiar with, and is clearly able to accomplish, each task on the hierarchy. Make each item as specific as possible, including any time limits and the number of prompts allowed. Arrange the list in order of increasing degrees of non-compliance. Then add to the beginning of the list one or two tasks that the student actually *likes* to do. The next one or two tasks should be ones that the student may not be thrilled about, but will usually comply with fairly easily. The subsequent task should be *slightly* more apt to produce noncompliance, the task after this should be a little more challenging than the previous one, and so forth. The final item should be a task with which the student rarely complies. Note that a compliance hierarchy also can be written for one specific task by breaking the task down into small steps.

Step Three: Prepare the student to begin the program.

Note: It is very important to work on the following steps only when the student is relaxed. Attempting to work on this program when she is stressed will undermine the success of the program.

Explain to the student that when she is working on this program, she will be earning a treat (or token, if applicable) for doing different tasks. (In some cases it is better to avoid the label "compliance program" when speaking with the child. Instead, choose an alternate, neutral name, such as "learning skills program" or "activity time," etc.) Tell the student that the tasks she will be asked to do will be very easy ones in the beginning of the program, and then will become more challenging as the sessions go on. Let the student choose the treat she will work for during each session. If possible, have the reinforcer visible before and during the time the student is working on the task, so that the student has a visual reminder of what she will earn for completing the task.

Step Four: "Hook the student in." Introduce the first item on the hierarchy.

Tell the student that you are going to give her a task to do, for which she will earn a reward from her reward menu. Explain the first task on her compliance hierarchy (see Step Two), making sure that she understands exactly what is expected of her in order to earn the treat. Ask the student to perform the task. Because the first item on the hierarchy is a task that the student already enjoys, it should take very little convincing for her to do it. Reinforce her for accomplishing it, using both verbal praise and the token or treat that she has previously chosen. The basic idea is to *hook the student in* to the program by reinforcing her initially *for doing something that she already likes to do.* In essence, you want the student to think, "Hey, this is a piece of cake. I just got rewarded for doing something I <u>like</u> doing!" In the subsequent two sessions, ask the student to do a slightly altered version of this task or another task that she enjoys, continuing with both verbal praise and a tangible reinforcer. Soon you will start introducing more challenging tasks, but in such small, incremental steps that the student will be *successful at complying with each task.*

A word of caution: Although all the items on the hierarchy should be ones that the student already *can* do without much difficulty, there inevitably will be times when her work is less than perfect. However, when working on compliance, be sure to respond to each reasonable effort to do the requested task with positive feedback and reinforcement, even if the work has flaws. A common error is for the teacher to correct the student's work during a compliance program, even when the student is trying in good faith to complete the task. Try to ignore the urge to correct the student's work in such situations. Remember that *you are working on the student's compliance rather than on the task itself.* It is essential for the student to feel successful at attempting the task. If she is corrected while or after making an honest attempt to do a task with which she already has problems complying, you are apt to lose her altogether. Keep in mind that you can go back and work on the quality of the tasks *after* the compliance program is finished.

Step Five: *Gradually* **introduce the remaining tasks on the hierarchy over several sessions.**

Introduce each subsequent task on the compliance list using the same method you used in Step Four. The tone of the sessions should be pleasant and without pressure, regardless of whether the student complies or not. If the student does not comply with a task, she simply does not receive her reinforcer for that session. Note that at this point the student may become quite unhappy with the teacher for withholding the reinforcer and she might decide to share how unhappy she is in a less than desirable manner. When working with a particularly non-compliant or temperamental student, it is easy for even the best teacher to react on an emotional level. However, once this happens, the teacher has entered into a power struggle with the student, and neither party will win in the long run. Instead, the beleaguered teacher needs to maintain at least an *outwardly neutral,* if not pleasant, attitude.

To make sure the student has mastered complying with each step, repeat each task (with minor variations if needed) until the student has complied with it three consecutive times, continuing to reinforce the student as noted in Step Four.[48] Note that it is acceptable to add, subtract, or make additions to items on the compliance hierarchy if the need arises. Once you have asked the student to do a particular task, you need to make sure that she does complete it, even if you must postpone the task until a later time. If the student does not comply with a task on the hierarchy, it is probably because a) the reinforcer is not attractive enough to outweigh the student's desire to avoid the task, b) the student's ability to work is being compromised by stress, not understanding the task, illness, etc., or, c) the task itself is too challenging for the student's current level of compliance. In the first case, it may be necessary to change the reinforcers being used. In the second case, the underlying problem needs to be addressed before the student re-attempts the task. In the last case, you will need to reevaluate the compliance hierarchy. You might consider adding easier tasks for a while, making them progressively more challenging until the student is ready to comply with the original task.

For example, when Ethan failed to comply with a request to do three math problems at his ability level, the teacher withheld the reinforcer for that session. Before the next session, she reviewed her hierarchy list and decided that that item was too challenging for his level of compliance at the time. She revamped the list, adding preliminary steps in which she broke down the task into smaller, easier steps. In the next session, he was asked to do *one* math problem that was *slightly below* his level. She reinforced him for complying with this, and then repeated the same step two more times to assure that he had mastered this level of compliance. In the next three sessions, he was asked

---

[48] See "A Brief Look at Reinforcement" on page 235 for the definition of "mastery" as it is used in this book.

to do *three* problems below his level followed by three sessions of one problem at his level, and so forth, until he worked up to complying with the original request to do three problems at his ability level.

Keep in mind that compliance problems often have developed over years, and may require a long time to overcome. *Expect* times when the student will not comply. (If the student <u>does</u> comply with every step in the program the first time through, chances are either that the tasks are not challenging enough, or that the actual problem is something other than non-compliance.)

Compliance Hierarchy

Student's name: _Amy Sutherland_   **Date:** _1/12/01_

1. One chapter preferred reading (Star Wars novel)

2. Give teacher one fact about Star Wars

3. Stop preferred reading after two prompts

4. Stop preferred reading after one prompt

5. Stop preferred activity (computer game) after two prompts

6. Stop preferred activity after one prompt

7. Unload plates from dishwasher (2 prompts maximum)

8. Unload plates and silverware from dishwasher (2 prompts maximum)

9. Unload entire dishwasher (2 prompts maximum)

10. Unload entire dishwasher (1 prompt maximum)

11. Complete one easy math problem within 5 minutes (with maximum 2 prompts)

12. Complete one easy math problem within 5 minutes with preferred book nearby on desk

13. Complete two easy math problems within 5 minutes (2 prompts maximum)

14. Complete two easy math problems within 5 minutes (1 prompt maximum)

15. Complete five easy math problems within 10 minutes (2 prompts maximum)

16. Write three spelling words (2 prompts maximum)

17. Write four spelling words (1 prompt maximum)

18. Write one simple sentence (noun-verb-adjective format, 2 prompts maximum)

19. Write two simple sentences (noun-verb-adjective format, 2 prompts maximum)

Figure 20a. <u>An example of a Compliance Hierarchy.</u> Note that this hierarchy is quite lengthy in order to include more examples of both the *types* of items and the *small, incremental steps* that this particular student required in order to achieve success. However, a compliance hierarchy can be as short as three items to begin with. The first two tasks on the hierarchy are ones that the student enjoys doing. Reinforcing her for doing these two tasks "hooked" her in to the reward system. This student had gone a few years without appropriate treatment of her learning disabilities in written language and math, and consequently had developed well-established avoidance behaviors in these areas. Notice that she was given a very small number of "easy" (below her ability level) math problems and writing tasks initially in order to allow her to experience success in these subjects. Note the inclusion of unloading the dishwasher, a chore that she disliked, but was able to do without problems. Further hierarchies were written for her as she progressed through the program, until she was compliant with academic tasks at her ability level 90% of the time. She still works intermittently on a compliance program for activities of daily living, although she has shown much improvement in this area.

Compliance Hierarchy –Taking a shower

Student's name: _Ian Blackwell_   **Date:** _2/11/01_

1. Take shower, including washing hair: 70 minutes, I prompt maximum (use timer)

2. As above: 60 minutes, I prompt max. (use timer)

3. As above: 50 minutes, I prompt max. (use timer)

4. As above: 40 minutes, 2 prompts max. (use timer)

5. As above: 30 minutes, I prompt max. (use timer)

6. As above: 20 minutes, I prompt max. (use timer)

7. As above: 15 minutes, I prompt max. (use timer)

8. As above: 15 minutes, 0 prompts (use timer)

Figure 20b. <u>An Example of a Compliance Hierarchy for a specific task.</u> This fourteen-year-old boy with HFA disliked showering due to tactile sensitivity to the feel of shampoo in his hair or soap on his skin. Both problems had been adequately addressed when he started using a shower gel recommended by his occupational therapist. Since then he had demonstrated the ability to both shower and wash his hair independently. However, it typically took him 60 minutes to do so. Because of this and other problems with self-help skills, Ian's parents had a very difficult time getting him out of the house on time in the morning. Their goal was for Ian to shower and wash his hair in 15 minutes, and to learn to depend on a timer instead of his parent's prompting to complete the task. Using the graded steps shown on the above hierarchy along with an effective reinforcement program, they were able to help Ian achieve this goal over a period of about one month. Even though the program required significant time and patience from the parents for that one-month period, they felt that it was well worth the effort in the long run. After Ian successfully completed this hierarchy, his parents designed and implemented a few more hierarchies that helped him with a complete morning routine, including making his bed, getting dressed, and eating breakfast. At this point, they also provided Ian with an easily read visual schedule, with room to check off each task as it was completed.

APPENDIX A

ADDITIONAL RESOURCE
MATERIALS

ADDITIONAL RESOURCE MATERIALS

Books and Other Publications

General books on Autism, Asperger's Syndrome, and related disorders

☞ **Asperger's Syndrome: A Guide for Parents and Professionals**
T. Attwood
Jessica Kingsley. 1998
ISBN 1-853-02557-1

☞ **Asperger Syndrome and Difficult Moments**
B. Smith Myles and J. Southwick
Autism Asperger Pub. Co. 1999
ISBN 0-967-25143-5

☞ **Asperger Syndrome**
A. Klin, F. Volkmar, S. Sparrow
Guilford Press. 2000
ISBN 1-572-30534-7

☞ **Asperger Syndrome: A Practical Guide for Teachers**
V. Cumine, J. Leach and G. Stevenson
David Fulton Pub. 1998
ISBN 1-85346-499-6

☞ **Autism and Asperger Syndrome**
U. Frith
Cambridge University Press. 1991
ISBN 0-521-38448-6

☞ **Autism – Preparing for Adulthood**
P. Howlin
Routledge. 1997
ISBN 0-415-11531-0

☞ **Children with Autism and Asperger Syndrome: A Guide for Practioners and Caregivers**
P. Howlin
John Wiley & Sons. 1998
ISBN 0-471-98328-4

☞ **High Functioning Individuals with Autism: Advice and Information for Parents and Others Who Care.** (Booklet).
S. Moreno
MAAP Services
chart@netnitco.net

☞ **Higher Functioning Adolescents and Young Adults with Autism: A Teacher's Guide**
A. Fullerton, J. Stratton, P. Coyne and C. Gray
Pro-Ed. 1996
ISBN 0-890-79681-5

☞ **Mindblindness: An Essay on Autism and Theory of Mind**
S. Baron-Cohen
The MIT Press. 1995
ISBN 0-262-02384-9

☞ **The Morning News** (a quarterly autism newsletter)
C. Gray, ed.
Jenison Public Schools
(616)457-8955

☞ **Teaching Children With Autism to Mind-Read**
P. Howlin, S. Baron-Cohen and J. Hadwin
John Wiley & Sons. 1999
ISBN 0-471-97623-7

☞ **What Does It Mean To Me?**
C. Faherty
Future Horizons. 2000
(817)277-0727

Social skills and pragmatics

☞ **Comic Strip Conversations**
Carol Gray. Jenison Public Schools.
Future Horizons. 1994
(817)277-0727

☞ **The New Social Story Book**
Jenison High School Students. Ed.: Carol Gray
Future Horizons. 1994
(817)277-0727

☞ **The Original Social Story Book**
Jenison High School Students. Ed.: Carol Gray
Future Horizons. 1993
(817)277-0727

☞ **Play and Imagination in Children with Autism**
P. Wolfberg
Teachers College Press. 1999.
ISBN 0-807-73814-X

☞ **Teach Me Language: A language manual for children with autism, Asperger's syndrome and related developmental disorders**
S. Freeman and L. Dake
SKF Books. 1996
ISBN 0-965-75650-5

☞ **Teaching Children with Autism: Strategies to Enhance Communication and Socialization**
Quill, K.
Delmar Pub, Inc. 1995
ISBN 0-827-36269-2

Sensory Integration

☞ **SensAbilities: Understanding Sensory Integration**
M. Colby Trott, M. Laurel and S. Windeck
Therapy Skill Builders. 1-800-228-0752

Autobiographies

☞ **Nobody Nowhere: The Extraordinary Autobiography of an Autistic.**
D. Williams
Avon Books. 1992
ISBN 0-380-72217-8

☞ **Pretending to be Normal**
L. Holliday Willey
Jessica Kingsley. 2000
ISBN 1-853-02721-9

☞ **Somebody Somewhere: Breaking Free from the World of Autism.**
D. Williams
Crown Publishing Group. 1995
ISBN 0-812-92524-6

Applied Behavioral Therapy

☞ **Behavior Modification, Basic Principles**
S. Axelrod, R. V. Hall
Pro-Ed. 2000
ISBN 0-890-79804-4

☞ **Don't Shoot the Dog!: The New Art of Teaching and Training**
K. Pryor
Bantam Books. 1999
ISBN 0-553-38039-7

☞ **Teaching the Tiger: A Handbook for Individuals Involved in the Education of Students with Attention Deficit Disorders, Tourette Syndrome or Obsessive-Compulsive Disorder**
M. Pierce Dornbush, S. Pruitt
Hope Press. 1995
ISBN 1-878-26734-5

Books for individuals with AS/HFA

☞ **The Care and Keeping of Friends**
N. Westcott
American Girl Library, Pleasant Co. Pub. 1996

☞ **What Does It Mean To Me?**
C. Faherty
Future Horizons, Inc. 2000
ISBN 1-885477-59-7

Idioms & Clichés

☞ **The American Heritage Dictionary of Idioms**
C. Ammer
Houghton Mifflin Co. 1997
ISBN 0-395-72774-X

☞ **The Dictionary of Clichés: Over 2,000 Popular and Amusing Clichés—Their Meanings and Origins**
J. Rogers
Random House, Inc. 1991
ISBN 0-517-06020-5

☞ **The Scholastic Dictionary of Idioms**
M. Terban
Scholastic, Inc. 1998
ISBN 0-590-38157-1

<u>*Web sites*</u>:

☞ **ABA Resources**
http://rsaffran.tripod.com/aba.utml

☞ **Autism-PDD Resources Network**
www.autism-pdd.net

☞ **Autism Resources**
www.autism-resources.com

☞ **Autism Society of America**
www.autism-society.org

☞ **Center for the Study of Autism**
www.autism.org

☞ **FEAT (Families for Early Autism Treatment)**
www.feat.org

☞ **Future Horizons**
www.futurehorizons-autism.com

☞ **Homeschool Zone**
http://www.homeschoolzone.com/add/autism.htm

☞ **The Idiom Connection**
www.geocities.com/Athens/Aegean/6720/#AB

☞ **Jeanie McAfee's Home Page**
www.jeaniemcafee.com

☞ **MAAP (More Advanced Individuals with Autism/Asperger's Syndrome and Pervasive Developmental Disorder)**
www.saintjoe.edu/~daved/MAAP/

☞ **OASIS (Online Asperger Syndrome Information and Support)**
www.udel.edu/bkirby/asperger

☞ **Oops...Wrong Planet Syndrome**
www.isn.net/~jypsy

☞ **Room 5's Autism Page**
http://members.aol.com/room5/welcome.html

☞ **TEACCH (Treatment and Education of Autistic and Related Communication Handicapped CHildren)**
www.teacch.com/teacch.htm

☞ **Tony Attwood's home page**
www.tonyattwood.com

☞ **UC Davis MIND Institute**
http://Mindinstitute.ucdmc.ucdavis.edu

☞ **Wayne Magnuson English Idioms, Sayings and Slang**
http://home.t-online.de/home/toni.goeller/idiom_wm/index.html

Computer Resources:

☞ **Gaining Face** (a computer program that helps children with Asperger's Syndrome to identify facial cues)
Team Asperger
www.ccoder.com/GainingFace

☞ **Smart Alex** (A computer program that is based upon a cartoon character who can change his facial expression. The student chooses an expression and observes Alex's face.)
Special Needs Computing
sncl@box42.com

Games:

☞ **Communicate: An educational activity to reinforce social communication skills during adolescence**
P. Mayo and P. Waldo
Thinking Publications. 1986
ISBN 0-030599-04-7

☞ **Communicate Junior: An educational activity to reinforce social skills in elementary-age children**
P. Mayo, P. Hirn, N. Gajewski and J. Kafka
Thinking Publications. 1991

APPENDIX B

STUDENT HANDOUTS

List of Emotions

AFRAID

Afraid
Anxious/Worried
Cautious
Frightened
Terrified
Uncertain

ANGRY

Angry
Enraged
Exasperated
Frustrated
Irritated

CONFIDENT

Confident
Courageous
Optimistic
Smug

CONFUSED

Confused
Perplexed
Puzzled

CURIOUS

Curious
Fascinated
Interested

HAPPY

Amused
Blissful
Contented
Ecstatic
Enthusiastic
Excited
Happy
Proud
Relieved
Satisfied
Silly

MISCELLANEOUS EMOTIONS

Bashful
Bored
Disgusted/Grossed out
Embarrassed/Sheepish
Guilty
Hopeful
Indifferent
Innocent
Jealous/ Envious
Love struck
Pleading
Self-conscious
Shocked
Shy

MENTAL STATE OF BEING

Arrogant/Vain
Bored
Concentrating
Determined
Disapproving
Disbelieving
Mischievous
Stubborn
Thoughtful

PHYSICAL STATE OF BEING

Cold
Exhausted
Hot
Miserable
Nauseated/Ill
Relaxed
Sleepy

SAD

Depressed
Disappointed
Grieving
Hurt
Lonely
Sorry
Sad

(From *Navigating the Social World*, Program 2.)

Student Handout

THE SECRET LANGUAGE

You probably know that people talk to other people with words. But have you ever noticed that people also "talk" with their faces (especially their eyes), their bodies, and their tone of voice? This type of talk is like a *secret language*. In this language, people give important messages with the expressions on their faces, the ways they hold or move their bodies, and the way their voices sound. Believe it or not, these messages are just as important as the words we use when we talk! In fact, we can totally change the meaning of words just by changing our tone of voice, the way we hold our body, or the expression on our face as we speak. For example, consider the following story:

There once was a boy named Peter who had a big sister named Jane, a lazy cat named Hairball, and a fat dog named Toothpick. Peter and Jane loved to eat fish and chips. They were thrilled one day when Mom decided to prepare her delicious, homemade fish and chips for dinner. That evening, Peter and Jane were helping to put dinner on the table, when Peter accidentally stumbled over Hairball, who was lying in the middle of the kitchen floor. Unfortunately, Peter was carrying the platter of fish and chips, which went flying across the room, landing squarely in front of Toothpick. In a flash Toothpick gobbled up all of the tasty fish and chips, leaving none for the family's dinner. At this, Jane looked over at Peter and said, "Good job, Peter!"

Did Peter think that Jane was complimenting him for tripping and letting Toothpick eat the fish and chips? The answer is no! Peter knew right away that Jane was really upset, and that her words actually meant "bad job," not "good job." How did Peter know this? Well, first of all, Peter heard Jane's angry and sarcastic tone of voice and saw her clenched fists, scrunched up eyebrows, and down-turned mouth.   **(continued)**

These were *nonverbal* clues that Jane was angry. Peter also knew that Jane loved fish and chips and therefore would be upset to lose her dinner. This was a *contextual clue* that helped Peter figure out that Jane probably was upset over losing her chance to eat Mom's fish and chips.

Some people seem to understand these types of clues easily. Other people need help to understand them. But one thing is for sure – a person needs to know how to figure out these clues in order to make sense of other people's words and actions. As a matter of fact, some people who have trouble doing this say that they feel like they live on another planet where everyone around them speaks a strange, secret language with their eyes and bodies, and that they understand only half of what these strange beings are trying to say!

If you have ever felt this way, help is on the way. This program will help you understand *how* people's facial expressions and body language can change the meaning of their words. You will get lots of practice using facial expression and body language "clues" to help figure out what other people may be feeling and thinking. This will help you learn to predict how other people might react to your words and actions, and what they are going to do next. If this sounds like it might be helpful, then it's time to get started on this program! Have fun!

(From *Navigating the Social World*, Program 8.)

Emotions and Facial Expressions

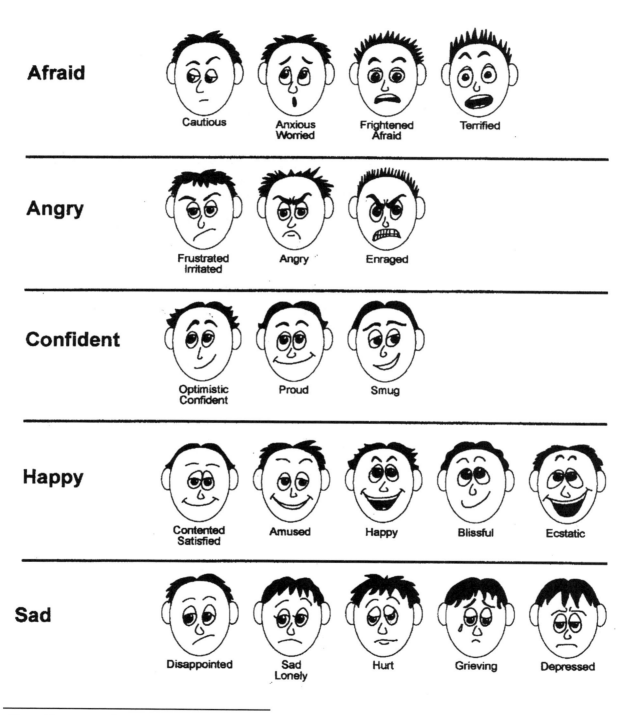

(From *Navigating the Social World*, Program 8.)
Graphics and layout by Dane Wilson. Artwork by Donna Burton.

EMOTIONS AND FACIAL EXPRESSIONS continued

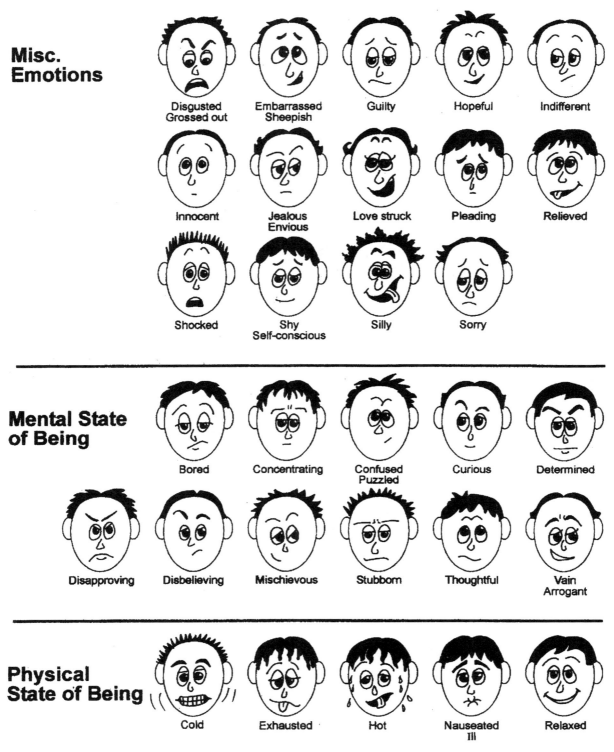

Misc. Emotions

Disgusted Grossed out · Embarrassed Sheepish · Guilty · Hopeful · Indifferent

Innocent · Jealous Envious · Love struck · Pleading · Relieved

Shocked · Shy Self-conscious · Silly · Sorry

Mental State of Being

Bored · Concentrating · Confused Puzzled · Curious · Determined

Disapproving · Disbelieving · Mischievous · Stubborn · Thoughtful · Vain Arrogant

Physical State of Being

Cold · Exhausted · Hot · Nauseated Ill · Relaxed

(From *Navigating the Social World*, Program 8.)
Graphics and layout by Dane Wilson. Artwork by Donna Burton.

STUDENT HANDOUT

RULES FOR HELLO AND GOOD-BYE

1. **Always start a conversation with a greeting.**
   (This is not necessary if you have already greeted the other person.)

2. **Always end a conversation with an appropriate form of good-bye.**

3. **Choose the right *type* of hello or good-bye.**

   The words that people use to say hello or good-bye are different, depending on the type of person they are talking to. In this program, we divide people into four categories: familiar adults, not-familiar adults, familiar kids and not-familiar kids.

4. **Use good nonverbal signals:**

   - face the other person
   - stand or sit up straight
   - make eye contact
   - smile (Exception: on certain serious occasions people do not smile when saying hello or good-bye.)

5. **Use a good handshake style.**

   Sometimes when people greet or say good-bye to each other, they also shake hands. If you are not sure whether or not to shake hands, it is usually best to shake only if the other person offers his or her hand. (Men and teenage boys shake hands more often than do women and girls.)

   When you do shake hands, try to:

   - Grip the other person's hand firmly, but not too hard.
   - Give two short shakes, and then let go.
   - Make eye contact.
   - Smile. (See exception in Step 4.)

(From *Navigating the Social World*, Program 9.)

PATHS to Starting Conversations

(Remember this mnemonic when you are about to start a conversation.)

Prepare ahead: keep "fact files" with important facts about the people you know. Most people who are good at conversations keep track of facts they know about other people. They use these facts in their conversations with the other person to: 1) use as conversational topics that will interest the other person, and 2) show the other person that they care about him or her. Start by keeping fact files on index cards. Write the name and personal *facts* such as birth date, family members, favorite color and favorite school subject, on one side, and interests, such as soccer, science fiction reading and computer games on the other side. Later on, you might want to keep invisible "files" in your head.

Ask yourself what you are going to say and how you are going to say it *before you start talking*. (You will be making a list of examples of conversation starters in Step 2.) Try to chose topics that:

1. Compliment the other person (compliments on appearance and achievements often work well with people you don't know well).
2. Show that you are interested in the other person by asking about a subject that is important to him even *if it is not important to you* (check your fact file).
3. Give information that the other person needs to know *or* ask for information that you need to know.
4. Offer or ask for help (see Program 10 for more help with this topic).

Time it right. Make sure that it looks like a good time to start a conversation with the other person.

   Some *not so great* times to start a conversation are when the other person is:

1. Having a private conversation with someone else (their voices are low and they are standing or sitting close together), or when he or she is in the middle of a phone conversation.
2. In a rush (walking fast, keeps his words very brief, looks at watch or tells you that he is on his way to somewhere).
3. Involved in an activity that requires his or her full attention (for example, reading, watching a movie, counting, working on a computer, etc.).

   *Exceptions: *true* emergencies or an urgent need to give or get information (such as telling Mom that she has a long-distance call waiting).

Hello. Start with a hello unless you have already greeted the other person (see Program 4 on Hellos and Good-byes).

Signals. Give good nonverbal signals:
1. smile (unless you are talking about a serious or sad subject)
2. keep your body turned toward the other person
3. use a friendly tone of voice
4. use eye contact to:
   - show the other person you are going to speak
   - show the other person you are interested and listening to him/her
   - check the other person's reaction to what you are saying
   - emphasize a point
   - close the conversation later on

(From *Navigating the Social World*, Program 10.)

Making *SENSE* in Conversations

Space

Remember personal ***space.*** Stand or sit at arm's length from the other person. *Exceptions:* You may sit or stand closer if the other person is a close relation, like a mom, dad, husband, wife, etc. Also, you may need to sit or stand closer in crowded conditions, such as on a crowded bus, etc.

Eye contact

Make ***eye contact*** intermittently throughout the conversation, and especially:
- when you or the other person is beginning to speak or is ending a conversation.
- to emphasize or acknowledge an important point.
- *to check the other person's reaction to your words* (check for nonverbal clues to the other person's reaction, such as facial expression and body language clues).

Nod

People ***nod*** while listening to another person to show agreement, disagreement, understanding, or sympathy. Nodding "yes" occasionally during a conversation shows other people that you understand or agree with what they are saying, or sympathize with how they feel. Nodding "no" shows disagreement, and should be done with a gentle shake of the head, if done at all. (In most cases, it is better to express disagreement using carefully chosen words.)

Statements of encouragement

Using the following kind of ***statements*** while listening to the other person will show that you care about what he or she is saying (note: even if what the other person is talking about is not one of your favorite subjects, he will think better of you if you take the time to listen to him carefully and make encouraging statements):

Hmmm. Uh-huh. I see. Cool! That must have been funny (or scary, awful, etc.).

Expression

Check the ***expression*** on *your* face. When listening, you usually will appear friendly and sympathetic if you smile from time to time during "small talk". Alternatively, you can convey surprise, disappointment, excitement, and countless other reactions to the speaker's words by using the corresponding facial expression. Also, remember to turn your body toward the other person during a conversation.

(From *Navigating the Social World*, Program 11.)

CONVERSATIONAL MANNERS

1. _T_ake turns talking.

Make sure you give the other person plenty of chances to talk.

2. _M_ake comments and ask questions to show the other person you are interested.

- Use comments like: _"Cool." "Wow." "Then what happened?" "Uh huh." "Really?" "I know what that feels like."_

- Time the comment or question well (when the speaker pauses for a moment).

3. _T_opics:

A) _Stay on topic_ until the other person has had enough time to finish talking about his subject.

B) _Change topics:_

- When there is a pause in the conversation.
- By linking the new topic to the old topic if possible. Use words like:

    "Speaking of . . ." ("Speaking of food, I had the best lunch yesterday!")
    "By the way . . ." (By the way, I saw Dave last week.")
    "Oh, guess what!" (Oh, guess what! I got a new computer program.")
    "Did you hear?" ("Did you hear? We're all going on a field trip next week.")
    "That reminds me . . ." ("That reminds me. Did you finish the book yet?)

4. _V_oice: Tone and Volume

Check to make sure that your volume and tone of voice fit the situation. (See Program 12 for more help.) Lots of practice will help with this one!

* If you like to use silly sayings to remember things, try this one for conversational manners: _T_ricky _M_icky _T_ickled _V_icky (for _T_ake turns, _M_ake comments, _T_opics, and _V_oice).

(From _Navigating the Social World_, Program 13.)

STUDENT HANDOUT-Advanced Version (Handout #2)

CONVERSATIONAL MANNERS

1. Turn-taking

A conversation is like a tennis game (only it moves slower). The chance to speak moves back and forth between the speakers in a conversation in the same way the ball moves back and forth between the players in a tennis match. If one player caught and held on to the ball, it would make for a very dull and frustrating game for the other player. Likewise, if one person does nearly all of the talking in a conversation, the other person may become bored and irritated. Each speaker in a conversation needs a chance to share his or her thoughts, feelings, or opinions. If people do not get this chance, it can make them feel frustrated with, and not valued by the other person.

2. Making Interjections

An interjection is a *brief* comment or question made by the listener during a pause in the other person's talking. If made in the right way, an interjection will show the other person that you are listening to him and that you care about what he is saying. To make a friendly interjection, do these three things: 1) time it for when the speaker pauses briefly, 2) keep it short, and 3) make sure the interjection is related to the current topic.* Here are some words that people often use as supportive interjections:

Cool; *Wow*; *Then what happened?*; *Uh-huh*; *Hmm*; *Really?*; *I know what that feels like*; and *I can't imagine how that must feel.*

*When an interjection cuts into another person's words, it is called an *interruption*. Interrupting another person's words, or making *long* interjections may cause that person to think that you do not care about what he is saying and that you are not acting in a friendly way.

3. Topics

Staying on topic

"Staying on topic" means continuing to talk about a topic until *both* speakers are finished saying what they want to say about that subject, or until a reasonable amount of time has been spent on that topic. If a person abruptly introduces a new topic before the previous topic is finished, listeners 1) may not be able to switch their attention quickly enough, and may therefore become confused by the new topic, or 2) may feel offended because they think the other person does not care about the topic that they brought up.

(From *Navigating the Social World*, Program 13.)

Recognizing when the other person has finished what he wants to say about a given topic can be tricky. It helps to realize that sometimes people bring up *topics that are very important to them*, and other times they bring up *topics that are <u>not</u> as important to them*. When two people talk about something that is not of great importance to them, this is called *small talk*. In our culture, making small talk serves to help people feel more comfortable with the other person and allows for the exchange of information. If you are acquainted with the other person, check your memory for information about what is important to him. This can help you decide if this is a topic of interest to him or simply small talk. *(Refer to Initiating Conversations on page 94 for information on keeping "fact files" to help you remember facts about other people.)* Also, check the other person's nonverbal and tone of voice clues. For example, if the person has an excited, sad, or upset facial expression, the subject probably is important to him. If, however, he has a neutral or bored expression or tone of voice, the topic probably is less important to him.

In general, if the other person brings up a topic that clearly is important to him, then you will need to spend more time on that topic than if he brings up a subject that is intended simply to fill silent periods in the conversation. If the topic is being used as *small talk*, people often share only two or three comments or questions about the topic (although more is acceptable). However, if the topic is *important* to the other person (i.e. it is a special interest to him, or he is excited or upset about the topic), then he generally will feel better about the conversation if you follow-up with several questions, comments, and statements of encouragement.

Making Topic Transitions (Changing topics)

A *topic transition* is a change from one topic to another within a conversation. Here are some rules for making successful transitions:

a) Time transition right.

If the other person is talking about something important to him, give him enough time to finish talking about it. When possible, let him be the one to change the topic. If, for some reason, you need to change the subject sooner, wait for a pause in the talking before you change topics. Likewise, if the other person is making small talk (see #2), you may change the topic during a pause, but first respond with at least one or two related comments or questions.

b) Link the new topic to the previous topic if possible.

Look for a way to relate the new topic to the old one. For example, if the first topic is about your friend's dog, you might choose to bring up the *related topic* of the dog show you just attended.

c) Use transition phrases.

These are phrases that let the other person know that you are about to introduce a new topic. A transition phrase can help link a new but *related* topic to the previous topic. For instance, in the above example, you might use the phrase *"speaking of dogs . . . "* ("I went to a dog show the other day," or "I am looking for a new dog" . . . etc.).

Another type of transition phrase lets the other person know that you are going to change to an *unrelated* topic. An example of this type of transition phrase is to use the words *"to change the subject".* . . *(for example: "To change the subject, I started classes yesterday," or "To change the subject, how is your mother doing?").*

Using Good Volume Control and Tone of Voice

Using the right volume in a conversation can make a big difference in how the other person accepts your words. When people speak too quietly, other people may not be able to hear what they are saying. On the other hand, speaking too loudly is likely to unnerve or irritate the listener. Good volume control means speaking at, but not above, a volume that allows listeners to hear the words clearly. You will have plenty of chances to practice the skill of volume control in this program.

Program 12 talks about how a simple change in tone of voice can completely change the meaning of the words spoken. In the same way that you interpret other people's words according to their tone of voice, other people will interpret *your* words according to *your* tone of voice. For example, when you are having a friendly or interesting chat, it usually works well to use a "neutral" or "friendly" tone of voice. In contrast, if you are upset about something, using an overly intense tone of voice can cause listeners to react negatively, or to stop listening to you altogether. (For more help with dealing with conflicts, see *Program 18, "Resolving Conflicts"* on page 182.)

RULES FOR MAKING INTRODUCTIONS

Have you ever felt like you did not know what to say when meeting someone new or when introducing other people? If you have, this program is for you. It will help you learn how to make great introductions!

Rule one: **Check your timing**.

If a person is already talking to someone else, wait for a pause in the conversation or for the end of the conversation before speaking.

Rule two: **Choose the right type of words for the introduction.**

The words used in an introduction are different for different types of people. For instance, you would use one set of words for introducing your teacher to your mom, and another set of words for introducing your friend to your little brother. When introducing your teacher to your mother, you might say: "Mom, I'd like you to meet my teacher, Mrs. Wagner. Mrs. Wagner, this is my mother, Mrs. Jensen." This is formal compared to the words you might use when introducing your friend to your younger brother: "Jim, this is my little brother, Dave. Dave, this is Jim."

Rule three: **Give good nonverbal signals.**

- face the other person
- stand or sit up straight
- make eye contact
- smile

Rule four: **Use a good handshake style.**

- Grip the other person's hand firmly, but do not overpower him or her.
- Shake hands for two shakes. (Avoid handshakes if you are not certain that the other person is a safe person to be physically close to. *See Program 15, Public vs. Private, page 143 for more help with this topic.*)
- In general, men and teenage boys shake hands during introductions. This is optional for women and girls.

(From *Navigating the Social World*, Program 14.)

OFFERING HELP

Offering to help someone can be a great thing to do. Many people like to offer to help others when they need it. People usually feel good about themselves when they help someone else. The person who is helped usually feels friendly toward the helper, too. Helping someone is good for both people. Here are some hints about how to offer help:

1) *Look for chances to help.*

People usually are most helpful when they *look for chances to help*. For example, John was very good at using computers. He knew that Sam often had problems with computer assignments. John glanced over at Sam during computer class from time to time to see if he could use some help. One time he saw Sam looking frustrated and confused. John knew this would be a good time to offer help.

2) *Ask first.*

Most people like to be *asked* if they could use some help before being helped. This is because sometimes people *don't* want help. They want to do it by themselves. In these cases, the other person normally will tell you that he doesn't want help. If this happens, it usually works well to say "okay" in a pleasant tone of voice, and let him finish the activity by himself. For example, Ken saw his sister trying to replace a tire on her bike. He asked her if she could use some help. When she said, "No thanks, not right now," Ken said, "Okay," and walked away. Ken's sister felt friendly toward him because he respected her wishes and let her work on the bike by herself.

3) *Wait for a pause in the conversation to offer help.*

The other person usually appreciates it when the helper *waits for a pause in the conversation* before offering to help. For example, Helen (who knew a lot about science) noticed that Sarah and Kim were having trouble with their science project. Helen waited for a pause in their conversation, and then said, "Can I help you with your project?" Because Helen waited for a good time to speak, Sarah and Kim were able to listen to, and appreciate her offer of help.

4) *Use a friendly and respectful tone of voice.*

People appreciate offers of help that are made in a *friendly and respectful tone of voice*. (Ask your teacher or a friend to help you with good vs. not-so-good tones of voice when offering help.)

(From *Navigating the Social World*, Program 16.)

NEWS BRIEF:

OFFERING HELP A BIG SUCCESS

A recent survey by a prominent polling firm indicates that offering to help another person benefits both the person *offering* help and the person *who is offered* help. Most people who received offers of help reported having friendly thoughts toward the person who had offered them aid. Likewise, individuals who had offered to help someone reported feeling both happier with themselves, and more friendly toward the person they had helped. The surveyors also found that offers of aid improved existing friendships, and sometimes even helped to start new friendships.

Further questioning of the respondents revealed some helpful ideas on how and when to offer help:

I. In most cases, it is best to <u>ask if the other person could use some help before starting to help</u>. One interviewee stated, "If you start right in helping, without asking first, the other person may be alarmed if your help was unexpected, or resent your assistance if he or she does not want your help at that moment."

However, another respondent gave this exception: *"In emergencies where the other person could get badly hurt or is so ill that he or she cannot communicate, and there is no one else already helping that person, you do not need to ask if you can help before giving aid."*

2. <u>Watch for opportunities</u> to help. One interviewee said, "If a person does not look for these opportunities he or she will rarely find them."

3. <u>Check your timing.</u> If it is not an emergency, it is usually best to offer help when there is a pause in the conversation or activity. Also, there are times when it is best to offer help in private. Check with a helper if you are not sure whether it is one of these times.

4. When you offer help, it is best to do so <u>willingly</u>. Both the helper and the one offered help usually end up feeling good about each other when the help is given freely and willingly. The respondents unanimously agreed that the knowledge that they were needed, and the warm feelings they experienced after helping someone usually made the experience a very positive one.

(From *Navigating the Social World*, Program 16.)

STUDENT HANDOUT

ASKING FOR HELP

Asking for help when you need it is a wise thing to do. First of all, if you don't ask for help, other people might not know that you *need* help. Also, people usually are glad to help if you ask them to. As a matter of fact, being asked for help often makes the other person feel good about himself and good *about you, too!* People often feel closer to someone they have helped and may admire that person for having enough confidence and intelligence to ask for help. Lastly, when you get the help you need, you will finish the job more easily and a whole lot sooner! Here are some ideas about *how* to ask for help.

1. First, try to figure out the answer for yourself.

When possible, spend a little time trying to find the answer on your own. For example, Justin was having trouble doing a math problem. Before he asked for help, he went back and reread the explanation in his math book, and was able to solve the problem without help. Another student, Keith, was not sure how to make an outline for his history report. After fifteen minutes he still had no idea how to start and wisely decided to ask his teacher for help. After she helped him, Keith was able to finish the outline in twenty minutes. Brad, on the other hand, did not understand his English assignment but sat through almost the entire class before asking his teacher for help. By this time, he was so frustrated and upset that he could not focus on what the teacher was saying and left class without understanding the assignment.

2. Decide who and when to ask for help.

Before asking for help, it is best to spend a minute or two deciding who is the best person to ask, and then wait for a good time to ask your question. If possible, make a list *in advance* of the people you can ask for help in different situations. It is usually best to choose someone you trust and who knows about the subject you need help with. Usually you will be okay asking a trusted friend, family member, teacher, or aide for help. In other cases, someone like a counselor, police officer, doctor, nurse, or clerk may be the best person to ask for help. Check with a parent or mentor to decide which people to ask for help in different situations. For example, Jim sometimes did not ask for help when he needed it because he did not know *whom* to ask. So with his counselor's help, Jim made up a list of different people he could ask for help in different situations. He decided that he would ask one of his classmates, Ted or Rick, for help in math class. If they were unable to help, then he would ask the teacher. He also listed Mrs. Hardy, the playground aide, and Mr. Simpson, the vice principal, to ask for help during lunch period, and so on. Then Jim reminded himself to wait for a pause in the conversation or activity before asking for help. (The exception to this rule was that if someone was in danger, it was okay to interrupt to ask for help!)

3. Practice how you will ask for help before you do it.

Spend a minute silently practicing the words and tone of voice you will use when you ask for help. For example, Jennifer had trouble getting the words out right when she needed to ask for help. Then her mom suggested saying the words to herself beforehand. Jennifer tried this and found (to her relief!) that asking for help went a lot smoother from then on.

(From *Navigating the Social World*, Program 16.)

NEWS BRIEF:
ASKING FOR HELP MAKES LIFE EASIER

In a study released late yesterday, researchers on the campuses of U. Noaskitt and U. Nogetitt found that people who asked for help at appropriate times tended to suffer less anxiety and confusion than those who did not. Of the people studied, those who asked for help when they needed it rated their lives as being significantly easier than those who rarely or never asked for help. When asked why some people avoid asking for help, Dr. Sol Eution stated that sometimes people do not know what words to use, or when and whom to ask for help. He added that sometimes people are afraid that others might think they are less intelligent if they ask for help. Nothing could be further from the truth, however, according to Dr. Eution. In his words, "Our study shows that people admire individuals who ask for help when necessary."

The study also revealed some ideas to help people determine how and when to ask for help. 943 participants judged by an independent panel to have the best help-seeking skills were asked for their advice on requesting help. Here are the results.

1. Before asking for help, it is a good idea to spend a few minutes trying to figure out the answer for yourself. This may entail looking for the answer in a book, for example. However, study participants advised the reader to not wait to request help until he or she is stressed or desperate. Participants unanimously agreed that when they waited to request help until they were stressed, they were often too frustrated to understand the response. (They also advised the reader to not wait to ask for help in emergencies when someone could get badly hurt or become seriously ill.)

2. Decide whom to ask for help. Participants recommended spending a few minutes deciding who is the best person to ask for help. Their recommendation: try to pick someone who you know is knowledgeable about the subject, and be sure that he or she is someone that you can trust (for example, a trusted friend, family member, teacher or aide, or in some cases a police officer, shop keeper, etc.) Check with a family member, teacher, or aide for help determining people you can ask for help in different types of situations.

3. Check the timing. Participants suggested that if the person you plan to ask for help is busy, wait until there is a pause in the conversation or activity. (Exception: do not wait to request help in cases where someone could get harmed or become seriously ill!)

4. Practice the words you will use before asking for help. Study participants said that they found asking for help to be much easier when they had practiced the words that they would use before requesting help. Dr. Eution added, "don't forget to use good eye contact and tone of voice."

(From *Navigating the Social World*, Program 16.)

STUDENT HANDOUT

FOUR TYPES OF COMPLIMENTS*

1. Personality or Character Compliments

Personality and character compliments are positive statements about a person's general personality or character traits. (For example, "You are such a helpful person!") Because they require in-depth knowledge of the recipient, these compliments usually are reserved for family members or friends.

2. Skills, Talents, and Achievements Compliments

This type of compliment is a positive statement about a person's skills, talents, achievements, or hard work. For example, "Wow, you got a really high score on that Play Station game!" These compliments can be paid to family members and friends. Also, they sometimes work with people with whom one is not acquainted, but in such cases one must be sure to state how he or she knows this information about the other person. For example, *"I saw you play soccer at the match.* You are a great goalie!"

3. Appearance Compliments

Appearance compliments are positive statements about the way someone looks, or about their clothes or accessories. For example, "Your new haircut looks good!" Because they do not require detailed knowledge of the recipient, these compliments often are appropriate for acquaintances as well for family members and friends.

4. Secondary Compliments

Secondary compliments make a positive statement about a person, place, or thing connected to the person being complimented. For example, "Your golden retriever is beautiful," or "You have great kids!" or "Your garden is lovely." This type of compliment requires the least amount of familiarity with the recipient, and therefore works well with most categories of people, including those whom you have not previously met.

(From *Navigating the Social World*, Program 17.) *With the exception of *secondary compliments,* the items on this list were adapted with permission from: Gray's Guide to Compliments: A Social Workbook. Gray, Carol. Jenison Public Schools, MI. 1999

HELPFUL HINTS ABOUT COMPLIMENTS[*]

1. While people usually pay compliments with their words, people also can give *silent compliments* by using facial expressions such as a special smile, or body signals such as a "thumbs up."

2. Compliments can be so powerful that they can change the way the other person thinks of himself, or change the way he does things. For example, a person who has been complimented for his or her smile may feel friendlier, and respond by smiling at others more frequently.

3. Some compliments give information that is already known. In these cases, the person giving the compliment tells the recipient something good about himself that he already knows. For example, John might say to Steve, "Steve, you are so talented on the computer!" Even though Steve already knows that his computer skills are good, he still likes to know that *John* notices how good he is on the computer. John's positive comment about Steve's computer skills makes Steve feel valued and recognized by John. As a result, Steve feels friendlier toward John.

4. True compliments are sincere. Carol Gray states, "sincerity . . . means that what a person is thinking and saying is the same thing." In other words, if a person says something nice about another person, but doesn't mean what he says, this is not a true compliment. More often than not, the other person will know that the words are not sincere, and may feel angry, hurt, or distrusting as a result. [People often know when someone is not sincere from the context of the situation, or from the nonverbal signals (tone of voice, body language, and facial expression) given by the person making the compliment.]

(continued)

(From *Navigating the Social World*, Program 17.) [*] This list has been adapted with permission from: <u>Gray's Guide to Compliments: A Social Workbook.</u> Gray, Carol. Jenison Public Schools. Michigan. 1999

5. How often one should compliment depends on the category of person being complimented. Complimenting *too often* can lead the other person to feel that the compliments are insincere. Complimenting a loved one or close friend *too infrequently* may cause the person to feel that he or she is unimportant to that person. Carol Gray suggests that it is good to compliment a loved one or *close* friend 1 – 5 times a day, a co-worker who is a friend 1 – 2 times a week, a co-worker who is not a friend 0 – 1 times/week, and a friend 1 – 3 times /week.

6. A compliment and the recipient's response can constitute the entire exchange between two people. Compliments also can open a conversation or start a new topic within a conversation. Appearance and secondary compliments can work especially well as conversation starters because they do not require in-depth knowledge about the other person. For example, a person could open a conversation with someone he or she has never met by saying, "Your dog is beautiful. How old is she?" or "That's a great hat. Where did you get it?"

A WORD ABOUT *RESPONDING* TO COMPLIMENTS

Always remember to acknowledge a compliment paid to you. This usually can be done with a smile and a thank you. This lets the other person know that you heard them, and that you appreciate the compliment. Sometimes, it works well to add an extra sentence to the "thank you." For example, in response to "Wow, you scored really high on that Play Station game," you might say "Thanks. I've been working really hard on this game!" Sometimes an additional comment like this can start a further conversation. For example, the other person might respond to this last comment with "I can tell you have put a lot of work into your game. Have you played for long?" As you can see, the two people now have something more to talk about, and they can choose to continue with a much longer conversation if they want to.

(From *Navigating the Social World*, Program 17.)

GUIDELINES for

DEALING WITH CONFLICT

Some Simple Rules For Handling Conflict
In a More Positive Way

(From *Navigating the Social World*, Program 18.)

Step One: Can Arguments Be Good?

Everyone has arguments and disagreements with other people from time to time. Sometimes we argue because one of us has made a mistake that hurt someone else. Other times we disagree because we have different opinions about what is right and wrong. And sometimes we simply misunderstand the facts, or we misinterpret the other person's actions, words, or intentions. One thing is for sure, though—disagreements and arguments are a fact of life. We all have them.

However, arguments and disagreements are not always bad. Believe it or not, there is such a thing as a good argument. It is an argument where the people involved try really hard not to worry too much about proving that they are right. Instead, they try to better understand each other's actions and words so that afterward their relationship will be as strong, or even a little stronger than it was before. This handout explains some things that people can do to understand each other better when they disagree and to make their arguments good arguments.

(From *Navigating the Social World*, Program 18.)

Step Two: Write It Down.

A. Journals

People sometimes find it helpful to take time out from a conflict to write about their feelings in a journal, before continuing to talk with the other person (both computer and book journals work well). This gives them time to "cool off" and figure out *what* their feelings are, *how strong* those feelings are, and *what events might have led* to the emotions. Also, it allows them time to use what they know about the other person to help figure out his intentions. Furthermore, by first writing his thoughts and feelings down in a journal, a person can practice what to say to the other person. Also, after writing in the journal, it can be very helpful to share the information in the journal with a trusted friend or family member to get their feedback and suggestions *before* talking to the other person in the conflict.

B. Notes or Letters

Next time you have an argument with someone, consider taking time out from the argument to write down your feelings and thoughts in a letter or note to the other person. Whenever possible, show the letter to a helper or a mentor to get feedback before sending it. (A mentor often can understand both sides of an argument more clearly than can the people directly involved in the disagreement, and may be able to offer invaluable advice about how best to approach the other person.) Also, reading about your thoughts and feelings in your note or letter gives the other person time to think about his own feelings and thoughts and how best to reply. When people have enough time to consider these things in advance, they often are able to calm down and think more clearly about how to talk with each other. They are less apt to say something that they might regret in the future. To make sure that you have

(From *Navigating the Social World*, Program 18.)

not said something that you later will be sorry for, it is often a good idea to wait a while (a few hours or a day or two) before sending the letter or note. After you have shared your thoughts and emotions in writing, it can be a lot easier to talk things over in person later on.

C. Comic Strip Conversations

Another excellent way to express your thoughts and feelings in writing is to use a technique called Comic Strip Conversations. You can use a Comic Strip Conversation to show what happened during an event that upset or confused you. First, draw stick figures to represent all of the people involved, and then add word and thought bubbles to show everyone's words and thoughts. You also can show what you think everyone was feeling by coloring their words and thoughts different colors for different feelings. You can do this activity with the person or people involved in the event, or you can draw the comic strips with a mentor who can help you figure out what went wrong and what to do next. This is a great way to "slow things down" and give you time to think about everyone's thoughts, feelings and intentions. It is also an excellent way to try out some possible solutions on paper to help you decide the best way to work things out.

For example, Mark loved to help people but he could not understand why he often got in trouble for helping. His mom had always taught him that it is important to help others. One time, Mark saw his brother trying to fix his broken bicycle. Mark, who was good at fixing things, went over to his brother, grabbed the wrench out of his hand and said, "Here, let me do it. You're doing it all wrong." Mark was surprised and hurt when his brother, instead of thanking him, yelled at him. Mark's mom suggested that Mark and his brother draw a Comic Strip Conversation with her help. In the drawing, Mark and his brother drew stick figures of themselves to show

(From *Navigating the Social World*, Program 18.)

they added word bubbles to show what words each boy had said. Each boy wrote the words in different colors to show how he felt during the episode. (Mark chose red for angry, orange for confused, and so on.) Finally, both boys added thought bubbles to show what they were thinking during the episode. Mark was very surprised when his brother wrote down "I wish Mark wouldn't barge in on me every time I try to fix something. I want to do it myself!" This helped Mark understand that instead of always appreciating his help, sometimes his brother wanted to do things on his own. After this, with the help of his mom and brother, Mark was able to draw a new Comic Strip Conversation that showed how he might handle the situation the next time someone looked like they needed help. In this comic strip, Mark drew himself standing a little distance away from this brother and asking, "Can I help you?" His brother wrote in the response, "Thanks for asking, but I want to try it myself." His thought bubble said, "I'm glad that Mark asked me first before trying to help me!" Since Mark learned better by seeing pictures and words, instead of listening to long explanations, he was able to see what had gone wrong and figure out a better way of doing it next time. *(See the illustrations of both of these Comic Strip Conversations on pages 211-212 of Navigating the Social World.)*

(From *Navigating the Social World*, Program 18.)

Step Three: Talk It Over With a Third Person.

It can be a great help to take time out of an argument to discuss the problem with a mentor who is not involved with the conflict (for example, a trusted family member or close friend). Many people find that this gives them a chance to figure out how they feel and how the other person may feel, and to plan what they want to say to the other person. Talking things over with a mentor often helps a person work things out more smoothly when it comes time to resume talking with the other person.

Here are five things to do when you discuss a conflict with an outside mentor:

1) Tell the mentor about the problem or conflict.

2) Discuss your feelings and thoughts about the conflict. (This is a good time to go over with your mentor any journal entries or letters you have written to the other person.)

3) Ask for and listen to your mentor's input.

4) Develop a plan for how to communicate with the other person.

5) Use your stress management techniques if you are stressed.

(From *Navigating the Social World*, Program 18.)

Step Four: Use Good Discussion Techniques.

Using good discussion techniques usually leads to a much better outcome in a dispute.

Here are **eight tips** that many people have found helpful when discussing feelings and opinions with another person.

1. Take time to calm down before speaking.

If you find yourself very angry with or hurt by another person, take a moment to use a relaxation technique to calm down before you speak, *whether this occurs at the beginning or in the middle* of the conversation. For example, some people count to ten before talking. Others briefly close their eyes and take three deep breaths, or picture themselves in a favorite place before they speak. It is helpful to practice these techniques regularly when you are *not* upset, as this will make it easier to use the techniques when you *are* upset. (Review the skills you learned in Program 5, page 33, for more help.)

2. Organize your thoughts before you speak.

If you need extra time to think things over, it often works to let the other person know this before trying to discuss the problem. (The time you need to think things over may vary from a few minutes to a week or more, depending on the circumstances.) *While you think it over, ask yourself these three questions*:

1) "What am I thinking and feeling?"

2) "What level of that emotion am I feeling and does it match what I am showing with my facial expression, body language and tone of voice?"

(From *Navigating the Social World*, Program 18.)

3) "What is the other person thinking and feeling?"

- *Check non-verbal, contextual and tone of voice clues.*
- *Compare how you have felt in similar situations.*

Take a moment to check the other person's non-verbal clues—does she look angry, sad, worried, afraid, etc.? What does her tone of voice tell you about what she is feeling? Are there contextual clues, such as she is irritated because you just bumped into her? Or she is worried because her school assignment is late? *(See Programs 8 and 12, on pages 71 and 109, respectively, for further help with recognizing nonverbal and tone of voice clues.)*

Compare how you have felt in similar situations. Ask yourself if you have ever been in a similar situation – if so, how did you feel? Often the other person is feeling the same way you felt when you were in that situation. Thinking how you have felt in similar circumstances can give you more *empathy* (the ability to actually feel what the other person is feeling) for the other person. The more empathy people have for one another, the easier it is to forgive each other's mistakes and find a solution that is good for both people.

3. Listen to the other person.

Most conflicts work out best if both people take turns listening to each other's words. Although it can be very difficult to really listen to the other person when you are upset with him, it is important to try your best to do so. Here are *three things* that people often remind themselves to do when they need *to listen* to the other person:

(From *Navigating the Social World*, Program 18.)

1) For a few minutes try to stop thinking about your own feelings and what you want to say next.

2) Focus on what the other person is saying.

3) As mentioned above, try to understand what the other person is feeling by imagining how *you* might feel if you were the other person.

4. Try your hardest to find something that the other person is saying, that you can agree with, even if it is something little.

(Most people need a lot of practice doing this before they learn to do it well.)

5. Avoid bringing up past gripes.

It usually is much better to try to solve only the current conflict rather than trying to solve past problems at the same time. Bringing up old grudges can lead other people to feel that you will never forgive them for past misdeeds, or that you think they are a bad person and that nothing they can do will change your opinion. So, for example, instead of saying, "Last month you ruined my best sweater, and now you've ripped my shirt!" consider simply saying, "I'm angry because you ripped my shirt."

6. Avoid the words "always" and "never" when talking about the other person's faults.

It is important to avoid the words "always" and "never" for a couple of reasons. First, most people don't *always* do the same thing wrong or *never* do a certain thing right, so the "never" or "always" statement probably is incorrect and the other person therefore is likely to feel unjustly accused. Second, being accused

(From *Navigating the Social World*, Program 18.)

of *always* doing something wrong can make the other person feel that he or she will *never* be able to meet your expectations, so why try to improve?

In one example, Carla was upset because even though she was sure Jeff had heard her ask him a question, he failed to reply. She knew that if she said, "You *always* ignore me!" or "You *never* listen to me!" Jeff would quite logically think that he often *did* listen to her, and he might therefore become defensive and angry. So, instead she said, "Sometimes you don't answer me and it makes me feel like you aren't listening." Jeff responded to this comment by explaining that sometimes he did not hear her because he was preoccupied with another thought. He asked Carla to make sure she got his attention before asking a question. Both Carla and Jeff understood each other better after this discussion, and the result was that their relationship actually improved after the argument.

7. Avoid accusations whenever you can.

The end result of a conflict almost always will be better if the participants avoid making accusations, and instead ask for clarification and talk about how the other person's actions make them feel.

Ask for clarification.

It is all too easy to accuse another person of something before we know *if* he actually did it, and if so, what his *intentions* were. For example, it is better to ask, "Did you spill juice on my report?" and "Did you do that on purpose?" in a calm tone of voice rather than to shout, "You spilled juice on my report on purpose!" Asking questions instead of accusing will help clarify whether the other person actually did spill the juice and whether it was intentional or an accident. This, in turn, will help you decide what to say next.

(From *Navigating the Social World*, Program 18.)

Talk about how the other person's actions make you feel.

Instead of accusing, tell the other person how you feel about their actions. Start sentences with phrases like "That makes me feel like . . ." or "I feel bad about . . . " For example, say, "It makes me feel like you don't care about me when you don't return my phone calls," instead of "You are not much of a friend. You never even return my calls!" Or, say, "I'm really upset about my ruined report. I worked so hard on it," instead of "Look what you did to my report! You always ruin everything!" Or "I feel hurt and angry when you yell at me like that," rather than yelling back, "All you do is yell! You just want everything your way!"

8. Avoid calling names.

As much as you might want to call the other person a "jerk" or an "idiot" (or some other unpleasant name), don't. Even though it might make you feel better momentarily to call the other person names, in the long run it will hurt your relationship with him or her.

(From *Navigating the Social World*, Program 18.)

Step Five: Admit your mistakes and apologize for them.

A. *Actively* look for what you could have done better, *admit it* and then *apologize*.

When you are feeling angry or hurt with someone, it can be very hard to stop and think about what *you* may have done to contribute to the problem. However, admitting what you did wrong almost always helps to resolve the problem, and it is a true sign of maturity to be able to do so. Although in some conflicts one person is completely wrong and the other blameless, it is *much* more common that both people "messed up" in one way or another. When you are having an argument, try to think of at least one thing that you could have done better and admit it to the other person. Then apologize. This can help him admit that he could have done things better, too. And, believe it or not, the other person is almost guaranteed to think more highly of you if you can admit to wrongdoing than if you act as if you are blameless.

B. Keep a list of ways to apologize in your head. (You never know when you may need them!)

Here are some examples of apologies that have worked well for many people. Notice that they are *short* and *to the point*. Also notice that sometimes a simple "I'm sorry" works well, and other times it is good to add a sentence or two admitting what you did wrong.

1) "I'm sorry."
2) "I'm sorry. I really blew it."
3) "I sure have been grouchy. Please forgive me."
4) "I was being careless when I broke your tape player. I'm really sorry."

(From *Navigating the Social World*, Program 18.)

Note: Avoid saying, "I'm sorry, but . . ." (and then adding an excuse or an accusation.) This is probably the most common cause of unsuccessful apologies!

C. Whenever possible, be the *first* to admit you did something wrong and the first to apologize.

Try being the *first* to admit making a mistake and the *first* to apologize. This is not to say that you should apologize without cause, but if you did do something wrong, admit it. You might be surprised at how refreshing this can be. In addition, *someone* has to be the first to apologize. After all, if no one is willing to take the first turn, chances are that the conflict will never be resolved, which obviously is not good for the relationship.

Note: It is also possible to apologize <u>too much</u>. If you find yourself apologizing for the same thing over and over, or saying, "I'm sorry," multiple times during the day, be sure and discuss this with a trusted mentor or counselor.

D. Show *sincerity* through your facial expression and tone of voice.

Apologies are *much* more successful when they are sincere. If you feel that you cannot apologize sincerely, it probably is better to tell the other person that you need to think things over before talking with her about it. Then take a break (anywhere from a few minutes to a few days) to calm down and consider the situation. If you wait to calm down, chances are that it will be much easier to see what you might have done better and to apologize. When you do apologize, make sure that your words, facial expression, body language, and tone of voice convey sincerity. Some people find it helpful to practice these with a helper or in front of a mirror before making the apology. *(Review Programs 11 and 12, pages 102 and 109, for more help using facial expression and tone of voice to communicate effectively.)*

(From *Navigating the Social World*, Program 18.)

Step Six: Make Up for Mistakes.

Ask yourself if you need to make *restitution* (do something for the other person to make up for a mistake you made). For example, if you have damaged something belonging to another person, it is important to offer to fix or replace it (and then follow through with this unless he or she *insists* that you do not need to). Another example is to write a short apology note (or send an apology card) when you have made a mistake. Sometimes adults even send flowers to the other person along with an apology note. All of these actions can help the other person forgive the mistake more easily, and can help you feel better about yourself, too.

(From *Navigating the Social World*, Program 18.)

Words That Don't Mean What They Are Supposed To Mean

People use words in different ways. Sometimes words mean just what you would expect. Other times words mean something very different from their usual meaning. When people use words to mean something different from their usual, or "literal" meaning, this is called *non-literal speech*. There are different types of non-literal speech—here are three that people often use.

1. Similes

These are phrases that often use the word "like" or "as" to show that one thing is similar to another. It usually is fairly easy to see how the two things are similar. For example, "her hair is *like* spun gold" is a simile that means that the lady in question has hair that is a golden color and is shiny like gold. ("*Spun* gold" means long strands of gold.)

2. Metaphors

Metaphors are words or phrases that have two very different meanings. One meaning is the expected, or "*literal*," meaning of the individual words. The other, *non-literal* meaning is something completely different from the expected meaning of the words. In some metaphors there is a hidden similarity between the literal meaning and the non-literal meaning, but a person has to search for that similarity. In other metaphors, there is no similarity at all between the two meanings. Here are two examples.

"I have a frog in my throat."

- The **expected, literal meaning** of these words would be that the speaker has a small, four-legged creature (that hops and croaks) in her throat. Imagine your aunt Martha announcing, "I have a frog in my throat!" and then picture a frog popping out of her mouth! This should be quite a startling image (unless, of course, your aunt Martha likes to eat frogs). When you are surprised or puzzled by the literal meaning of someone's words, and the literal meaning simply does not *fit* the situation, this often is a *clue* that those words are being used as a metaphor. In other words, they are being used in an **unexpected, non-literal way**.

- The **unexpected, non-literal meaning** of these words is that the speaker is hoarse. When someone is hoarse, his or her voice sounds "croaky." A frog sounds croaky, too, and so in this case there is a connection between the literal meaning and the non-literal meaning of the metaphor. (Unfortunately, this is not always the case. Sometimes there is *no* similarity or connection between the literal and non-literal meanings of a metaphor. These metaphors tend to be more difficult to interpret.)

(continued)

(From *Navigating the Social World*, Program 19.)

"I'm in a pickle."

- The ***expected, literal meaning*** of these words is that the speaker is *inside* of a small, long, green vegetable that has been soaked in vinegar, garlic, and salt. But, whoa—wait a minute, how could this be? That would have to be one very small person or one extremely long pickle! Besides, how many people do you know who could survive being soaked in vinegar, salt, and garlic? (Well, okay, I admit there is my great uncle George, but he is an exception . . .)

- The ***unexpected, non-literal meaning*** of these words is that the speaker is in a difficult or awkward situation. For example, your mom says, "I'm in a real pickle— I have to be at the dentist's office and the bank at the same time." She certainly cannot mean that she is stuck inside a salty cucumber! This gives you a *clue* that the literal meaning can't be the right one! Now, if you look, you might see a look of worry on your mom's face. *(See Program 8, page 71 for more help with recognizing facial expressions.)* This gives you another *clue*—she might be telling you that she is worried. You know from the context (she has to be two places at once) that she is in a difficult situation, so you might guess that she really means that she is worried because she is in a difficult situation. If this is what you guessed, you are right! (By the way, you *can* find a similarity between the literal meaning and the non-literal one here if you really look for it. After all, being stuck inside a pickle would be a difficult situation!)

3. Ironic or sarcastic phrases

These are phrases that mean the *opposite* of the normal meaning of the words. For example, consider the following scene: Mary is a girl who loves chocolate. One evening, the family is having chocolate cake for dessert, but unfortunately Mary's brother drops the chocolate cake on the floor. Mary glares at him and says, *"That was really good!"* What Mary *really* means is the opposite of what she said. In other words, what she really means is "That was really bad!" Mary has used sarcasm to show her brother that she is not happy with him for dropping her cake on the floor.

- The ***expected, literal meaning*** of the phrase "That was really good!" is that the other person did something well and is to be complimented.

- The ***unexpected, non-literal meaning*** of the phrase "That was really good!" is exactly the opposite. What Mary really means is "That was really bad!" We know from the context that Mary loves chocolate cake, and therefore probably was *not* happy to have the cake land on the floor! This is a *clue* that the literal meaning does not fit the situation. If we could look at Mary's face we would see that she is frowning. This is another *clue*—one that tells us that probably what Mary *really* means is that she is angry.

(From *Navigating the Social World*, Program 19.)

What To Do When Words Don't Mean What They Are Supposed To Mean

1. Similes*

How to recognize one:
- Ask: Does the phrase compare two things, using the words "like" or "as"? If so, chances are it is a simile.

Example:
- That old dog is *as slow as molasses in winter.*

How to figure it out:
- *Look for similarities* between the two things being compared. For example, winter is the coldest time of the year. Molasses flows very slowly when it is cold, so slowly, in fact, that we sometimes get impatient and wish it would flow faster. So if an old dog is as slow as molasses in winter, this means that the dog moves so slowly that sometimes people wish he would move faster.

2. Metaphors*

How to recognize one:
- Ask: Does the usual (or literal) meaning of the phrase make sense *in that situation?* If the answer is no, then this may be a metaphor.

Example:
- A man named John just tried his new skis and he likes them a lot. Afterward, John says, "I'm *hooked* on my new skis!"

How to figure it out:
- **Use *contextual clues:***
  For example: John just tried out his new skis for the first time. Afterward he exclaimed, "I'm hooked on these new skis!" The context is that John just used his new skis for the first time. His clothes are not "hooked" on his skis and as a matter of fact, there are no hooks anywhere on or near him. Therefore, the context tells you that he is not *literally* hooked on anything.

(continued)

(*When many different people use the same similes or metaphors to mean the same thing over a long period of time, these are called **idioms.** Idioms also are called *figures of speech.*)

(From *Navigating the Social World*, Program 19.)

- **Use *nonverbal* and *tone of voice* clues:**
  Check John's facial expression and body language. He is standing up tall, and he makes a "victory" fist as he talks. His mouth is turned up in a big smile, he looks right at you as he talks, and his eyes are crinkled up. His tone of voice sounds excited and happy. All of these clues tell you that he is happy. He is talking about his skis, so it is reasonable to assume that he is happy about his skis.

- **Check the usual (or literal) meaning of the word or phrase for hints to the "hidden" meaning:**
  (Note: This works sometimes, but not always.)
  For example, the word to "hook" literally means to "firmly attach to" or to "fasten together" so that whatever is fastened won't separate. So, if John is *hooked* on his new skis, then this *could* mean that he won't separate from his skis.

- **Put it all together:**
  So, here is what you know so far:
  1. John is not physically hooked on or caught on his skis, so this must be an idiom about the subject of his new skis.
  2. He is happy and excited about something—most likely his skis.
  3. *Hooked on* means "firmly attached to."

  Therefore, a reasonable interpretation of this idiom is that he is happy with, and very attached to, his new skis.

3. Ironic or Sarcastic Words

How to recognize them:
- Ask: Does the literal or usual meaning of the words fit in that situation? If not, and if the *opposite* meaning would fit better, then this probably is sarcasm or irony.

Example:
- Sue burns her finger on a hot burner. She exclaims, "Ouch! That sure was clever of me!"

How to figure it out:
- **Use *contextual, nonverbal* and *tone of voice* clues.** If the situation and the speaker's facial expression, body language, or tone of voice make you think that she must mean the <u>opposite</u> of what her words normally would mean, then you probably are right. In this example, what the speaker really means is that it was <u>not</u> very clever of her to touch the hot burner on the stove.

(From *Navigating the Social World*, Program 19.)

APPENDIX C

TEMPLATES

ANGER THERMOMETER

For: _____

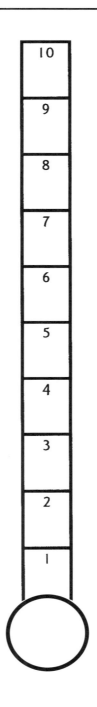

EMOTIONS SCALES

For: _____

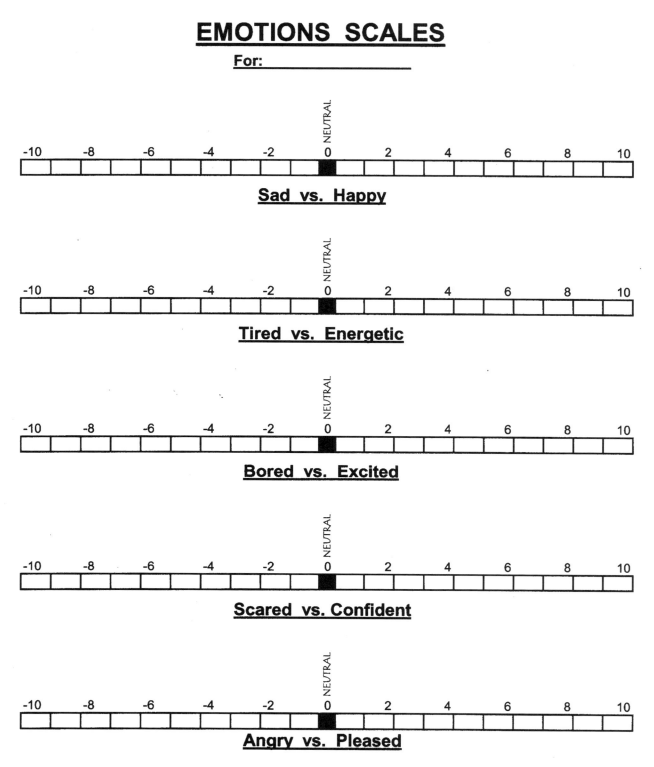

Sad vs. Happy

Tired vs. Energetic

Bored vs. Excited

Scared vs. Confident

Angry vs. Pleased

Scales showing 5 different opposites of emotions, each on a continuum. Have the student label the scales with his own choice of words. The words &/or scales can be colored with colors which the student has chosen to match the various emotions. [Note: it may be useful to enlarge this chart when photcopying it for use.]

From *Navigating the Social World*, Program 3.)

Stress Tracking Chart

Home / School   Student: _____

Date & Time	Precipitating event (trigger)	Underlying or "hidden" stressor(s) & related emotions	Stress signals		Stress level: -Low -Moderate -High	Outcome
			Body language, facial expressions & verbal clues (as observed)	Physical symptoms (by student report)		

(From *Navigating the Social World*, Program 4)

Summary of Stress Signals

Student:_____

	Low stress	Moderate stress	High stress
Verbal & nonverbal clues: Body language, facial expressions & verbal clues (As observed by others. Data from Stress Tracking Charts)			
Physical symptoms (As reported by student. Data from Stress Tracking Charts)			

(From *Navigating the Social World*, Program 4)

Summary of Common Stressors

Student:_____

	Low stress	Moderate stress	High stress
Common stressors			

(From *Navigating the Social World*, Program 4)

Student:_____

STRESS HIERARCHY

1. _____

2. _____

3. _____

4. _____

5. _____

6. _____

7. _____

8. _____

9. _____

10. _____

11. _____

12. _____

13. _____

14. _____

15. _____

16. _____

17. _____

18. _____

19. _____

20. _____

Instructions for completing Stress Hierarchy Form: List a very mildly stressful activity as #1, a slightly more stressful activity as #2, and so forth. The last item should be an activity that induces a significant amount of stress in the student. Items on the list should be activities that can be realistically carried out in a controlled setting at home and/or school. It is helpful to fill out this form in pencil to allow for changes later on. Additions to the list can be made at any time.

_____

(From *Navigating the Social World,* Program 5)

STRESS THERMOMETER[1]

For: _____

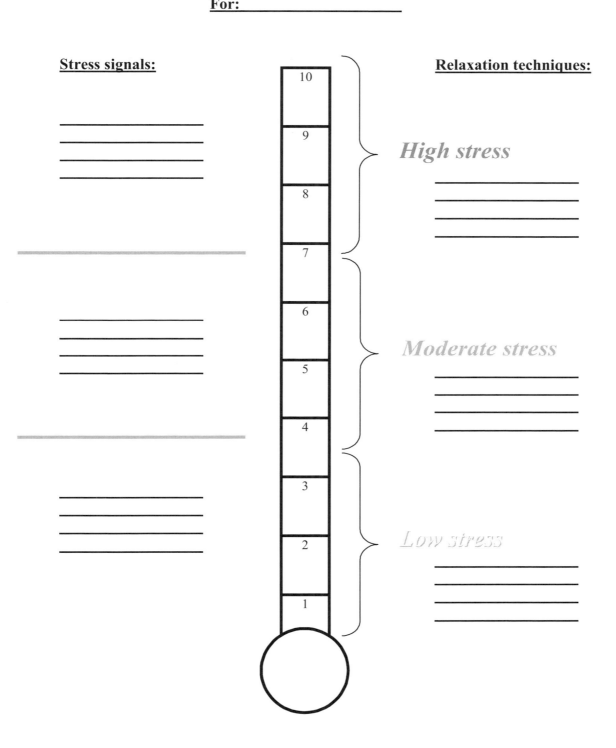

Stress signals:

Relaxation techniques:

High stress

Moderate stress

Low stress

10
9
8
7
6
5
4
3
2
1

---

[1] Adapted with permission from Attwood, Tony. Personal communication, 2000.

(From *Navigating the Social World,* Program

Student: _____

Words to use for *Hello*

Adults		Kids	
Familiar*	Not familiar*	Familiar*	Not familiar*

Words to use for *Good-bye*

Adults		Kids	
Familiar*	Not familiar*	Familiar*	Not familiar*

*A "familiar" adult means a family member or a close friend of the family.

A "not familiar" adult is someone you do not know well, or someone you need to treat more formally because of his/her position (such as a teacher, doctor, store keeper, policeman, etc.).

A "familiar" kid is a kid whom you know well.

A "not familiar" kid is a kid whom you do not know well.

(From *Navigating the Social World*, Program 9.)

Student: _____

CONVERSATION STARTERS

Scenario	P Recall info from Personal file	A Ask yourself what you are going to say	T Check Timing	H Start with a Hello	S Use good nonverbal Signals	Start the conversation

(From *Navigating the Social World*, Program 10.)

SCRIPTS FOR MAKING INTRODUCTIONS

Student:_____

People being introduced	Examples of phrases to use	Possible responses
Introducing self to another person or to a group		
Introducing two other people to each other		
Introducing someone to a group		

(From *Navigating the Social World*, Program 14.)

__Privacy Circles Chart__

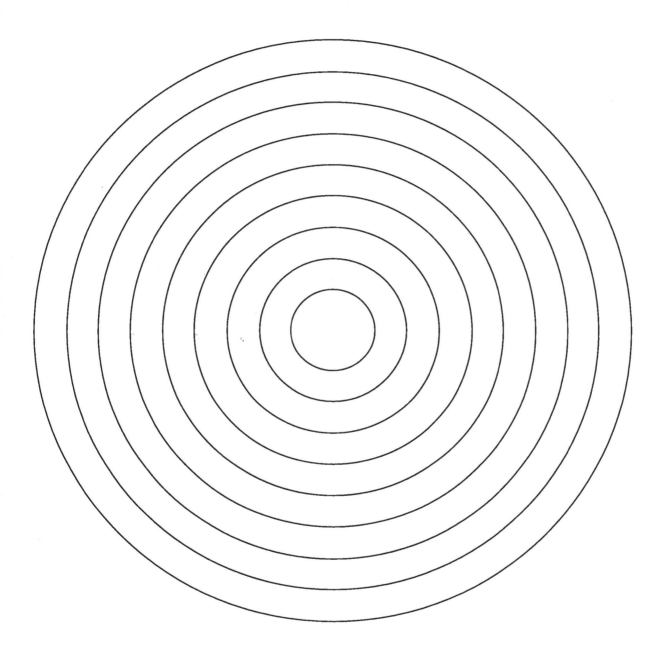

__Note:__ Any conversations/activities/etc. that are appropriate for a given circle are also usually appropriate for all of the circles inside of that given circle (e.g. any conversational topic that the student can share with grandparents/best friends could also be shared with siblings and mom/dad).

(From *Navigating the Social World*, Program 15.)

Offering to Help Worksheet

Situations in which to offer help	Timing	Script (what to say)

(From *Navigating the Social World*, Program 16.)

Asking for Help Worksheet

Situations in which to ask for help	Whom to ask	When to ask	Script (what to say)

(From *Navigating the Social World*, Program 16.)

COMPLIMENTS SCRIPTS

Date:_____ Student:_____.

Person to be complimented	Type of compliment -Skills/Efforts -Appearance -Personality -Secondary	When & Where	Script

(From *Navigating the Social World*, Program 17.)

APPENDIX D

PROGRAM TRACKING FORMS

Program Tracking Log

Student: _____

Item	Date	#Unprompted Correct Responses	#Prompted Correct Responses	Total #Trials	Notes

A generic program tracking log that can be used to track the student's progress for most of the programs in the book.

(From *Navigating the Social World: A Curriculum for Individuals with Asperger's Syndrome, High Functioning Autism and Related Disorders.*)

Tracking Sheet
Program 5: Stress Management II

Student

Item (from student's stress hierarchy)	Date	#Times used Stress Mgment. #Times stressed	Reinforcer (Note type of reinforcer, or "0" if none given.)	Notes

(From Navigating the Social World: A Curriculum for Individuals with Asperger's Syndrome, High Functioning Autism and Related Disorders.)

Basic Conversational Skills Tracking Sheet

Program 7: *Basic* **Conversational Responses**

P = Prompted
I (tally mark) = Used skill appropriately
e = Error in using skill

Student: _____

	Date worked on:	9/5/01							
	Length of conversation:	15 min.							
1	Y/N Questions	PP IIII							
2	Simple Questions	P LHT I e							
3	Open-ended Questions	III e							
4	Reciprocal Questions	P II							
5	Statement/Statement	LHT e							
6	Statement/Question	PPP II e							
7	Statement/Statement/Question	PPPP I eeee							

(Note: The first column is filled in as an example.)

(From *Navigating the Social World: A Curriculum for Individuals with Asperger's Syndrome, High Functioning Autism and Related Disorders.*)

Advanced Conversational Skills Tracking Sheet
Programs 8 – 13: *Advanced* Conversational Skills

Student:

| P = Prompted |
| I (tally mark) = Used skill appropriately |
| e = Error in using skill |

	Date worked on:							
	Length of conversation:							
1	Body Language							
2	Proximity							
3	Eye Contact							
4	Tone of Voice							
5	Volume							
6	Stays on Topic							
7	Transitions							
8	Takes Turns							
9	Chooses Topic of Interest to Others							
10	Responds to Other Peoples Cues							
11	Facial Expression							
12	Nodding							
13	Interjecting							
14	Recalls Previous Conversations							
15	Uses "Rescue Terms" for Pauses							
16	Asks for Clarification							
17	Closes Conversations Appropriately							
18	Makes Encouraging Statements							
19	Hello & Goodbye							

(Note: See the *Basic* Conversational Responses Tracking Sheet for an example of how to fill out this form.)

(From *Navigating the Social World: A Curriculum for Individuals with Asperger's Syndrome, High Functioning Autism and Related Disorders.*)

Tracking Sheet
Program 20: Compliance

Student _____

Item (from student's compliance hierarchy)	Date	#Times off Task / #Allowable Times off Task*	Reinforcer (Note type of reinforcer, or "0" if none given).	Notes

*The number of times a student is allowed to be off task may stay constant, or, if desired, a beginning student may be allowed more times off task early on. In the latter case, it is important to explain to the student that he will be allowed more times off task in the beginning, but that this number will decrease over time. Note: Ideally, the student should be prompted once, or at most twice, each time he gets off task.

(From *Navigating the Social World: A Curriculum for Individuals with Asperger's Syndrome, High Functioning Autism and Related Disorders*.)

APPENDIX E

GLOSSARY

GLOSSARY

Abstract thinking skills – The ability to think in terms of ideas and concepts vs. concrete facts.

Advisory visiting teacher (AVT) – In Australia, special education teachers who specialize in a particular field, such as autism or cognitive impairments. These teachers visit several different school sites, serving as consultants to classroom teachers and aides and working directly with students in that area of disability.

Applied behavioral therapy – A type of psychological therapy in which the recipient is helped to replace dysfunctional behaviors with functional behaviors through the use of shaping and positive reinforcement.

Asperger's Syndrome (AS) – A neurologically-based disorder that causes: 1) problems with developing normal peer relationships, 2) impaired ability to recognize or use appropriate nonverbal communication, 3) impairments in social interactions such as problems recognizing and responding to other people's emotions and inappropriate social and emotional behavior and 4) restricted and intense interests in certain subjects or activities. There are significant problems with social, occupational or other important areas of functioning. By the DSM IV criteria (see reference to the DSM IV below), there are no significant delays in cognitive development apparent during the first three years of life, and the child uses single non-echoed words by age two years and spontaneous communicative phrases by age three years.

Attention deficit/hyperactivity disorder (AD/HD) – A neurologically-based disorder characterized by deficits in attention and/or hyperactivity/compulsivity. Under the DSM IV criteria, there are three subtypes: 1) Attention-Deficit/Hyperactivity Disorder,

Combined Type, 2) Attention-Deficit/Hyperactivity Disorder, Predominantly Inattentive Type and 3) Attention-Deficit/Hyperactivity Disorder, Predominantly Hyperactive-Impulsive Type.

Auditory discrimination – The ability to recognize and identify sounds and words as well as to hear similarities and differences between them.

Autism – The term "autism" sometimes is used to refer to the autism spectrum [also called the Pervasive Developmental Disorders (PDD) spectrum]. Alternatively, the term autism often is used loosely in lieu of the terms autistic disorder, classic autism, Kanner's autism, childhood autism or early infantile autism. These terms apply to a neurologically based disorder that causes striking impairments in social interaction and a remarkably restricted, repetitive range of interests and activities. In contrast to Asperger's syndrome, there are also significant delays in verbal communication as well as non-verbal communication. Mild to profound mental retardation is found in the majority of cases.

Autism spectrum – Autism is not a single diagnosis, but comprises various diagnoses along a continuum. The "autism spectrum" refers to all of the different autism diagnoses along that continuum. An alternate term for the "autism spectrum" is the "PDD spectrum."

Behaviorist – Someone who specializes in analyzing the functions of difficult or challenging behaviors and in designing and implementing treatment programs for such behaviors.

Central auditory processing deficit – An impairment in the ability to discriminate, recognize, or comprehend auditory information despite normal hearing ability. The CAPD individual will experience greater problems when listening to distorted speech and in poor acoustic environments such as listening in the presence of competing background noise.

Childhood Disintegrative Disorder – A neurologically based disorder in which there is a marked regression in several areas of functioning after at least two years of normal development. Regression occurs in at least two of the following areas: expressive or receptive language, social skills or adaptive behavior, bowel or bladder control, play or motor skills. Onset is before age ten and severe cognitive deficits usually are present. The social, communication and behavioral manifestations of this disorder are comparable to those seen in autistic disorder.

Chunking – Breaking down a complex task into smaller incremental steps ("chunks"). By mastering each step individually, the student can more easily master the larger task.

Cognitive – Relating to intelligence or the ability to think abstractly, to reason and to problem solve.

Cognitive ability – Intellectual ability, or the ability to know and understand.

Cognitive behavioral therapy (CBT) – A form of psychological therapy in which the therapist looks for misperceptions and distortions in the patient's thinking that cause inappropriate responses and helps the patient to correct these distortions.

Compliance – The act of participating in a task or activity in response to someone else's request to do so.

Compliance hierarchy – As used in a program to teach a student to comply with reasonable requests, a compliance hierarchy is a list of tasks that begins with a task that usually elicits compliance from a particular student, and then progresses through tasks that typically cause increasing levels of non-compliance.

Concrete thinking – Thinking that focuses on details and facts in contrast to ideas or concepts.

Contextual clues – As used in this book, these are clues to another person's thoughts, feelings or intentions that are found either in preceding events or in a body of knowledge that one has already collected about the other person. For example, the knowledge that Jane loves chocolate is a contextual clue that can help another person predict what Jane might feel, think and do if Jane were offered a piece of chocolate cake. Likewise, the knowledge that David was just reprimanded by his boss is a contextual clue that can be used to help understand why he is frowning and what he might be feeling and thinking at that moment.

Deductive reasoning – To start with an overarching principle or meaning and use that to draw a conclusion about a specific individual fact or event (i.e. to reason from the general to the specific). Example: Knowing that *in general* autistic children dislike changes in routine, Mrs. Davis deduced that her autistic student's temper tantrum had been caused by changing the time his art lesson started. (Contrast with "inductive reasoning".)

Delayed gratification - The ability to put off receiving a reward or reinforcer until a later time.

Diagnostic and Statistical Manual of Mental Disorders (DSM IV) – The diagnostic text of the American Psychiatric Association that describes and categorizes all currently accepted psychiatric diagnoses of mental disorders. Note that many of the disorders included in the DSM IV are *neurodevelopmental* disorders (for example autism, Asperger's syndrome, AD/HD, and mental retardation) and as such the term "mental disorders" may at times be misleading. The DSM IV is the fourth and most current edition.

Emotionally disturbed – According to the Code of Federal Regulations the label "emotionally disturbed" refers to "a condition exhibiting one or more of the following characteristics over a long period of time and to a significant degree, which adversely affects educational performance and requires small group instruction, supervision, and group counseling: (i) an inability to learn which cannot be explained by intellectual, sensory, or health factors; (ii) an inability to build or maintain satisfactory interpersonal relationships with peers and teachers; (iii) inappropriate types of behavior or feelings under normal circumstances; (iv) a general pervasive mood of unhappiness or depression; or (v) a tendency to develop physical symptoms or fears associated with personal or school problems."[50]

Etiology – Cause. Example: The etiology of his headache was meningitis.

Executive functioning: - The ability to plan and organize tasks, monitor one's own performance, inhibit inappropriate responses, utilize feedback and suppress distracting stimuli.

---

[50] Code of Federal Regulations: 300.7 b-4, p. 13.

Extrinsic reinforcement - The use of a reinforcer that is desirable to the recipient and encourages him to perform a target task or engage in a particular behavior. Extrinsic reinforcement can take the form of praise, a desired object or food item, participation in a favored activity, or a token that later can be traded for a desired object or activity. (Contrast with "intrinsic reinforcement.")

Fade - To gradually withdraw either prompts or reinforcers in order to encourage the student to do a task without the need for outside influence.

Figurative language – Language that conveys a meaning that is different from the literal meaning of the words or phrases being used.

Generalization - The transference of skills learned in one context to different contexts, including the ability to use those skills in different locations with varying stimuli, with different people, and at different times.

Graded approach – To teach a skill by starting with small, easily achievable steps, and gradually increasing the difficulty or number of steps until the skill is mastered. Also known as "shaping."

Hidden stressors – Stressors that affect an individual, but are not recognized by him or by others around him.

High functioning autism (HFA) – Although HFA is not officially recognized as a diagnostic category in the DSM IV, it nonetheless is a term that is in common usage. HFA typically refers to individuals on the autism spectrum who have near-normal to above average cognitive abilities, and who are able to communicate effectively through the use of receptive and expressive language. There currently is much debate about whether HFA and AS represent the same or different entities on the PDD spectrum.

ICD 10 – The International Classification of Diseases, Tenth Edition. The international diagnostic manual published by the World Health Organization in 1992.

Idiom – A figure of speech that is commonly known and used within a culture or subculture, in which the intended meaning is different from the literal meaning of the words (e.g., "You're *skating on thin ice.*" Or "He's *head over heels* in love.").

IEP – (Individualized education plan.) By California standards, a written special education plan that is created for an individual student by a team that includes (at the minimum) a parent or guardian, a teacher, and an administrator or specialist who is qualified to provide or supervise the child's program. The team may include other members as necessary. The IEP must include, but is not limited to the following: 1) the student's present levels of performance, 2) annual goals and short-term instructional objectives, 3) the specific educational instruction and related services required by the student, 4) provisions for participation in regular educational programs when possible, 5) the projected date for initiation and the anticipated duration of the programs and services included in the IEP and 6) specific criteria and procedures for determining whether the short-term objectives are being met. [51]

Inductive reasoning – To consider specific individual facts and draw an overall conclusion or meaning from those facts (i.e., to reason from the specific to the general). Example: After observing over several years of teaching that her third grade students took about twice as long to learn to write in cursive as did her fourth grade students, the teacher *induced* that third graders as a group are not developmentally ready to learn cursive. (Contrast with "deductive reasoning.")

Intrinsic reinforcement – The positive reinforcement that comes from an inner sense of achievement or pride in having completed a task. Alternatively, a feeling of pleasure or happiness associated with doing an activity.

Irony – The use of words in writing or speaking to convey the opposite meaning of the usual or expected meaning of the words.

---

[51] California Department of Education (1997). *California Special Education Programs. A Composite of Laws: Education Code – Part 30,Other Related Laws, and California Code of Regulations – Title 5* (19th Edition). Sacramento: CDE.

Kanner autism – So-called "classic autism" as described by Leo Kanner in 1943. See also "Autism."

Learning disability – A compromised ability to learn, manifested by a severe discrepancy between the student's intellectual ability and his level of achievement in one or more of the following areas: oral expression, listening comprehension, written expression, basic reading skills, reading comprehension, mathematics calculation or mathematics reasoning.[52]

Mastery (of a skill) - The point at which the student can accomplish a task correctly nine out of ten times. (It is generally accepted that this is the point at which the student will be able to *retain* the ability to independently accomplish the skill in the future.) An alternate definition sometimes used in this book is the point at which a student can do a task correctly three times in a row.

Mentor – For the purposes of this book, a person who is available to the individual with AS/HFA as an advisor, friend and confidant.

Metaphor – A form of figurative language in which there is an implied comparison between two different things without the use of the words *like* or *as*. *"He is a chip off the old block," "She is pouring her heart out,"* and *"He is a sly fox"* are examples of metaphors.

Negative stimulus - A situation or task which a person finds repellent, and which he will avoid if possible.

Neurodevelopmental disorder – A biological disorder in the development of the neurological system of a person, resulting in one or more clinically discernible deficits in that person.

Neurotypical (NT) –A popular term that refers to a person who does not suffer from a neurodevelopmental disorder such as autism.

---

[52] California Department of Education (1997).

Noncompliance – As used in this book, a person's refusal to comply with a reasonable request to engage in an activity or task that is necessary for his own well-being, growth, or independence.

Non-preferred activity – An activity that a person does not enjoy doing.

Nonverbal clue – A non-vocal clue (such as body language and facial expression) to the thoughts, feelings or intentions of another person.

Nonverbal learning disorder (NLD) – A disorder thought to be due to damage to or dysfunction of the right cerebral hemisphere, which causes relative strengths in verbal skills vs. significant weaknesses in non-verbal skills. Specifically, NLD causes dysfunction in three areas: 1) social skills (problems reading non verbal clues, adjusting to changes and transitions, and/or deficits in social interactions and social judgment); 2) visual-spatial and organizational skills (problems with visual recall, spatial perception, and forming images); and 3) motor skills (problems with coordination, balance and/or fine motor skills).

Obsessive-compulsive disorder (OCD) – A neurologically-based psychiatric disorder characterized by recurrent obsessions or compulsions that interfere with the individual's daily life (i.e., they occupy more than one hour a day, cause marked distress, or interfere with the person's normal routine, social life, work, or school performance).[53]

Oppositional defiant disorder (ODD) – A disorder characterized by recurrent defiance, disobedience and hostility over a period of at least six months, that is not due to another disorder such as depression, psychosis or antisocial personality disorder. At least four of the following eight behaviors must frequently be present for the diagnosis to be made: 1) losing temper, 2) arguing with adults, 3) actively defying or refusing to comply with the requests or rules of adults, 4) deliberately doing things to annoy other people, 5) blaming others for his own or her own mistakes, 6) being easily annoyed, 7) being angry or

---

[53] California Department of Education (1997).

resentful, or 8) being spiteful or vindictive. These behaviors must occur significantly more frequently than is normal for the individual's age and developmental level, and must interfere with his or her social, academic, or occupational functioning.[54]

Pedantic speech – Speech in which the speaker demonstrates his knowledge in an unnecessarily long or tiresome way, often dwelling on minor, narrow points.

Pervasive Development Disorders (PDD) – An "umbrella" term that refers to a spectrum of disorders that includes Autistic Disorder, Asperger's Disorder (Syndrome), Pervasive Developmental Disorder Not Otherwise Specified (PDD-NOS), Rett's Disorder and Childhood Disintegrative Disorder. Individuals with these disorders have severe impairments in reciprocal social interactions and communication skills and frequently have stereotyped behavior, interests and activities.

Pragmatics – The social use of language.

Preferred activity – An activity that a person enjoys doing.

Prompt – To encourage, remind or "cue" someone to do something. Prompts can take several forms, ranging from physically guiding the student through a task (e.g., placing one's hand over the student's hand to guide him to pick up a pencil) to a verbal reminder or a slight gesture (such as pointing or nodding one's head) that reminds the student to start or continue a task. In general, it is best to use the least intrusive and least noticeable prompt that will work for the particular situation. Also, it is important to fade prompting by slowly decreasing the number of prompts and by moving from more intrusive and noticeable prompts to those that are more subtle, until the student requires only that amount and type of prompting that is appropriate for his age.

Prosody – As it applies to speech, prosody is comprised of the pitch (or "intonation"), loudness and tempo of the spoken words.

---

[54] Ibid.

Psychoanalysis – A method used in psychiatry to search a person's mind for unconscious fears, anxieties or desires that may be causing a particular mental or emotional disorder.

Psychotic – Referring to symptoms such as delusions, hallucinations, disorganized speech, or severely disorganized or catatonic behavior.

Reinforcement menu – A list of extrinsic reinforcers from which the student may choose a reinforcer for desirable behavior or for successfully completing an assigned task.

Reinforcer – Anything that follows a behavior and increases that behavior. A *negative reinforcer* is something that a person will try to avoid. In the process of avoiding a negative reinforcer, the individual increases a desirable behavior. For example, the loud beeping sound made by a phone left off the hook is something that people typically want to avoid. The obnoxious noise increases the likelihood that people will hang up their phones. (In this example, the loud noise made by the phone is the negative reinforcer and hanging up the phone is the desirable behavior that results.) A *positive reinforcer* is something that is desirable to the recipient. The expectation of receiving a positive reinforcer motivates the recipient to increase the desired behavior. Types of positive reinforcers include social praise, preferred activities, edible reinforcers and tangible reinforcers (e.g., stickers, toys, tokens, etc).

Remediation – In special education, the process of providing appropriate programming to improve the student's performance in a particular area.

Rett's disorder – Categorized in the DSM IV as one of the pervasive developmental disorders, Rett's Disorder is found only in females and is characterized by a period of about five months of apparently normal development followed by a loss of multiple previously achieved milestones: Between five and thirty months of age functional hand movements are replaced with hand-wringing movements. Head growth decelerates between five and forty-eight months of age. Subsequently there is a loss of social interaction (some of this may be regained later) and the development of severe delays in expressive and receptive language, psychomotor skills, and coordination of gait and trunk movements. Significant mental retardation is present in most cases.

Semantics – The meanings of words and expressions.

SENSE skills – An acronym used in teaching nonverbal social skills. The letters stand for the following words: **S**pace—Maintaining the right physical distance from the other person. **E**ye contact—Making appropriate eye contact. **N**odding—Nodding the head to show attention, agreement and disagreement. **S**tatements of encouragement—Making standard, brief comments such as "hmm," "uh huh," or "really!" to show encouragement or attention. **E**xpressions—Using appropriate facial expression and body language.

Shaping – To teach the student a completely new behavior in a graded, stepwise fashion by: a) first reinforcing the student for a preexisting behavior that is close to the ultimate goal behavior, and b) then reinforcing successively closer approximations of the desired behavior until it is mastered. (See also "Graded Approach.")

Simile – A figure of speech in which one thing is compared to another thing. Similes always use the words "like" or "as." (Examples: *"She is as light as a feather,"* or *"She sings like a bird."*)

Social story –As developed by Carol Gray: A brief story that is used to teach a student an important lesson that would be difficult to explain to the student using usual teaching methods.

Stress hierarchy – A hierarchy that lists tasks that cause the student varying degrees of stress. The tasks are ranked in order from least to most stressful. The student is reinforced for accomplishing each task on the hierarchy, starting with the least stressful and then working up the hierarchy in a slow, methodical way to allow the student to succeed at each successive task before moving on to the more difficult task that follows.

Stress prevention – To reduce stress in a student's life by proactively preventing causes of stress in the student's daily life whenever possible.

Syntax – Sentence structure. The arrangement and function of words, phrases or clauses in a sentence.

Target task – An isolated task that the teacher or student designates for the student to accomplish.

Theory of mind skills –

First order theory of mind skills: The ability to understand or predict what another person thinks, feels, desires, intends, or believes about something (person, place, thing, event, etc.). For example, when packing for a trip, Megan packs her son's coat in a suitcase while he is at school. Later, she finds him looking for his coat in the closet. Megan *knows* that her son *believes* that the coat is in the closet because that is where he always puts it. She realizes this because she knows that her son was absent when she packed the coat; he did not see the coat being moved, and he therefore would believe that the coat was still in the closet.

Second order theory of mind skills – A person's ability to understand or predict what a second person thinks or believes about the *thoughts, beliefs, feelings, desires, or intentions* of a *third* person. For example, when Ted sees Justin frown angrily at Hilary (who is holding Justin's broken toy), Ted *thinks* that Justin *believes* that Hilary *intended* to break his toy.

Token economy – A system of reinforcement in which the student earns different numbers of tokens, or tokens of differing values, for doing various types or numbers of tasks. The student then "cashes in" the tokens (either immediately or at a later time) for a reward of corresponding value. Many different items can be used as tokens, including tickets, poker chips, and "play" money, to mention a few.

Tone of voice clues – Clues to the speaker's feelings, thoughts or intentions that are conveyed by his tone of voice.

Triggers (or triggering events) – An event that precipitates a certain behavior or response.

INDEX

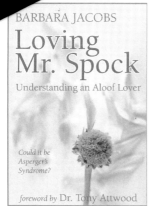
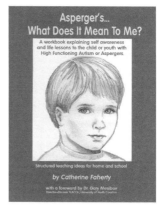

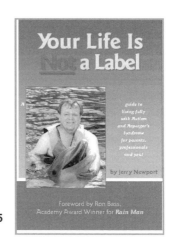

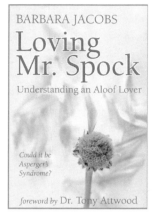
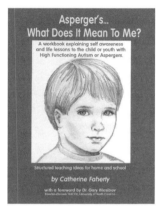